Dr.

Lost Boy Found

One man's account of surviving childhood sexual abuse, and how he turned his life around.

Life to Paper Publishing Inc.
Toronto, Canada | Miami, U.S.

LOST BOY FOUND

Copyright © 2019 Dr. Peter Gregg

All rights reserved.

All rights reserved. No part of this book may be reproduced or used in any manner without written permission of the copyright owner except for the use of quotations in a book review.

For more information, tabitha@lifetopaper.com

FIRST EDITION

www.lostboyfound.ca

ISBN: 978-1-5136-5572-7

For Anita,

who proves every day,

love bridges all differences.

LOST BOY FOUND

PRAISE FOR LOST BOY FOUND

Thank you for entrusting me with your story Lost Boy Found. I am just finished my second time through and the second reading was just as intense as the first. Your tale was gripping and visceral and raw. I am left saddened that someone I love and care about had to endure these experiences but also filled with even more admiration for what you've done with your life. You are one of the kindest and most compassionate people I know and I'm proud to be your friend.

Darren Lamothe, CEO & President, Novamen

An incredibly brave and honest account of a most difficult childhood, with countless important messages throughout. As the father of two teenaged girls, I can say that this is a must read for all parents to ensure they are vigilant in ensuring their children's safety. Moreover, Lost Boy Found, is a story of the remarkable human spirit, as Peter overcame countless tribulations to lead a most impactful existence, while touching the lives of many.

Jeremy Jablonski, friend and CEO at The Coverall Shop Ltd.

A powerful story that speaks to the essence of the human spirit. Peter takes us on dual-track a journey of how parental leadership is the most important thing we impart on our children while at the same time articulates how pliable and adaptable children can be when circumstances demand it.

Horrific things happen to amazing people and the role parents play as teacher and mentor are the critical building blocks that equip our children to set boundaries, seek out and surround themselves with good people, build friendships, and foster resiliency. When parents don't step up to the plate their children teeter between catastrophe and fulfilment – thankfully Peter's is a story of the latter. Intertwined is a powerful story of how we overcome adversity, play to our strengths, and look for the path forward through the most basic of human needs – relationship. This is a must-read for parents looking to understand how their behaviours and practices become the blueprint, whether subtle or obvious, for how their children will respond to the circumstances of life. We can leave them to their own devices or be there to guide the way, shape their choices, and provide the attachment they need to lead strong, healthy and emotionally vibrant lives. Peter, thank you for sharing your journey of fear, deception, trauma, hope, connection, and resiliency!

Darcy Mykytyshyn, Dean, Donald School of Business

A powerful read. While its pages are haunted with sorrow and tragedy, Dr. Gregg's story is also a testament to resiliency, healing and hope.

Dr. Mike Kroetsch, M.D.

An emotional read knowing that great success was achieved from such a troubling start. As a father of two daughters it's clear how, as parents, we need to be vigilant. Dr. Gregg reminds us of our great responsibility in raising our children through his story of what can occur when a compounding set of circumstances and events collide. I was drawn in to the story and wanted so much to meet little Peter and be there for him. Whether despite, or due to, these events, a great person and respected leader and mentor emerged.

Damian Zapisocky, CEO, Proform

Gripping story of strength, courage and how young Pete on his own, with no support from his parents, rose above tragic circumstances at age 9. As I am a father of two sons, and a son, our home is our refuge, and our parents protect and prepare us for the evils in the world. Peter's story will change the lives of many, so they don't have to suffer alone, and I'm sure all parents will hug their children after reading this book."

Don Sutherland, Entrepreneur

Lost Boy Found opened my eyes to the power of predators, and the vulnerability of our children in this world. I wouldn't consider myself naive, but I would say I didn't fully understand this aspect of society before reading this book. I have known Peter and Anita for several years, and credit them with helping me become the person I am today. I have nothing but the utmost respect for Peter and the amazing life he has led, I never thought this level of traumatic experience could have been a part of shaping such an incredible man.

This goes to show you how little I knew, of what is possible. This story has opened my eyes and made me reflect on how I raise my three young boys. We must always protect our children, ensure they know how loved and supported they are, and build the trust and openness in our relationships with them so that we might prevent a similar situation from happening to any child in our lives. Peter, thank you for sharing your story with all of us.

Keegan McLevin

Dr. Pete, thank you for trusting and sharing this time in your life with me, my heart aches for young Pete. As a mother of five children, four of them boys, I felt a wide range of emotions while reading your book. I was excited for the Pirates in their fun escapades, proud for the way they demonstrated friendship and loyalty and sad for the pain, guilt and shame felt by so many people. I also feel frustrated for the disregard towards the importance of parenting and the absolute privilege it is to have, protect and raise children. My emotions have not stopped since I closed the cover, I continue to reflect. Your story gives insight to the behavior of a child that is being abused and the lifelong impact of the emotional triggers because of the abuse they've experienced. It is powerful to know the manipulation tactics that a pedophile uses to groom their victims. I can't imagine the awareness this book inspires would ever diminish. Young Pete grew to be a kind, gentle and loving soul who shares these gifts with everyone whose journey in life intersects with his. You, my friend, are an inspiration and I am eternally grateful for how you have contributed to my life.

Kerri Tisdale, General Manager, Novamen

I am amazed that my respected friend, mentor and coach became the person he became after his childhood that is described in this book. Peter is so worldly, so connected and so full of experience. His gift to all of us Success Lab members is his patience and his perseverance as he accompanies us on our journey to become much better leaders for our organizations. We are all blessed that he survived his horrific start in this world and then develop into a thriving and contributing member of the business and academic communities across North America.

Jim Dixon

LOST BOY FOUND

TABLE OF CONTENTS:

Authors Notes

Chapter 1: Boy Rape

Chapter 2: Davey's Game / Grooming

Chapter 3: The Project

Chapter 4: Brothers

Chapter 5: B-47, Prelude to Disaster

Chapter 6: The Lye

Chapter 7: Hello, Davey

Chapter 8: Pyjama Game

Chapter 9: Goodbye, Mrs. Bear

Chapter 10: Bridges

Chapter 11: Hooked

Chapter 12: Snake Fight

Chapter 13: Getting it on with Jesus

Chapter 14: Don't be a Rat

Chapter 15: Switchblade

Chapter 16: On a Roll

Chapter 17: It's All in the Landing

Chapter 18: Dead Cat-Gone

Chapter 19: Satan's in the House

Chapter 20: Bitter Truths

Chapter 21: Route 66

Epilogue

Acknowledgements

About the Author

LOST BOY FOUND

AUTHOR'S NOTES

This is my story. It's based on true events that occurred when I was nine. These situations were so horrific that they changed my life forever and remain seared into my memory.

In writing this memoir I created a work of literary creative nonfiction, complete with story, plot, character, texture, and dialogue, which wraps around true events, bringing them to life. I have relied on this often-used writing technique because at a distance of over fifty years, some of the facts have slipped through the web of memory and I have no means to reconstruct them. In these cases, I have reimagined events and scenes in ways I believe reflects the true reality of what took place, and an honest portrayal of my story.

I have changed the identities of all the people in the book except for my own and my wife, Anita. I have created new names for the organizations I included.

Lastly, a thought on language. This book describes the underbelly of poor people living in America's Midwest. It reflects the thoughts and feelings of primarily young boys talking their talk, and the vile acts and descriptions of sexual assault perpetrated by a disturbed fifteen-year old paedophile. Consequently, I have used real language, with all its colour and depravity, to bring to life how it felt to be in this world. If I offend anyone, I apologize in advance. However, to sugar coat those experiences would have led to a dishonest book.

Thank you for reading.

CHAPTER 1: BOY RAPE

We heard strange male voices downstairs. "Where do you have the kids stashed, pervert?" one of the voices demanded.

Jerry Kaye and I started screaming. "Help us! Help us! We're up here!" The sounds of boots rushing up the stairs gave us hope.

Our captor was a fifteen-year-old male paedophile named, Davey. Davey was living with his aunt in our World War II government housing project, in the Midwest of the United States. Davey ended up with his aunt as part of his release agreement, while awaiting sentencing on child abuse charges.

Jerry Kaye and I were both nine. She and I lived in an area we called, The Project. We were founding members of the Pirates, an exclusive club modelled after Peter Pan, Wendy, and the lost boys. There are five of us Pirates and for us it is "one for all and all for one" as we tear through the neighbourhood playing games we invented and generally harassing the adults in our lives.

For the past several months, Davey has spent time shaping and grooming me for today's final performance. Up until now, I was the only kid he sexually assaulted, but today he had coerced Jerry Kaye into participating in his demented play. For whatever reason, Davey had sensed he was about to be caught so he locked us into the cavernous dark linen closet on the upper floor of his aunt's house. He had made Jerry Kaye and I take off our clothes and then he sexually molested us and raped me.

Then we heard our moms' voices.

"Where's are our kids?" I heard my mom shout. We heard Jerry Kaye's mom demanding to see her daughter and proclaiming the death of Davey. "I've got to see Jerry Kaye immediately, and I'm going to kill that pervert, Davey." Their voices got closer, then . . . CRASH! The wooden door of the closet, where Jerry Kaye and I were being held, was smashed by one of the cops.

Jerry Kaye and I rushed out of the closet, naked and overwhelmed at being found. We were greeted by the sight of two cops, a nurse, and our mothers. The nurse saw how exposed we were and ran past the cops to Davey's room and grabbed two blankets. She came back and quickly covered our bodies. Our moms rushed to us, grabbing and hugging us tight.

In the next room, we heard yelling, a loud crash on the floor, a voice of protest, and a deep baritone shouting, "Shut up! Get up and put your hands behind your back. You have the right to remain silent. Anything you say may be used against you. You have the right to counsel, if you can't afford a lawyer one will be provided for you at no expense."

The nurse and our moms helped Jerry Kaye and I get our clothes on. Just as we finished dressing, we saw Davey in handcuffs being hauled by the police officers down the stairs towards the front door. As Davey went by us, he yelled. "Peter, you ratted me out! I can't wait to tell the cops and your parents how much you enjoyed our playtime together."

***

This life shattering experience, and all that led up to it, created a profound wounding of my soul. My abuse was made even more impactful because my parents, and other adults around me, provided no safety or protection that every nine-year old deserves.

These events have affected every aspect of my life from that day Davey abused Jerry Kaye and I, until now, as a seventy-five-year old living in the shadow of my diminished self. In fact, I have lived a divided existence. My outward persona is driven by images and actions of success and achievement. The other part of me devolved through learned self-loathing, guilt, and lack of trust.

Let me explain further. On one hand, I've had a great life as a young adult and mature professional. My experiences were punctuated by being an outstanding university scholarship football player and becoming an up and coming executive at a major movie studio and entertainment conglomerate. I earned a PhD in behavioural sciences from a top US university, graduated *magna cum laude* and built an enduring legacy as a university professor, clinician, and founder of a highly respected leadership consulting firm.

But like an evil twin, lurking beneath all this success was an underbelly of a lack of confidence, poor personal relationships, interpersonal chaos, and at times lack of impulse control. I've had only a few close friends in my life. Although, I feel I was a good father, my son hasn't talked to me in years. I became a pleaser, fulfilling others' needs as opposed to what was good for me. I've been married several times, and only in my last relationship of ten years, have I felt love for and from the women I've lived with.

I'm embarrassed and loath the diminished part of me hidden beneath my successful public self. But finally, I want to share my story of rape and abuse. I have only told a handful of people my story, including my wife, Anita. I want to free myself of the lingering guilt I have felt every day since Davey destroyed my childhood. In addition to my excavation of my inner demons, I hope to give readers a glimpse of an unreported but very important aspect of the world of child abuse: namely boy rape.

Boy rape is not as prevalent as the perversion done to girls and women, but by being in the shadows, we miss the profound consequences of what happens when boys, who have been subjected to the forces of molestation, grow up to become men. Abused men are over represented in mental health hospitals, prison cells, gangs, suicides, bankruptcies, spousal and child abuse, and sadly the molestation and rape of children. This is not to say every boy subjected to rape becomes socially maladapted. Indeed, the preponderance of boy rape victims grow up suffering diminished lives but do not cross over to the dark side. But the few, in proportion, that act out, create an immense cost to society, families, and individual victims.

Through my story, I hope to shed light on how boys become victims, to show the cunning ways predators recruit boys to participate. I want to show how even the slightest parental neglect can set the stage for abuse, and the utter destruction of ego a raped boy experiences when he suffers in silence and fear.

The rape of a boy sets off a cascade of forces that focus like a laser on his relations with his parents. As Erik Erickson, the eminent developmental psychologist points out in his masterwork, *Childhood and Society*, the male ego structures are built around accomplishment. A boy's energy is laser focused on dominating their play and environment with rambunctious power to compete and win. Boys become friends with their playground brothers and sisters on the field of tribal cooperation, competition, bruised knees, and smelly jeans.

When boys are sexually abused, they lose their self-worth and dignity, and they end up feeling like damaged goods. All of this leads to a web of stigma found in phrases like, "I must be awful for someone to pick me to beat." "I must be awful to be fondled and groped." "I must be awful for an adult to want to penetrate me." "I must be really awful so that adults want to grind me into nothing."

Parents are an abused boy's safe harbour. When the rape of their son is first reported, most parents freeze. They ask what took place? Who did this? Who knows what happened to my son? Let's not tell anyone. In most cases, parents are dazed, angry, and embarrassed. All they want is for all of this bad stuff to be out of their son's life. But most parents soon get over this introspective phase and they kick their unconditional love into high gear.

The empathetic parents sound like this. "There's no fault nor guilt. I embrace my son. I hold him in a cocoon of enveloping love. We will get through this together."

It's essential to understand that supportive parents are an abused boy's saviour. If there are no parents, or neglectful parents, in the picture, then it's very hard for a raped boy to survive unscathed.

Unfortunately, there are some parents who don't know, or want to be bothered with the facts of their son's rape. Most parents panic when they find out about the abuse done to their son. In most cases, parents don't know what to do. Their first response is usually to withdraw, pretending silence will make everything go away. But time and the grievous nature of the abuse to their son forces parents to respond. Usually grieving parents start their confrontation with the reality of their son's rape by asking a series of questions.

- My son has been raped, is he now damaged goods?
- What did my son do to provoke his attacker?
- How do I express the love and fear I'm feeling without sinking into weakness?
- Can I remain silent and maybe it will go away?

Parents who withdraw, showing little love or empathy for their son's horrendous situation, foster the seeds of future psychological problems. Parents must remember that their sons, too, are asking questions of themselves. In interviews with abused boys, when asked about what they secretly wanted to ask their parents, they said:

- Do you really care about me? Do you love me?
- Why did you let this happen to me?
- Will you ever be proud of me again?
- Do you really want me as your son?
- Did I embarrass you?
- Will you ever take me to the game after this?

How parents answer these questions, either verbally or through action, produce long-term effects for themselves, their relationship with their son, and the entire family. Parents that stay missing in this tornado of a family crisis leave a wake of destructive guilt and anger experienced by all parties. But the parents who plunge directly into their son's life of trauma show up with unconditional love, nurturance, and support, builds the bridge for parents and son and family to heal.

CHAPTER 2: DAVEY'S GAME / GROOMING

At the heart of a family's anguish of the rape of a son is how these monstrous events were allowed to happen. That is, how do boys fall prey to predatory paedophiles? For years, social scientists have attempted to answer this question. We know parental care, or the lack thereof, plays a crucial role in the incubation of the predatory targeting and rape of a child. But when you dig deeper, there is a complex process of social influence that wily and cunning paedophiles use to target and lure children.

To fully understand what happened to me, and what happens to most boys who are raped, I have to give you a quick overview of the science of grooming and socialization. A basic understanding of how paedophiles get kids to join in their deadly and sadistic games of sexual abuse is essential to make sense of what follows.

***

I was forty-three in 1985 and about to give a presentation at Police Plaza One. It was a hot and cloudy summer day, smack in the heart of downtown. I welcomed the air-conditioned comfort as I got off the elevator and walked into one of the Plaza's large conference rooms. This one was decked out in faux maple tables and chairs, with about fifty seats set in neat rows. I was the guest speaker, invited by Captain Mike Collins to address his team, a group of Special Victims Unit detectives.

My presentation covered the process of grooming, how to recognize it, and how law enforcement officers must respond to its victims. I had consulted with Mike for years, both individually, and with his detective teams. The focus of our work together was the improvement of the mental health and operational effectiveness of those working in environments loaded with stress and conflict. No one in that room, or any other presentation or consulting assignment I'd been involved in, knew anything about my personal story of rape and abuse. I kept quiet because I did not want pity. I didn't want to come across as a whiny victim, and I didn't want to suffer the embarrassment my self-disclosure would provoke.

The fifty detectives in attendance were primarily white men, but there were some women, and other ethnicities. All were about thirty-five and up in age. These folks were earnest, with little of the cynicism usually associated with cops. They were eager to learn, while at the same time, slightly reserved.

It seemed like years ago that Mike and I met. At the time I was working as a special consultant to the Board of Policing. I had built, in addition to my research and teaching in all aspects of social influence, a secondary specialization working with police organizations. I was involved in the national commission on police practices and worked to improve leadership within the criminal justice system. I was first brought into Mike's unit to help remediate the horrible atmosphere created by the family murder-suicide of a beloved detective in the Special Victims Unit (SVU). Mike had been good friends with the man and up until that point, he'd been a hard-charging detective well on his way up the professional ladder. Understandably, this event nearly destroyed Mike and many of his close team members, leaving a wake of depression, and ripples of poor performance. As a result, I was asked by the Chief of Police to intervene with Mike and his team and conduct individual coaching sessions and lead team-building events.

Mike invited me to the front of the room and introduced me to the members of his detective team.

"How many of you have been involved in cases involving paedophilia?"

Almost all hands went up. I went on.

"What do you look for when investigating paedophiles? What do we mean by the term grooming, and how do you think sexual predators use these techniques on their victims?"

The detectives and I had a spirited discussion on grooming and predatory behaviour. They asked lots of questions and then I suggested we summarize the scientific literature focused on grooming and socialization. I grabbed a marker and wrote my first three words in all caps on an oversized pad of paper on the easel at the front of the room.

"WHAT IS GROOMING?" My pen squeaked. I cleared my throat. "Grooming is a predictable, step-by-step process sexual predators use to convert their targets into compliant victims. The best way to understand grooming is to visualize it. I like to use the metaphor of the frog in hot water to help you understand grooming. Imagine an unwitting frog, invited to bathe in a warm, comfortable pot of water. Unbeknownst to the frog, however, the pot is set on top of a lighted burner. As time goes by, the frog's bathwater gradually becomes hotter and hotter. The frog doesn't realize what is happening to him until it's too late and he's boiled to death without knowing it.

"Grooming is like the slowly raising the temperature of the bathwater. The predator slowly increases incentive and gifts, trading them for gradual sexual favours until a victim is completely enveloped into a full-blown sexual relationship. Here are a few escalating actions that a paedophile might use, in combination, to trap their victims."

I continued to talk and scrawled the key points on my easel as they came up. These were important punctuations I wanted the crowd to remember.

"Paedophiles look for opportunities to have TIME ALONE with the target. For example, babysitting, picking up the target from school, and scheduling secret meetings are some of the ways the predator achieves this alone time with their victim. There are also sleepovers, where the predator finds opportunities for bed-sharing.

"GIVING GIFTS and money for small intimate FAVOURS. SHOWING PORNOGRAPHY to the child while talking about sexual topics. Engaging in HUGGING, KISSING, or other INAPPROPRIATE TOUCHING. Targeting CHILDREN with BEHAVIOURAL ISSUES such as loneliness, high attention-seeking, and lack of self-worth.

"So, as a detective, when you are approaching a sexual abuse case, look for these indicators that deserve more in-depth investigation. But we can be even more precise in our understanding of boy rape if we establish the specific steps the predator uses to complete his full vanquishing of the victim. Here's what the paedophile, either through thought-out action or instinctive whim, does to turn targets into participants. There are six steps to grooming victims."

I peeled back the large paper to reveal a fresh page.

"Number one. TARGETING AND CULLING. Paedophiles look for targets susceptible to attention, praise, and reward. Once identified, the paedophile works hard for relationship exclusivity by separating the target from his friends.

"Number two. ESTABLISHMENT OF TRUST. They create and keep secrets, make promises and honour them, and make sure parents are the enemy.

"Number three. FULFILMENT OF NEEDS. Paedophiles look for ways to satisfy their target's needs. Whether it's gifts, clothes, food, or excitement, the paedophile seeks bridges to the victim by providing sources of payoff, whether these be material or experiential.

"Number four. ISOLATION OF THE CHILD. Once culling from friends takes place, then isolation through manipulation of parents, family, and friends is top of the paedophile's list. Paedophiles will continually look for ways to insert themselves between the target and their core relationships. Especially important for child separation are the actions the paedophile takes to get the parents to trust him or her, so that they can carry out their grooming actions without arousing parental suspicion.

"Number five. SEXUALIZATION OF THE RELATIONSHIP. Slowly the paedophile will progress the target from gentle touching and hugging, to kissing and exposing them to pornography, sensual fondling, exhibitionist masturbation, and finally, sexual foreplay and intercourse.

"And number six. MAINTENANCE OF CONTROL. The paedophile will use the withdrawal of rewards, physical punishment, and even in extreme cases, torture, to keep the target in line."

Once I finished my presentation there was even more discussion and questions. One young female detective stood and said, "Dr. Gregg, I think I can speak for my colleagues—this was the best presentation we've had related to doing our jobs more effectively. We want to thank you for your insight and knowledge."

I put the lid on my marker. Little did my audience know that I personally lived through every step I mentioned. I do recognize that it would give my scientific presentation greater credibility if I owned and discussed my personal history of abuse and rape. But I wasn't ready to climb from the observation perch of the bleachers to the playing field of my concrete experience.

I answered their questions for a few more minutes. When the energy left the room, I said goodbye to Mike, grabbed my lecture notes, and headed for the door. As I got to my car, I stopped for a moment before charging into the crush of the freeway in the afternoon.

***

Years later I was driving home with my wife and business partner from a presentation to about a hundred people on the power of values-based negotiations. Anita's cell phone rang. It was our son, Lars. He asked his mom if she'd seen the morning paper. She hadn't, so he told her to look at it when she got home and then once she'd read it, to call him.

Immediately upon arriving home we grabbed a copy of The Times. I couldn't believe what I saw. There on the front page, above the crease, was a large colour photo of our accountant. The caption read: *Lawrence von Stadler arrested and charged for sexual child abuse and rape, and the production and distribution of child pornography.*

Lawrence von Stadler had been our accountant for over ten years. He was in his early fifties, divorced, the father of two adult children. He reminds me of a lumberjack at six-foot-two-inches with a burly beard and bushy eyebrows. Von Stadler was certainly eccentric, non-conventional. He wore short pants throughout winter. He refused the suits and ties that his profession might regularly dictate and rode massive BMW motorcycles all over North America and Europe. There was nothing wrong with these personal proclivities, and to top it off, von Stadler was a superb accountant. But paedophile? Child rapist? Pornographer? Well, you could have knocked me over with a feather.

A quick and profound lesson hit us in the face. It was a reminder that paedophiles come from every stratum of society, every neighbourhood, and even every church.

He met his victims online through a sexual chat room. The kid was eleven at the time Von Stadler wrote his first email to him. Then, for the next four years, he plied his victim with gifts, money, and praise. Once the kid hit fifteen, von Stadler initiated sexual contact and proceeded for the next year to assault and rape this young man.

The victim's parents discovered von Stadler's sexual messages, photos, and videos on their son's computer. They confronted their son and called the police. The police took six months to secretly investigate von Stadler. At the end of their surveillance, the police arrested him. At the time of this arrest, they found sixty-eight electronic devices used to produce child pornography.

Von Stadler was charged with, sexual assault, sexual interference, luring a child for sexual assault, luring a child to make pornography, making child pornography, and making sexually explicit materials available to a child.

He was convicted on all counts and jailed. At the heart of his case, according to detectives and prosecutors, was the sophisticated and systematic process he used to lure his target and turn him into a victim. It was the exact same process I'd outlined to the SVU detectives.

***

I had thought that one day I would feel free enough to muster the confidence to tell my story. Finally, in 2019, I'm ready to describe how Davey raped me and sexually assaulted Jerry Kaye. I hope my honest depiction of my experience will help others to understand and act on the crisis of boy sexual assault. Only by shining a light on it can we snuff out this darkness.

CHAPTER 3: THE PROJECT

It was a cloudy day at the end of August. You could tell summer was coming to a close. There was that slight pre-autumn sting in the air. School hadn't started yet, so the Pirates still had time to raise a little more hell until they traded cut-off jeans for clean pants, T-shirts, and tied sneakers.

We were playing one of our favourite games, I Dare You. Long before the popstar, Madonna, made Truth or Dare a fashionable parlour game of the rich and bored, we played I Dare You. We took turns identifying our favourite dare. We rated our dares on a ten-point scale. One was for pussies and tens created legends. We swore we would never do a dare that wasn't a seven or above. We took the risk spelled out in one of these diabolical plots and played it through to its logical conclusion—often contusions, cuts, and utter joy.

I stood on the roof of one of the four plexes where we lived. Strategically placed on the ground, directly below me, was a well-used mattress we had liberated from the trash. As I looked down, the height from the roof to the ground appeared to be on par with

Mount Everest. I was pretty sure that when I jumped I would kill myself.

"Come on, Pete! You can do it!" Benny Tail-Feather shouted. After all, it was my turn to jump. Benny prodded some more. "Pete, if you don't jump, we're going to kick you out of the Pirates!"

Then Jerry Kaye yelled out, "Yeah, Pete! I jumped. I had the guts to do it. You can, too. Don't be a *girl!*"

That did it. I was increasingly convinced that my mother wanted to turn me into one of those—a *girl*. Once, she gave me a perm so I would have hair like Shirley Temple. She pushed me into dance lessons so she could revel at the picture of her son as the Curly Blond Prince. I was actively committed to discouraging any more of this nonsense.

So, I launched into space. My arms and legs wind-milled as I fought for stability. I crashed onto the mattress, safe. Then I flew ass-over-teakettle off the safe landing zone. My jeans ripped and my limbs were thrashed by the turf. Despite all that I yelled, "I'm the king of the Flying Pirates! Nobody does it better than Pete!"

As soon as I stood, Mike slugged me in the arm and Benny jumped on top of me, knocking me to the ground while yelling for everyone to pile on. In seconds, the rest of the Pirates were on top of us. Because I was laughing so hard, I couldn't breathe from the weight of all my friends.

Our celebratory mirth-making at the edge of our mattress was interrupted by the voice of Old Man Williams, the neighbourhood curmudgeon. He tended to loiter and gripe about anything outside his realm of comfort. On occasion, we tried to entice him with our antics, to coax some rebuke out of him. We doubt that he realized the entertainment he offered, that he unwittingly played the important role of villain in our japes.

"You kids had better clear out of here before I call your parents. By the way, Pete, your jump was really a stupid thing to do." Then he added, "But it was exciting to watch."

Mr. Williams missed everybody's jump but mine. Actually, all our jumps were mediocre save for the wild, wounded-bird flight of Jerry Kaye, and Benny's incredible effort where he flew over the mattress and landed squarely on his ass in hard-packed dirt.

We grabbed our landing pad and headed for the sanctuary of a stealthy place we'd carved out of a clump of hidden bushes and trees. This hiding spot was at the far side of a rundown park that sat adjacent to the housing project where we lived. We called this park, The Plaza. It was home our outdoor games, meetups, and shared suffering. After storing the mattress under the trees that provided our cover, we sat in a tight circle and started to chat about our fears, apprehensions, and curiosities, and about school starting in a couple of weeks. We were all in the same grade, having finished fourth last June. For whatever reason, our climb into fifth grade felt like it was going to be really difficult.

"I've heard Mrs. Bear, our new fifth grade teacher, is really tough," Jerry Kaye said.

Bill chimed in, "Yeah, I've heard that, too. My older brother Lance said Mrs. Bear was so tough on him that she threatened to hold him back for a repeat. Sure, he's no genius, but still."

I decided to share my thoughts as well. "I know Mrs. Bear really hates boys. I've heard that anyway. But what freaks me out the most is Larry Schultz's story of going into fifth last year and how the biggest boys from sixth jumped him on the first day of school, beat the hell out of him, and stole his lunch money."

Things went silent. Benny had a small stick in his hand and used it to doodle in the dirt just in front of where he sat. He stopped drawing and looked up to say, "I dare any of those bastard sixth graders to lay a hand on any of us. If they do, my family and I will make sure it's the last time they try to pick on kids younger and smaller than they are." All of us breathed a collective sigh of relief. The Muscle had our backs.

***

I met Benny and Jerry Kaye when I was in kindergarten. I started a year early, as no doubt my mother's competitive spirit had encouraged her to debut her brilliant son while he'd stick out. I expect she saw it as a feather in her cap to have one of her offspring in school at four-years old. Really, it was just that my birthday fell in September, a bit of a grey area for registration and admissions. She failed, however, to take into account that I was small, scrawny, and poorly-prepared to launch my school career alongside kids a year older, more physically developed, and more able to handle challenges both social and academic.

I was forced into kindergarten as well, and subsequently bullied, beaten up, ostracized, and proved a poor student to boot. But near the year's end, I began to adjust. I was the fastest runner in my class, so I got chosen for a lot of games in the yard and during Phys. Ed. I also wrote funny little essays and excelled at reading. But my biggest success that year was the formation of The Pirates. Here, I could put my imagination to work inventing games and hijinks for the group to get up to, from dawn to dusk.

Benny was two years older than me, making him the oldest Pirate. Benny stood out because he wore his hair in a stunning, full Mohawk, a proud salute to his American Indian heritage. He was strong and big for his age and loved to fight, so he was the Pirate muscle. Bullies did not mess with us when Benny was around.

Jerry Kaye was a small, skinny girl—the only girl, in fact, who felt strong enough to join us. She was always dressed like a girly model, prim and proper. Jerry Kaye was a supreme tomboy who could outrun, out punch, and outthink all the Pirates put together. She was an instigator who also knew how to sweet talk teachers and parents if the situation called for it.

The rest of the crew was made up of Mike Anderson, a chubby kid, but a supreme brainiac, and Bill Thompson whose claim to fame was he could build anything out of anything. They were officially recruited into the group after pouring a tin of red paint all over a bully who terrorized the entire school. Benny and I played field cops —basically, reconnaissance and security—while Mike, Bill, and Jerry Kaye marked their man while he napped. Parents were called and teachers mobilized to provide facts and punishment for the juvenile delinquents so awful to have committed such a dastardly deed against a defenseless, sleeping student. After a few days it became clear that the bully had such a bad reputation that most of the adults laughed and turned a blind eye to our prank.

The five of us were galvanized as a unit. The year I was nine, we were going on five years strong. A real kick-ass team always primed for adventure (and adult torment). It didn't hurt that we all lived in the same small neighbourhood, stuck squarely in the middle of the United States. Our name for where we lived was not clever. We just called it, The Project.

***

The World War II Housing Project sat atop a large, flat plateau, shrouded in a haze of grey and brown. The surrounding area was littered with discarded junk, and sparse clumps of grass and weeds. The identical fourplexes were painted a tawdry grey and sat on scant stilts. The muted tones gave the whole place an aura of sadness.

The plateau gave way to a series of sharp cliffs that steeply transitioned several hundred feet below to a narrow half-mile-long river valley. Running smack down the spine of the gulch was a creek. The creek flowed full in spring and summer, and in fall and winter it dwindled to a trickle. The water looked fresh and clean, but our moms warned us to stay out of it, and to *absolutely not* drink it, because it was full of discarded toxins from the sewage plants upstream. Running along the banks of the creek were very thick stands of willows, pine, and aspen trees. This was Pirate Country.

All the families living in The Project were housed in one of the identical four plex units. Each four plex sat on top of a raised foundation with six large steps leading up to a front porch and entry. The units all had two storeys. Downstairs was a kitchen, a furnace room, and a living area. Upstairs there was a large linen closet, the one and only bathroom, and two bedrooms. My family lived in an end unit. I had one of the bedrooms, and my parents the other, which they shared with my baby sister. We had no money for furnishings, so our living space was very sparse. The residents there were all poor. After all, it was subsidized government housing for returning WWII vets. Without this leg up, we would have probably all been living on the streets. In the end, because most of our families had so little money, we didn't feel like we were missing much: we were all in the same boat and living our lives as best we could.

The Project was a mulligan stew of ethnicity, religion, and opinions. There was Joseph Tail-Feather (Benny's dad), and his family of full-blooded Chickasaw who came from Oklahoma. It was the first house they'd lived in outside their reservation. There was Ellen Kit, a black, single, war bride from Haiti and her kids (the gossip around The Project was that her husband had died on his second deployment), and Ray Esposito, a member of The Big Red One, and his family from Los Angeles, via Mexico City.

Blended into this multi-racial mix were the Pirates and their families. Only the colour of our skin separated us from the common plight of poverty and little opportunity.

And of course, there was my family; me, my sister, my dad, Thomas, and my mom, Louise. My sister was much younger than me, just a baby, and for the most part, I saw her as intrusive and boring. My dad didn't have much to do with me. My mom, on the other hand, gave me a lot of attention, though not all of it pleasant. She didn't work outside the home, but she burned with passion and anger as if it was her full-time job. My father had returned home from a stint in Patton's Army. He fought in such theatres as The Battle of the Bulge and was there for the Liberation of Paris. My mom, like my dad, came from a background of bone-shattering poverty, she said it was not unlike that described in Steinbeck's, *Grapes of Wrath*.

My parents were good-looking, though. Scottish-Irish heritage was responsible for my father's wavy raven-black hair, and Scottish-German for my mother's curly red hair. Her high cheekbones left men breathless. Physical appearance was where their similarities stopped. My father was a passive man, who always had eyes for beautiful women. He lived his life in constant desperation and was starting to drown as an emerging alcoholic. He had no ambition other than his weekend runaways to bars to commune with friends of the opposite sex. With Monday mornings came lipstick-stained collars and a recurrent prelude to the Five-Day War that arose after his weekend binge.

My mother, on the other hand, was not passive. She spent most weekends calling her sisters to complain about her husband, the rum hound, and worked herself into a real lather so that by the time he got home, she was raring for a fight. He'd smell like a brewery and other women. Often the neighbours came out onto their porches to catch some of the Gregg Family Dispute show. Because the demographic shaded to the low-income, multi-ethnic, and drug-abusing population, these weekly battles were neither surprising, nor anything to get upset about. Instead, they were considered entertainment. Sometimes something noteworthy enough would happen and Benny

Tail-Feather's mom would call the cops to come separate my parents. These cooling-off periods didn't take long, and the psychological debris spilled over only as far as Wednesday when we returned to Normal Gregg Family. Those were the days when the silent treatment between my mom and dad turned to the necessary dialogue of family routine.

    I tried not to spend much of my time there. I even went out of my way to ensure my friends never came to my house. I wanted to spare them the humiliating reality of that environment. The goings-on of my indoor life were what drove me outside, into the whole wide world. From the moment I woke, until bedtime, I surrendered to games and mischief with my gang of friends. Parents, adults, and their conflicts, were left back behind closed doors.

CHAPTER 4: BROTHERS

Earlier that summer I had a big surprise. It was a late afternoon, hot and humid. There was an odour in the air from the incinerator of a smelting plant about a mile from The Project, one of the culprits behind our creek's pollution. I was hot, sticky, and sweaty from an afternoon of Pirate stickball. As I climbed the steps of our front porch, I heard my mom talking to someone inside. I couldn't believe my ears—it was my Uncle Jimmy. I burst through the door and there he sat, larger than life. He wore gleaming cowboy boots, fresh-pressed jeans, an amazing white western shirt with silver collar tabs, and a belt buckle larger than Texas. He had the kind of grin that stopped everyone in their tracks.

My Uncle Jimmy was my father's oldest brother. He was good looking in his western duds with a few extra pounds on his frame, but men and women seemed to flock to him. He and his wife, my Aunt Florence, built a bit of an empire comprising large-scale cattle ranching, huge land holdings, and a robust oil-drilling business.

Uncle Jimmy and Aunt Florence had no children. My sister and I were the closest thing they had to a family of their own. They were rich, with all the accompanying material and experiential goodies rich people enjoy. Compared to my mom and dad's economic existence in working poverty, the contrast couldn't be more striking and profound. Because of this visible discrepancy between our world and my uncle and aunt's, they were always seeking to help us in any way they could. They brought gifts for the family, and summers at the ranch for me and my sister (replete with our own horses and cowboy garb). My uncle would eventually teach me to drive (at thirteen), and give me a car for my use on the ranch (but I mostly used it to tear unimpeded from one county town to the next).

When Uncle Jimmy or Aunt Florence were in town, the good times rolled. Even at nine, I couldn't help but feel sorry for my dad when I looked into his eyes as they were filled with envy. There was also shame for his meagre professional reality and lack of accomplishment when compared to his big brother.

Only Uncle Jimmy had come this time. Aunt Florence must have stayed at home. Uncle Jimmy jumped up and rushed over to give me a huge bear hug.

"Hey little man, where have you been? We've really missed you at the ranch this summer. There's still time, Pete—you could come for a couple of weeks before school starts."

I wriggled out of his paws. "I can't, Uncle Jimmy. School's starting soon, and besides, I thought you didn't really want me at the ranch anymore since I spooked Lucky. Remember? You sent me home early."

My uncle chuckled. "Pete, what you're saying is silly. We just had a misunderstanding. Next summer I want to see you at the ranch. Stay June through August. Your Aunt and I will buy you new boots. I think it's time we got you riding a full-sized cattle horse. We might even teach you how to drive. What do you say?"

"Does my sister have to be there?" I asked.

"Of course she does, but she'll be out of the way with your aunt." He looked towards my mom. "Isn't that right, Louise?"

"Jimmy, if you say so," Mom said. "I'm sure that's the way it will work out. But next summer's a ways off, so let's talk ranch details later. Now, tell Pete why you showed up on his doorstep out of the blue."

Uncle Jimmy nodded, then took a sip of the iced tea Mom had put out for him. There were cookies, too.

"Okay, little man, here's what's going on. The Plain Dealer, Dorset's weekly paper, held a contest to identify the best-looking local WWII vet. The idea was to call attention to all the guys who served from the area and find a fun way to recognize them. At the same time, they ran pictures of all the other bands of brothers from around Dorset. Long story short, your dad won. They looked at old yearbook photographs, newspaper shots, and a whole bunch of other pictures they got their hands on, and he proved to be the Clark Gable of the bunch." My uncle paused as the news sank in.

"Now here's where it gets tough. They want more pictures, but this time of your dad, your mom, and you and your sister. Your aunt and I don't have anything else to give them, and I had nothing better to do, so I jumped in the truck and cruised the four hours to see you guys and grab a bunch of photographs I know your mom has kept. The paper's going to run the spread next Sunday, so I have to get on this, pronto." My uncle leaned in closer.

"This is really important, Pete. Your grandfather, the one you've never met, is dying and it will be a great surprise for him to see your dad in a good light. Our dad and your dad never really got along. This might be an opportunity to open a door for your grandfather to forgive your dad before the grave calls."

My head was spinning. I couldn't believe this. So much new information, and I couldn't help but think this was a bogus excuse my uncle used to come and see us. There had to be more going on than a pretty-boy mugshot of my dad. I could have been wrong. My uncle could have been acting in good faith, but that wasn't really like him. My mom interrupted my train of thought.

"My God, Pete. You really smell. Get upstairs and grab a bath, put on some clean clothes, and get ready for dinner. Your uncle is only going to stay for a short time. He's spending the night with a friend, so we have to get going and find the photos he wants."

I assumed I was going to help look through the photos with my uncle, but my mom's tone implied I was not invited. My uncle and I exchanged glances.

"Okay Louise, enough. Hurry up, Pete—I have another lucky silver dollar I want to give you for your collection. I'll show it to you when you come back down."

I hustled up the stairs, got into my room, ripped off my dirty clothes, and stuffed them into the laundry basket. I started my bathwater and quietly moved to the head of the stairs where I could get within earshot of my mom and uncle's conversation.

"Have you told him yet?" Uncle Jimmy asked.

"Jimmy. He's still a little boy, he won't understand. And besides, Thomas has no idea. I'm going to let sleeping dogs lie. And so are you."

"Louise, this is not just your party. I have interests here. Florence and I have no children. You know she can't conceive, so this is as close as I'm ever going to get to having my own son. I'll keep quiet for now, but I want you to know I'm going to say something to Pete and Thomas in the next couple of years. Get ready for it."

"Jimmy, you do what you have to do." Her voice was an urgent whisper. "I beg of you, let's approach this together. I do not want you to destroy my marriage or my son's life."

"Okay, okay." He took a deep breath. "I hear you, Louise. Let's get those pictures out so we can choose a few. I'll say hello to Thomas when he gets home and tell him the news—let him bask in his Clark Gable-ness—and then I'll be on my way."

I couldn't believe what I'd heard. Were my mom and uncle saying I wasn't my dad's son, but rather that my *Uncle Jimmy* was my real father? The tub was about to spill over as I'd let it run too long. I trod carefully back to the bathroom and jumped in. The water sloshed over the edge. I lay soaking in the hot soothing liquid and focused on the stunning news I'd just heard. What would happen now?

After a good soak and scrubbing, I got out of the bath. The used water was a dark brown, accurately reflecting the passion of our stick ball game. I took my favourite big yellow towel to dry off and jammed on clean jeans and a bright red polo. I didn't want to go downstairs and face my mom and uncle, even if they had no suspicion that I was now on to them. These circumstances were so much like what happened this past May.

***

It was a bright spring day at The Project. Wispy clouds floated by in the amazing blue sky, and a light wind fluffed the leaves of the trees. The Pirates had just finished another game of I Dare You and I was heading home. My mom yelled at me from our front porch, and insisted I get ready in a hurry. It was the familiar, "Pete, get upstairs, grab a quick bath, clean clothes, so-and-so is coming over!"

That time it was my Aunt Thelma and she was coming by in her new car.

"Where we going? When are we coming home? I promised Jerry Kaye that I would do ice cream scoops from the fun wagon at four. I don't want to miss that."

"Stop worrying about your friends and give me some of your time. We'll get home when we get home, and if you miss licking ice cream cones with Jerry Kaye, then that's the way it goes. Get over here and get going."

I tore home, following my mom's command. In about twenty minutes I was presentable and waited by the front door for Aunt Thelma to show up. When she did, she looked just like Marilyn Monroe with a flourish of blond hair. She had her new Ford convertible waiting for us in The Project's parking lot.

My Aunt Thelma was the complete opposite of my mom. She was single, stylish, and highly-educated, with a very important corporate job. She had a BA and an MBA from a top university and was Vice President of Finance at a large telecom that had its corporate headquarters in the city. That day she was dressed in peach-coloured pedal-pushers, a bright teal, silk, sleeveless blouse, and white Chuck Taylor sneakers. In contrast, my mom was wearing the best she could afford: khaki slacks, a white shirt, and some bright red pumps to provide a sassy splash of colour.

My mom took my sister to a neighbour's house, then herded the three of us to Thelma's car and off we went. I had never ridden in her convertible before. Riding in the convertible was a blast. Our hair flew up and we had to yell to hear each other over the engine and be-bop jazz (as my aunt called it) on the radio. Then we arrived at a graveyard. It was old, dank, and grey in colour cast by the shadows of hundreds of tombstones.

"Mom, why are we here?" I asked.

My Aunt Thelma piped up instead. "Pete, your mom is going to take you and me to the grave of a very special person that she wants us to pay our respects to."

My mom was silent. She motioned for Thelma and me to follow her. We wove in and out of the headstones of vets' where they had been buried, families of settlements, and finally to the special children's grave sites. I could tell Mom was on a mission. She looked around and shook her head. "I know it's right around here."

It became clear that she was searching for a specific child, a child she knew. Finally, she stopped in front of a flat, pinkish-grey marble marker. "This is it!" she exclaimed.

The inscription on the stone read:

Leroy Jones

Beloved Son

Dead at Birth

I took a deep breath. I knew my mom's maiden name was Jones. I wondered to myself if Leroy was my mom's son, my unknown brother?

Aunt Thelma moved closer to her older sister. She took her in her arms. Both women sobbed quietly. Eventually, my mom turned to me and through her tears managed to say, "Peter, this is your brother by another father. He never had the chance to live. I wanted you to be here, so you knew of Leroy, and how I hope you appreciate your life and all that your dad and I give you."

The first thing that crossed my mind was who this other father was, and why my mom would have a kid with him and not my dad. I started to say something, but I compelled myself to keep my mouth shut all the way home. I suffered in silence amid and despite all the questions that jumped into my mind. An encounter with a dead brother raised a lot of questions, but so far, the most important question seemed to be, "Who the hell is my mother and what was her life like before she had me?"

***

My mother and I didn't ever recount the visit to Leroy, but the image of my mom and Aunt Thelma sobbing by his little marker still haunted me months later. And now, here I was again, after such a short time, being made to consider another secret from my mom's life. From the words exchanged between my mother and uncle in the conversation I overheard, I could only infer that I was his bastard son, and it didn't seem like my dad had a clue. My mom was proving to have quite the sordid past.

By the time I decided to come back downstairs, my dad had arrived home from work. My uncle has regaled him with the news that he was the newly-anointed *hunk* of the county, and predicted he was about to achieve celebrity status among all the milkmaids looking for husbands. My dad didn't get many compliments, or much recognition (at work, and for sure, at home), so he was pleased and proud about the news. My mom, for the first time in a long time, looked at him with love in her eyes.

The adults pawed through the extra photographs and culled a small grouping of images of my dad that might be good for the paper's Sunday spread. There were several pictures of him and my uncle ploughing fields behind a mule rig, of my dad in WWII fighting gear, and a beautiful portrait of my mom and dad taken on the day they were married. There were no pictures of him with us kids, even though my uncle made a point of asking for some. This only furthered my conviction that I was a bastard. My uncle seemed satisfied with the haul and shuffled the collection into a manila envelope. He headed for the door on his way to spend the night, not with my aunt, but as I came to learn, a lady friend.

"Well, I'm off. Thanks for the snack, Louise." He winked and tossed me a silver dollar. Then he nodded to my dad. "Thomas, you son of a gun. You had better watch yourself around those ladies. They're a-comin'."

Then it was time for dinner. Dad brought home Chinese take-out. After dinner, I drifted back upstairs, dazed by all that I'd heard. I could hear my mom and dad chirping on about his sudden fame. But I had other things on my mind. This newly-minted bastard could hardly wait for tomorrow. Some Pirate reality was just the ticket to get me out of my own head.

CHAPTER 5: B-47, PRELUDE TO DISASTER

I jumped out of bed, got dressed, and headed for the door. Even though a few months had passed, I was still stunned and actively processing the visit to Leroy's grave. It had been weeks since the conversation I overheard between my mother and uncle. The thought of my mother harbouring a secret past continued to encourage a lot of introspection. I grappled with a far bigger question, much beyond the scope of a nine-year-old: "Who am I, anyway?"

I knew one thing for certain. I was a Pirate.

I rushed past my parents, drinking tea at the kitchen table. I didn't stop. I yelled out for no one in particular, "Playing B-47 this morning—the Pirates are going to have baloney sandwiches down by the creek, so I won't be home until after lunch."

Last night Jerry Kaye told me she'd scammed the lunch meat, along with some mayo, bread, and chips from her family's refrigerator and pantry, leaving us set for a feast after the Pirates' B-47 game. I hoped we would chat some more about our expectations of fifth grade.

I headed to our meet-up place at the far end of the Plaza. We had cut and stacked trees and bushes into a cool hideout. The other

Pirates were already there, blending into our vegetation of stealth. Just seeing my gang, getting outdoors, smelling fresh air, and not listening to my parents drone on and on, allowed Leroy and his bastard brother to drift away, slowly, but surely, on the receding waves of anxiety.

Everybody was glad to see me. Before I got a chance to sit on the dirt like the others, Mike Anderson shouted, "Hey Gregg! You take Jerry Kaye and Benny Tail-Feather. You guys are the American Supersonic Jets Squadron. I've got Bill. We are the Deadly Russian Attackers. The Russians need thirty minutes to find our ambush place. You Americans try to find us. The battle will explode by either a direct American attack, or a crafty Russian sneak-up. This time Bill and I are going to kick some American ass."

Our substitute planes in this game of hide-and-crash were our old bikes. The hide aspect was self-explanatory. For the crash, we rammed into each other over and over again. Winners were the pilots and planes/bikes left standing. We collectively wheeled our make-believe warplanes to the edge of the cliff leading to the river valley. Bill and Mike launched off the steep incline, hooting all the way, "American blood is ours today!"

***

B-47 was one of our favourite games. It grew out of our proximity to Summers Air Force Base. Summers was the home of the largest squadron of B-47s (nuclear-capable bombers) in the country. Their crews were billeted here as well. The B-47 was the precursor of the much larger B-52. The B-52 still flies, but for a while, the B-47 was the prime delivery system for A-bombs targeting the Soviet Union. Every day, at all hours, and throughout the year, you had only to look upwards and it was likely you would see several of these condor-like war machines flying in formation with the contrails from their jet engines blowing white ribbons across the sky.

Duck-and-cover was the culture of the day for all American kids. On secret days, known only to our school's principal, and at the signal of our teacher, we would simulate a nuclear attack by the Russians. We would all squirm under our desk hoping this was not the real thing.

Living so near to the home of the B-47s created an atmosphere in which the wild imagination of kids could create all sorts of possibilities of play, especially good vs. evil. This was how we went about inventing B-47. We would look up to the sky and see these gigantic, swooping delivery systems of A-bombs and imagine what would happen if American planes attacked Russian aircraft, or vice versa. And to make it more real, what would happen if this explosive warfare took place over the skies of our housing project?

***

That particular B-47 day was *alive*. It was one of the last warm days of summer with the sky an azure blue, free of clouds. Mosquitoes were still seeking their pound of flesh. As Mike and Bill disappeared into the heart of the river valley (on their way to find a powerful ambush site), Benny Tail-Feather, Jerry Kaye, and I messed with our bikes, making sure they were ready for the simulated dogfights to come.

The Pirates took playing B-47 very seriously. All of us wanted to look as close as we could to real pilots, flying real planes. We did this with flyboy costumes of long pants, jackets, goggles, and gloves. We simulated flight by stuffing dirt in our hands and when we were on the attack, we slowly released our crumbly brown fuel to create an artificial exhaust that would billow behind us for a few almighty seconds.

Russians or Americans (we rotated each time we played) took time hiding and planning an elegant ambush. The waiting team, still on top of the plateau, spent their time going over their attack strategy.

Jerry Kaye laid the groundwork of our plot. "Pete, when we find them, since there's only two of them, and three of us, let's catch them in a vice grip like we did last month—you charge them right up the middle, and Benny, you come in from the rear. I'll catch one of them on the side."

Let me just say that back then, I thought Jerry Kaye ruled. She was so smart, and it was the perfect plan.

We took our time perfecting what we were going to do. Thirty minutes later we charged into action, tearing down the cliff to start our search of the gulch.

Benny hollered, "Pete, are they on the other side of the creek?"

"No!" Jerry yelled before I can answer. "I think they travelled up the valley to the badlands!"

The badlands were the part of the river valley that was dangerous. Poisonous snakes, dangerous discarded junk, and the occasional big hairy monster roamed there.

I yelled, "I'm sure they haven't hightailed it to the badlands. Mike is a big sissy. You won't catch him anywhere near that evil forest!"

We kept searching. We were The Americans and we were on the prowl. And then it happened. Mike and Bill attacked. Mike went after us from the front. Bill came at us from behind. So much for our three-pronged pincer plan.

Mike crashed his much heavier beast into me, knocking me, my bike, and my dirt-fuel to the ground. I was ejected from my plane and my head hit a stump, opening a small cut in my scalp. I was wounded. Benny Tail-Feather circled behind Mike and Bill, looking for a clean kill shot. Benny stood on his pedals and pumped madly, flying at The Russians. Mike and Bill saw Benny coming at them. They swerved and Benny missed. Mike and Bill immediately changed the momentum by setting their sights on Jerry Kaye.

"Pete, get out of the way!" Jerry Kaye yelled. She quickly spun her bike 180 degrees and was positioned so she could T-bone Mike. She pedalled furiously and caught Mike and his bike squarely in the middle of its frame. Jerry Kaye's attack sent him flying into the swampy weeds next to the creek.

Mike jumped up, looking pissed off. "Goddamn it, Jerry Kaye! You've ruined my bike and my knee is bleeding like a stuck pig." Mike made a menacing move towards her.

Benny jumped in front of him and yelled, "Mike, you're such a baby—even a girl can knock you on your ass. If you can't play clean B-47, I don't want to play with you anymore."

This post B-47 conflict was a regular part of our America vs. Russia ritual. In the end we would limp home, always good friends as ever, all the while engaging in geopolitical gossip on how the Real US would kick the Real Russia's ass in a Real War.

But on this late August afternoon, we seemed different. All of us were a bit more wounded, and harboured hurt feelings. I got my bike up and rolling again, despite the broken spokes and bent wheel that the battle had produced.

"Let's go home," I suggested soberly.

Jerry Kaye looked sad, but being the good sport she was, she asked, "Does anyone want baloney sandwiches?"

We all shook our heads no.

Benny spoke up. "Come on, guys. Shake it off. Today's B-47 was great. It was just a little tougher than we're used to. When we play next week, let's make it even more fun. Jerry Kaye and I will be The Russians and we promise not to pick on anyone."

Everyone laughed. We continued the slow crawl back to The Project. I casually glanced up. There, against the brilliant blue sky, even more radiant than it was this morning, I saw two B-47s, flying in formation. One plane's nose was just below the tail of the other. The white contrails from the collective engines of the planes mixed together to form a loose set of waves.

I yelled, as most of us had at some time or other, "Look! They're crashing!" It was a joke. We all laughed.

Before we moved much farther, Bill screamed out hysterically, "Jesus—they really *are* crashing!"

I whipped around and turned my gaze back to the planes. The B-47 on top in the formation was on fire heading nose-down towards the fields north of the river valley. "He's going straight in," I shouted. The second B-47 twisted in a tight corkscrew close behind. With each turn, he was out of control, and like his brother, sure to meet his destiny crashing into the same fields.

I couldn't help myself. I panicked, and yelled, "Look what I've done! My stupid shout caused this. People will be dead because of me."

The rest of the Pirates were silent. Then Jerry Kaye tried to provide me with some grace. "Pete, you didn't cause the crash—you know that's not possible. Give yourself a break, man. We've all yelled, 'They're crashing, they're crashing,' and nothing happened. Let's head home. I'm sure the crash will be on TV tonight, so we can figure out what happened then."

***

We behavioural scientists call what my nine-year-old self was engaged in as Magical Thinking. It's a term first coined by the renowned child-developmental psychologist, Jean Piaget. He posited, and through scientific observation found, there are four steps in a child's development cycle. The stage from the age of two through seven, and even up to nine years in boys, is ripe for magical thinking.

Magical thinking is the belief that thoughts, by themselves, can bring about actions directly linked to those thoughts. If I command a plane to crash and it does, then it must be my fault. Most people older than the child experiencing magical thinking, will recognize this (perceived to be) causal link between thought and action as irrational. But some children (or in some cases the mentally ill or delusional) within this stage of early development, are absolutely convinced their thinking causes events to transpire.

In the short term, this type of thought can result in guilt and self-deprecation. Once a child matures and Reality Thinking overtakes its Magical counterpart, these feelings of causality recede. In some cases, especially when death is involved, there's an operating conclusion by the child, that their thoughts about this person (or people) caused their death(s). The feelings of guilt and shame these dramatic circumstances produce can linger throughout a lifetime.

***

We ran our bikes home. There was no conversation. We were all anxious to see if others saw the crash, and what they were saying about the catastrophe. Since I was transfixed by the belief that the fate of the B-47s was my doing, I was particularly driven to find out the specifics of what happened. We trudged up the cliff and onto the plateau. We were sweaty and out of breath, and all driven by fear and wonder. We each peeled off from the group and made our ways to our separate homes (and the safety of parental rationality). Little did I know, I was about to put my magical thinking on steroids.

Our house was at the end of the block. I had to run a bit farther than the rest of the Pirates. The first person I bumped into before getting home was Chip Fisher. Chip was an electrician who somehow wormed his way into The Project so he could score a lower, subsidized rent. He was in his late twenties and good looking. He had a continuous string of young women coming and going from his house. The Pirates often made rude comments about Chip's *daughters* coming to see him.

Chip's pride and joy was his pink-and-grey '52 Chevy. The Chevy was a two-door coupe with tuck n' roll seats of gleaming white leather. Often, Chip's afore-mentioned daughters adorned the car, sitting on his lap as he drove by. It appeared that his favourite sport was tearing around the neighbourhood showing off his bachelor lifestyle.

"Hey Chip," I hollered as loud as I could. "Did you see the crash? Let's go check it out. They went down in the fields just north of the river valley."

He obliged me. "Sure Pete. Come on, jump in the car. We should be there in just a few minutes."

Chip and I trotted to The Project's parking lot. His Chevy was parked on an angle, taking up two spots, so no one could park close to Chip's dream. He didn't want anyone to blemish the finish with an errant door opening. I jumped in. The upholstery was *pluu-uush!* It was something I noticed, even though (or perhaps, because) I was running on adrenaline. Chip started the Chevy. What a sweet sound that V8 made as it throbbed to life. We tore out of the lot with a roar.

In the near distance, above the gulch, plumes of dark black smoke billowed up into the sky. The shroud of smoke muffled everything with a grey-and-white patina. It took only ten minutes to find the fields, which were now serving as coffins to the magnificent flying machines and their crews. The Chevy didn't like the rough terrain we were navigating to get closer to the wreckage. I heard a hubcap fly off, and there were some bumps so big, we bottomed out. But Chip didn't stop as he seemed to be on a mission.

The gate to the first field was locked. Chip gunned the Chevy, breaking through the barbwire barrier aimed at keeping poachers and thieves out and commodities in. I could tell the Chevy, our battering ram, suffered major hits. One headlight was cracked, and a side mirror was shorn off. I heard the barbwire tear into the paint in its refusal to yield to Chip's assault. The tires weren't faring much better.

We were immediately confronted with a raging fire that consumed the remains of the B-47s. The smell of jet fuel overwhelmed me. Then I was made aware of an even more pungent and noxious order. I couldn't recall ever smelling anything like it before. This smell made me gag, and I had to hold back the urge to vomit. Chip saw my disgust.

"Burning flesh!" he shouted. "Cover your nose with your hand! Breathe through your mouth!"

I moved closer to the fuselages of the planes. I looked closer, too. I saw severed body parts from the B-47's crews. There was an arm here, a torso there, and a hand dangling from a tree, all torn and smoldering from its rendezvous with death. The sight was grotesque and unbearable. What had I done? This was all my fault. Not only was I a bastard, I was a murderer, too.

The onslaught of rescuers and scavengers began to arrive. I saw several grown men navigate belching pools of fire to grab plane parts, only to stuff them into the back of their pickups and roar off. It was despicable. Chip darted off to confront one of them.

The rescuers reached critical mass and the site was starting to resemble a beehive. It was a mix of concerned civilians and Air Force personnel, combing through the ash and magma for life—or what remained of it.

There were cops, too, on their bullhorns, trying to control the crowd. "Anyone making off with plane parts will be found and arrested." Their artificially-magnified voices only added to the surrealistic feeling of the scene.

Bright-red fire trucks arrived with their huge illuminating lights, now needed because the sun was setting. They sprayed gallons of water through the brass nozzles of their pressure hoses onto the burning carnage of the crash. I heard one of the firemen shout, "We have to back off a bit. There's no one alive inside the planes. The fire is burning extra hot and dirty."

Some more Air Force men, in their grey-blue jumpsuits, with masks covering their noses and mouths, scoured the few areas cool enough for discovery and excavation. I surmised they were on the hunt for important, secret equipment thrown from the planes' innards.

A voice called out. "Over here! There's a transponder we can't let out of our hands, and here are the bombsights we have to get back to Washington for safekeeping."

My gaze drifted back to the other Air Force operatives that were looking for and finding bodies (and parts of them). It was a grisly scene to take in. I was overwhelmed. The cops pushed me away from all the action. They wanted to know where my parents were. They told me that if they couldn't find them, they were going to take me home and give my mom and dad trouble. Just as one of the cops laid his judicial pen to paper to mark my delinquency, Chip returned from trying to get the plane parts back. He smelled of sweat, jet fuel, and burning bodies. It was all mingled into an aromatic soup that was hard to stomach.

He yelled over the cacophony of the now-teeming crash site, "Come on, Pete, it's time to go. Your mom is going to kill me. She doesn't know where you are. I'm sure I'm in for a tongue-lashing from her."

I followed him and we jumped into Chip's wounded Chevy and headed home. As we retraced our route from the killing fields of the burning B-47s and their crews, I turned and looked over my shoulder. It looked like War of the Worlds. The aliens had landed.

CHAPTER 6: THE LYE

My mom plopped me down on one of our kitchen chairs. "Peter Gregg. I've told you a million times, *You are not to leave The Project without my express permission!* I'm going to kill that Chip Arden. I have a right mind to call up Family Services to investigate him. Taking you over to that plane crash . . . you could have been hurt—even killed—and I would know nothing about it."

My dad sat silently, watching and listening as Mom yelled at me for what she called my thoughtless acts.

"Louise, you're too hard on that boy," he piped in. "When the crash happened, you were nowhere to be found. And besides, if Pete did find you, he knew you would have automatically said no. Give him a break. You can't control everything. Pete's growing up. We need to let him experience the world. You can't tie him to your apron strings forever."

My dad's comments really pissed my mom off. Rather than argue, she violently yanked on the hot water tap and started to fill the small kitchen sink. As soon as she got the water going, she ripped off my clothes.

"Mom, don't do this," I begged. "I'm really sorry I didn't tell you I was going to see the crash with Chip. I won't do it again. Ground me, but don't hurt me."

I noticed my mother's normally immaculately coiffed hair was beginning to lose its shape. Thin loops of strawberry blond were unravelling themselves in the hot steam rising from the sink. She looked deranged.

"Pete, get your shoes off. You're going to be severely punished. You're out of control. You're a bad kid. When I'm finished with you, you'll never do this again, and if you do, you won't be living under this roof anymore."

My dad jumped up. "Louise, you're a total bitch. If you hurt him, I'm calling the cops. I'm not going to fight with you, but I can't let your sick need for punishment drive you to physically destroy our son."

My mom turned on my dad. "Get out of here, Thomas. You don't know what you're talking about, and don't start trying to be a father now. You've been missing in action all Pete's life. Go ahead and call the cops and let's see who they side with. The cops that show up will probably be the ones that come on Sundays, when you're drunk, out of control, and attacking Pete, his sister, and me. Who are they going to believe, Thomas? Get out of here right now, you loser."

My dad stormed out of the kitchen, leaving me alone, in the hands of my mom and her medieval ideas of child discipline. "Get in the sink, Pete!" she screamed.

I refused, so she grabbed my arm, yanked me to my feet, and shoved me to the enamel basin herself. I continued to fight back because I knew what was coming. Our small, single kitchen sink was used for cleaning vegetables, laundering diapers, washing dishes, bathing babies, and on occasion, for torturing me. She slapped me across the face, grabbed my bottom, lifted me onto the kitchen countertop, and forced me into the steaming cauldron. The water was so hot I screamed.

"Dad! Help me! *You can stop her.* Don't let her do this to me."

I heard nothing from my dad. I was scalding. I didn't know what to do. I had no idea what was coming next. Fear now dominated. I wondered, *was she going to kill me?*

I took one more crack at pleading my case. "Mom, you're burning me. Let me out of the sink and I will do anything you want."

"Shut up, Peter. Open your mouth." Again, I refused. She forcibly grabbed my jaw and got some leverage by pushing back my forehead, eventually prying open my mouth while I resisted. I shook my head back and forth and grabbed her hands to force her off me. No dice. Her steel grip prevailed.

My mouth gaped. My mom took a washcloth and loaded it with some kind of soap from a can with an image of a skull and crossbones on it. Below this stark graphic warning, in bright red letters, was the word LYE.

She ground the cloth throughout my mouth, scrubbing my lips, gums, teeth, tongue, and throat. My mouth was immediately on fire. The taste was vile. She pushed the cloth so far down my throat that I gagged and threw up.

"See, you're getting what you deserve, Peter. Don't you *ever* go behind my back again." Then she dropped her face next to mine. Her tone was different, but no less menacing. "Peter, I had to do this. I want you to know it hurts me as much as it hurts you when you make me punish you this way."

"I hate you. I wish you were dead," I yelled from my perch in the kitchen sink. I pulled myself out of the water and grabbed a towel my mother laid beside me. She tried to grab my hand. I shoved her away.

"Peter, you will thank me for this someday. You can't run wild, all over the country, all the time. If you do, you're going to end up getting hurt. It could've happened this afternoon. It didn't. You're so lucky. Now your memory of the lye in your mouth will make you think twice before you disobey me and get yourself in situations that will injure you."

I climbed out of the sink, jumped to the kitchen floor, and ran sobbing up to my room. I could feel the lye blistering my lips, tongue, and throat. My legs, feet, and bottom were burned from the hot water. That, combined with the excruciating pain shooting from my mouth, made me feel like I was on the verge of death. I laid down, still naked, on my little, fake-maple twin bed. I was a boy with a vengeful mother and a missing father. I was alone.

I couldn't sleep. I was up all night. My dad popped into my room around two in the morning. "Pete, you okay? Is there anything I can do to help you? I'm so sorry your mom did this. I couldn't do anything. It would have been World War III. We all would lose. I don't want to leave you, your sister, or your mom. I'll see if we can get you to the doctor tomorrow. We have to be careful going to a hospital or medical clinic. Your mom could get in trouble. She might even be charged with a crime."

My dad didn't say anything more. He slipped out the door and I was left with my thoughts. I didn't know if my mom was a monster, or not. When she was stressed and taken for granted, she overreacted. It couldn't be easy being her. Her husband was an out-of-control alcoholic, she had no education, no job, few friends, and lived a life of poverty. To top it all off, she had a strong-willed son, who at times could seem out of control. Still, even with those pressures, she had no right to engage in child abuse.

***

The lye attack wasn't the first time she lost control and crossed the line. Several years before, I had a pet hamster I named Oscar. My mom hated him. She thought he was dirty and creepy. Some days I would find her watching Oscar run in his exercise wheel, going round and round, getting nowhere.

"Oscar looks like your dad, running like mad, nothing good happening," she'd say.

In what started as a funny situation, it eventually turned disastrous, I woke up one morning and went to feed Oscar. The little gate that opens and closes his cage was ajar. There was no Oscar to be seen anywhere. I scoured the house. I looked under and through the couch, behind curtains, in the pantry—in every room. Oscar was nowhere to be found.

Once school was over, I ditched the Pirates and raced home to continue the search for my furry friend. I busted through the front door and didn't see my mom anywhere. I ran upstairs and found her and my sister taking a nap. Where was Oscar? I looked some more. And then I heard a blood-curdling scream coming from my mom's bedroom.

"It's attacking me! Peter, come and get this monster. It's biting my neck!"

I rushed into my mom's room. There was Oscar, quite comfortable, snuggled against my mom's breast. I grabbed the little critter off of her. This was the funniest thing I had ever seen. I laughed hysterically as I ran back to my room to put Oscar in his cage. I was still laughing when Mom burst in.

"Peter, you little asshole, stop laughing and get that rat thing out of this house! *You are in trouble!*"

I peeled out of my room and ran for the front door. I couldn't believe it—my mom was chasing me! She was screaming, totally out of control, and acting bizarre. She caught me, threw me to the ground, and started beating my head into the dirt. Jerry Kaye's mom was nearby and saw what was going on.

"Louise! Leave Peter alone! If you don't stop hurting him, I'm calling the cops."

"Shut up, Helen," my mom snarled. "Mind your own business." She turned back to me. "Get up, Peter. Hightail it to your room. I don't want to see your face the rest of the day. No dinner for you tonight, mister. I'm not a joke for you to laugh at. Get that animal out of the house right now. If you don't, I'll kill it in the morning."

I got Oscar a reprieve from my mom for a couple of days. In that time, Benny Tail-Feather got permission from his parents to add Oscar to his already robust little critter zoo. And every so often I went to Benny's house for a furry visit.

That was when I was seven, and there I was, two years later at nine-years-old, in pain from my mother's attack and unable to sleep. I drifted further into my thoughts. I realized my mom was not the only culprit in the chaos of our house. My dad was a raging weekend alcoholic. He didn't come home from his work on Fridays. Instead he headed to his favourite bars and beer halls and didn't show up at the house until about five p.m. Sunday evening. Just a few months prior to this incident, the geography for his debauchery was contained within a specific perimeter. He had no car, so he got to his watering holes either by taxi or on foot. It was a good thing, too, because this limited locomotion didn't give him much of a chance to cause a drunken, catastrophic automobile accident.

But his transportation equation had recently changed. Several months ago, my dad showed up at the house on a Wednesday after work with a new car: a black four-door Chevy, Belair. The car's exterior was in surprisingly good shape. The interior seats were worn, but not torn, and it smelled of cigarettes. This didn't bother my dad, though, as he was a smoker. With his new ride, my dad's drinking territory had dramatically expanded. The chance of a killer car wreck was a real possibility.

My mom spent the weekends when my dad was out on the town, commiserating her plight, in long phone calls to her sisters, and my Uncle Jimmy. She was so sad, lamenting her situation, and my father, the Rum Hound, that she didn't eat. My sister and I were left to fend for ourselves. We struggled to fashion three square meals a day from things about the house. We survived on sandwiches, chips, Kool-Aid, and candy.

By Sunday morning my mom's grief would give way to a fireball of targeted anger. "When your dad gets home, if he does, I'm going to smash him in the mouth—really kick his sorry ass. The three of us are leaving. We will move in with one of my sisters. Who needs this shit."

These threats escalated throughout the day. My mom shouted them to no one in particular. By the time Sunday evening rolled around, she had worked herself into a real lather and was raring for a fight. Dad would stumble into the house, still drunk as a skunk, and smelling like a brewery and other women. He would stagger into the kitchen and then the war was on. Pushing, shoving, name-calling, sometimes a punch (usually by my mom to my dad's face). On it went for hours. I would grab my sister, hustle upstairs, rush into my room, and wait for the storm to pass.

Neighbours tuned in every weekend to the Gregg Family Dispute. In the summer, those living closest to us even came out on their porches so they could be closer to the action. Because the demographic shades to the low-income, multi-ethnic, and drug-abusing population, these weekly battles were not surprising, nor anything to get upset about. Rather, they were entertainment—a thrilling serial. Several times the fights between my mom and dad flew completely out of control and my dad would venture out onto the front porch with a torn shirt and bloody nose. Apparently, this was noteworthy enough for the Porch Bleacher Crew, because whenever they saw that, they would panic and call the cops.

It wasn't long before two people in blue would show up. They'd jump in between my mom and dad and get them to separate rooms. They'd threaten each of them with a visit to the police station downtown if they didn't control themselves. They'd check in with me and my sister to see if we were hurt. And then, when they were satisfied there was no more blood or threats about to flow, they'd disappear back into the night.

My mom, dad, sister, and I were left to cope with the blowback. These cooling-off periods didn't take long. The psychological debris spilled over only as far as Wednesday when we returned to Gregg Normal. The silent treatment between my parents turned to the necessary dialogue (well, grunts) of family routine. Armistice. Wounds, physical and emotional, had time to heal, or at least become less obvious, and we settled back into our rhythms until the wheels came off again the following weekend.

I found it all embarrassing. I was embarrassed. For all the time I lived in my parents' house, even up until I left home at sixteen, I would never have a friend over for weekend play, meals, or such. Who knew what would happen to Benny Tail-Feather or Jerry Kaye if they were caught in my family's warzone? Besides, all my friends' moms and dads knew what was going on. They would never allow their kids to come to my house.

***

I barely slept all night. When morning arrived, I heard someone downstairs, clanging pots. I jumped up, put on my dirty jeans and T-shirt, slipped on my gym socks, and padded down the hallway to the bathroom. I wanted to do a damage assessment. I dropped my pants to examine the scalding. Splotches of bright red greeted me. No blisters, but my skin was close to being crispy.

I looked in the mirror, to see what was going on with my mouth. I was shocked. My lips were a deep red, and swollen, cracked, and blistered. I looked inside my mouth. My tongue was twice its normal size, a dark grey, and with white blisters all over it. The insides of my cheeks were abraded and peeling. I tried to say something, but I could only muster a groan. Words weren't coming out of this mouth for some time. And then there was the pain—I couldn't believe how bad it hurt. I left the bathroom and went back to my bed, where I promptly crawled under the covers. As tears ran down my cheeks, I hoped I could find some way to escape the madness.

CHAPTER 7: HELLO, DAVEY

My parents didn't take me to the doctor. Instead, I spent three days in bed being cared for by my mother. Her primary therapies were warm salt water for my mouth, and bandages laced with butter for the burns on my behind, legs, and feet.

"Pete, I'm so sorry you made me hurt you. I'll never forgive us for what we did to you. Please never make me do something like this again. If you start to behave and your dad stops drinking, we'll have a great family."

What the hell did she mean? I made *her* torture *me*? *We* are responsible for her actions? It was such a crock, but even at my young age, I was sure this delusional thinking was the only way she could rationalize her behaviour. Each day of my convalescence I heard more of this crazy talk. I didn't respond. I just sunk further into my disgust and fear. The Pirates kept coming by, wondering when I'd be ready for more chills and thrills, or at least when I'd be ready to assault fifth grade.

My mom didn't dare let me be seen by anyone until I was healed. Finally, on the morning of the fourth day, I couldn't stand being anchored to my bed any longer. I got up to check my wounds.

My lips were no longer liver-red, and the swelling was down. They were still cracked and bleeding, but they looked a damn sight better than they did when I first checked the mirror a few days before. I could now speak a few words without exploding in searing pain. I looked at the scalding I took on my behind, legs, and feet. I was amazed they were no longer red, just somewhat blistered. It seemed my mom's old-fashioned butter remedy for burns was working. I was ready to join the world again.

Once dressed, I headed for the front door. My mom was at the kitchen table with my dad, and both were having breakfast. She was eating toast and tea—he was working on his usual eggs and bacon. "A real rancher's breakfast!" as he put it. He was also smoking a cigarette. He tapped his ashes onto the plate, and when he was done, he stamped out the finished stick in what remained of his egg yolk. This really bothered me. The smell was putrid and I found the gesture revolting. The grey ash from his doused butt would swirl into the curdled, yellow goo and languish there until my mom cleared his plate.

Despite the normal appearance of a family meal, eating breakfast together was not routine in our family. Nor had our household fostered other conventions, like the basics of personal hygiene: brushing my teeth, washing my hands, or taking a regular shower or bath. I knew something was not quite right, because when I spent time at friends' homes, their families regularly engaged in habits of health, cleanliness, and social wellbeing. Once I became aware of the radical discrepancy between my family's unhealthy patterns and the more positive lifestyles of my friends, I started to change my ways. I was wise to the fact that some of my friends' parents viewed me, the Gregg boy, as riff raff, and I was eager to incline their opinions of me in a more positive direction. I began to brush my teeth twice a day, shower regularly, and wash my hands for consistent hygiene.

Once I questioned my mom about this. "Why didn't you teach me how to brush my teeth? Why didn't you insist I take a regular shower—not just when I was covered in mud? Why don't we wash our hands before eating and after using the washroom? And why don't we have clean underwear and clothes to wear each day? My friends' parents make sure their kids do all these good things. I never heard a word about any of this from you."

"Peter," she had shouted. "We are not country club people. We are the working class. We don't have the money and didn't have the folks, to teach us those fancy ways of living. It's all I can do to get food on the table, raise your little sister, and deal with your dad's drinking and your bad behaviour. I don't have time to worry about your little needs, like brushing your teeth, or taking a shower. You're on your own. Don't blame me for being a grimy kid."

After breakfast, I brushed past them. My mom turned around in her chair. "Peter, I forgot to mention it to you, but while you were in bed resting up, we were supposed to go to a student/teacher orientation with Mrs. Bear, your new teacher. I called her and explained how your cold had forced you to bedrest, and asked if we could come at another time. She understood completely and we set the new meeting for tomorrow. I think your friends are seeing Mrs. Bear today. So, you will be pretty much on your own this afternoon—and that's a good thing. You don't need to be running around the neighbourhood with those hooligans just yet."

I couldn't believe it. In bed, resting? Sick from a cold? My mom really couldn't face the reality of the havoc she caused. She had graduated to trying to convince other people of her confabulations. Not just me. I was determined to get outside and not waste my time arguing. Maybe I could catch the Pirates before they headed to school.

I spotted them clumped together at the far end of the Plaza. I caught Bill's eye. He shouted, "Gregg, get your ass over here. You've been gone so long we thought you were dead."

I cruised over to my tribe, a sudden feeling of peace washing over me. I was where I belonged.

Benny stared at me. "My God man, what happened to your lips? You look like you went fifteen rounds with the world champ, and you came out on the short end of the stick."

"Shut up, Benny!" Jerry Kaye said. "Pete's mom did this to him. She blew a gasket because Peter went to the B-47 crash site with Chip Arden without telling her."

Then Mike said, "My mom is always saying she can't understand why Pete's mom is always laying into him. She says Pete is no worse than the rest of us. She thinks it's criminal what Pete's mom does to him."

I was relieved to hear I wasn't so far gone in some parents' eyes after all—that I wasn't completely lumped-in with my family's drama. Since I had launched my self-imposed redemption campaign, my new hygiene regimen, it looked like there was some hope for my case.

I had trouble talking, swollen lips, thick tongue and all, but managed a raspy, "It's really not that bad, guys. My mom just loses her temper easily. She can fly off the handle, crush anybody or anything in sight. I was just unlucky enough to get in her way the other night. I paid the price."

My friends looked unconvinced. Benny jumped in again. "Pete, are your mom or dad taking you to the doctor?"

Jerry responded quickly. "If Pete's mom takes him to the doctor, they're going to be suspicious of his injuries. They might even call in the cops. Pete's mom could get in real trouble."

No one said anything in response to Jerry Kaye's insight. She was a good mediator and I was relieved for her efforts. I didn't like too much of this kind of attention on me. Mike caught on and changed the subject. "In just a few minutes we're all going to the orientation to meet Mrs. Bear. Are you coming?"

I explained that my mom called Mrs. Bear to postpone our meeting until tomorrow. I told them I wasn't sure how she was going to explain my mouth. The group looked a bit worried again.

Benny put his arm around me. "Okay, pal. Well, we'll see you when we get home. You better get well soon. We have a vicious game of I Dare You coming up on Saturday."

The Pirates scattered so they could get to school on time with their moms. I drifted back to the house. My dad had gone to work, and my mom was making a quick trip to the store with my sister. I was on my own again. Instead of going inside, I sat down on the top step of our front porch. I'd created a game to play to keep my head busy (a common protocol of mine), for when I was alone, had time to kill, and could sit on something high off the ground. The steps of my porch were perfect. I call this particular game, Jac-Ball.

It was a simple game. I always carried a Jac-Ball in my jean's front pocket, just for times like this. The thunk-thunk sound the ball made on the cement and the comfort of the catch, soothed me. The required concentration and repetitive rhythms always reduced my stress and anxiety.

I taught the Pirates the game, too, and we had several tournaments. Benny always won. He had great numbers and his ball flew higher on each bounce than any of ours. We admired the level of difficulty with which he engaged the game. On that day, I was satisfied with easy Jac-Ball.

I was thunking along in my court space when an older kid I had never seen before came up and just plopped down beside me. The intrusion really bothered me. First, I had to stop my game, and then I had to deal with this stranger. The guy is short and fat with brown hair. Dark stubble covered his face and he had some pimples on his forehead and cheeks. He was dressed in a white polo shirt, dark blue jeans with ironed-in creases, and well-worn blue sneakers. I guessed he was fifteen or sixteen.

"Hey," I said. "Can't you see I've got a game going here? You sorta ruined my play. What's the story? And oh, what did you say your name was?" I had a hard time hiding my annoyance. This kid didn't seem to pick up on my undertone of, "Please leave me be. I'm busy."

"Sorry. My name is Davey Watson," he said. "And I jumped on your step 'cause you looked so lonely. What the hell happened to your mouth? Swallow poison? And yeah, who the hell are you?"

I was a little baffled by his candour, offended even. "I'm Peter Gregg. You might say I tangled with poison, but that's another story."

"Are you the kid that Mike Anderson told me about? The one that thinks he caused those two B-47s to crash. Crazy thinking, man."

"Yeah, I guess that's me," I said. "I don't think it's wacky to think you may have caused it when you yell 'they're crashing' and then some planes bite the biscuit."

He went on. "My Aunt Peaches lives here in The Project and is taking care of me while my mom and dad complete their divorce."

I knew his Aunt Peaches. She was very nice. But I wondered how she could take care of this kid when she worked all day and tended bar four nights a week.

He elaborated as if he'd read my mind. "I'm old enough to take care of myself, though. All I need is a place to sleep, food in the refrigerator, and the adults in my life off my back. Since my aunt is never around, it's perfect."

"Wow," I thought. I really admired Davey's freedom, but I wasn't sure I was ready to face the big world on my own, even though things at home were rough. I squeezed my Jac-Ball.

"Hey, Pete. Do you like comic books? I saved a bunch of money over the summer and bought new editions of Superman, Tarzan, and Batman. I haven't read any of them yet. How about you come over tomorrow morning after my Aunt Peaches goes to work? We can check out the comics, feast on baloney-and-chip sandwiches, and swig it all down with Cokes. But we can only do the eating part of our comic book party if your mouth can stand food. Whaddaya think? Sounds great, right?"

I paused. I did like comic books. But it was a bit weird that this teenage kid wanted to spend his time with me. Maybe his friends just weren't that into comics.

"Gee, Davey, I don't know," I said. "I'll have to check it out with my mom. We have student/teacher orientation tomorrow and I'm not sure what time it starts. Plus, I'm in heaps of trouble over going to the B-47 crash site. But if I can sweet-talk my mom into an okay, the comic book party sounds like a ton of fun. I'll let you know in the morning. My friends and I hang out on the far side of the Plaza most mornings. Stop by there, and I'll have an answer for you."

"Okay, Pete. I'm sure you can make it happen." Davey got up, shook my hand, and left.

A short time later, Mom and my sister returned from the store. Once my sister was securely stowed in her playpen, my mom scurried from pantry, to refrigerator, to flour bin, to Lazy Susan, to stow the groceries in their proper places. I had come inside to scour the pantry for snacks.

A box of frozen fish sticks and two cans of creamed corn were left out on the table, signalling the menu for another fast food supper. It wasn't that my mom was a bad cook, but rather that she saw preparing meals was akin to watching paint dry on the wall—a boring waste of time. The least effort for the desired result was her operating rule.

"Hey, Mom?" I try to catch her attention in mid-flight from the pantry to the refrigerator. "What time is our meeting with Mrs. Bear tomorrow?"

"It's at three p.m. Why do you ask?"

"Well, I met this kid today. He's Peaches' nephew and he's staying with her for a while. You know Peaches, right?"

"Of course, I do. I didn't know she had family in the area."

"Well, anyway, he invited me over to Peaches' house for a comic book party. He has new editions of some of my favourite superheroes. You know, like *Superman*, *Batman*? He wants me to come over at about ten in the morning, and we'll check out his collection until about 12:30. I'll be back home with plenty of time to make our meeting with Mrs. Bear. Can I do it?"

My mom had gotten out the step-stool and was putting away a box of Premium Plus soda crackers above the refrigerator. She rummaged a bit in the cupboards to make room. "I don't know this Davey kid, do I? Is Peaches, or any other kids, going to be there? What about your other friends, are they going to feel jilted?" It was rare for her to ask after them.

"I'm sure you don't know Davey," I replied, "but he seems like a good guy. I don't know if anyone else is going to be there, and the Pirates are going to be busy shopping for school supplies, so they'll be out of the picture."

She looked down for a moment.

"Okay, Pete. You can go, but I want to meet this Davey c̶ ter tomorrow when you come back from Peaches' house. I'm not completely comfortable with you hanging around strange kids I don't know."

I was so lucky my mom didn't ask how old Davey was, but I thought she was clear on Peaches' work schedule. I heard about it from her while she gossiped with some neighbours in The Project. You see, my dad goes to her bar. She must have been aware of the high probability that Davey and I would be alone together in our comic book frenzy. Perhaps she'd forgotten because if she had zeroed-in on any of these factors there would have been no way she'd be okay with such a dubious venture.

I spent the day catching up on some of my own comic books. I wanted to brush up on my All-Star Western strips, as well as my copies of the action, adventure, and detective comic series, so I'd be primed for my morning at Davey's.

Later, my dad arrived home. He was quickly out of his work duds and sitting at the kitchen table with his attention focused squarely on a series of his own; a three-ring binder of modules. Not comics, though. He was taking an insurance sales course. I'm sure, despite his reticence, that his low-paying, suffocating work as an aerospace engineering technician heightened his obvious depression, alcoholism, and social deviance. It was bewildering, but encouraging, to see him aspiring to a new path in life. Maybe he just needed a little encouragement. His boss, for whatever reason, had taken a real shine to him and helped him find and enrol in the course. He even promised that if my dad passed his state qualification exams, he would make sure he got a real shot at a new job selling insurance.

My dad had the right idea in keeping busy, because my mom, although she hated cooking, could not stand anyone intruding on her meal prep. I was very hungry, so I tried to pitch in to speed the process along, but in two nanoseconds she pushed me out of the way. No harm done, though, because a few minutes later, our plates were filled with breaded fish sticks, golden mounds of creamed corn, boiled frozen peas, and salad with sweet French dressing on it.

My dad didn't lift his head, eating while he studied. My mom was trying to spoon a concoction of processed peas into my sister's mouth as quickly as she could, before being made a target for the green slime spit from the highchair. As for me, I just crammed the food on my plate down as fast as I could so I could escape. The only sounds were our clinking cutlery. I finished quickly and pushed myself away from the table with a cursory, "May I be excused?" This is one of the few fancy phrases we did engage in with my family.

The Cisco Kid was going to be on, and I wanted to be in front of the television to avoid missing the start of the episode. Just as I was about to push past my mom on my way to the front room and the television set—a new extravagance in our home, bought on credit from the local Co-Op—she pulled me aside and motioned for me to join her in the furnace room.

All the houses located in The Project were heated by coal, so coal management was a constant for the families who lived there. It started with coal delivery to big concrete coal bins situated in the back of The Project's parking lot. Families came to the coal bins with collecting buckets, which they filled and took back to their houses. Each house had a furnace room. Each furnace room contained a large coal container and a furnace. Individual family members took turns filling the furnace with coal so there was constant heat. Furnace rooms were usually blighted with coal dust and soot and tracked in dirt. A trip to the furnace room, if you were not filling the furnace, was a signal of sharing dark secrets, or dire admonitions.

I followed my mom into the dungeon, with dread. What was she going to do to me? Was another lye job coming? I cowered against the wall to the side of the furnace's stuffing door. I felt like I was about to melt into a hot puddle.

"Pete, I wanted to talk to you before we meet Mrs. Bear tomorrow. I think it's best we tell her your mouth's blisters and cracks were caused by you mistakenly eating too much hot sauce. If we told the truth, Mrs. Bear might overreact and tell someone who might want to punish me."

Punish you? Not a bad idea! I thought. But I pushed these ideas of retribution out of my mind as I was focused on getting to my television show and didn't want to start another row.

"Pete, you understand me?"

I said nothing. I was awaiting some physical retaliation for something or another. But instead she just said, "Okay, well, tomorrow we leave for our meeting at 2:45. Wear your new jeans and red polo. You have to look sharp for Mrs. Bear."

I stumbled out of the furnace room. I was relieved that I got off easy that time. But there was no *Cisco Kid* coming from the front room. Instead, it was my dad's favourite radio show, *The Grand Ole Opry*. There was no way I could shake him from his recliner, a beer, and Minnie Pearl's plucky hillbilly routine. I knew from experience that no matter how much I pleaded, *The Grand Ole Opry* always trumped *The Cisco Kid*. Sadly, I went upstairs. Despite his recent studiousness, old habits die hard, and I heard the clink of another bottle and a, "How-Deeeee!" from both my father and Minnie on the main floor.

I was lucky there was another radio in my room. I could catch *Sergeant Preston of the Yukon*. It was a good alternative to my preferred Western—not the same as the TV, but exciting nonetheless. I listened to Preston and his dog King fight really bad guys, while I got ready for bed. Once my PJs were on and my mouth was gargled with salt water, I climbed under the sheets and looked out my bedroom window from my pillow.

I looked deeply into the darkening sky. Things were changing. Summer was giving way to autumn. The sky was a cold, sharp blue, with clouds ripping by at top speed. The wind moved slow, but there was a slight nip in the air. Leaves would fall from the trees, birds would go away, butterflies would leave or die, and the world would turn brown before the refreshing white of the first snowfall. For the first time, I felt the hot breath of time, of life, moving by. Like my natural world, I too, was changing. The crash of the B-47, my mom's lye attack, the anxious inquiries of the Pirates—all worked in a flurry of opposites to provide a catalyst for some great change around the corner.

***

Later in my life, music offered me much meaning and joy. It painted many tapestries, and pointed poetic pathways to the answers of life's great questions. When I think back to these lonely, early September days, it's music that filled my memories. What I hear is Neil Young's plaintive song, "Helpless." The stark imagery and haunting melody capture my mood when I remember the days that came after meeting Davey.

Helpless, helpless, helpless …

CHAPTER 8: PYJAMA GAME

The next morning, I woke and followed my mom's directions to look sharp and dive directly into my new jeans and red polo. I knew I'd gotten gussied up a couple of hours early, but since I was playing with Davey in his house (and not with the Pirates, outside, where rolling in the dirt was a must), I was sure I'd be presentable for Mrs. Bear later. I headed downstairs. My mom and dad were nowhere in sight. This was the breakfast routine I was more accustomed to. I grabbed an apple and a piece of toast, and made a beeline for the door, hoping against all hope I would not run into my parents.

Then I was out on the porch. Davey was slouching in the same spot where I'd met him yesterday.

"Sleep in, Peter? Do you always get up this late? School is starting next week, so you'd better get used to an early start. Thank God, the school thing is over for me. As soon as I'm eighteen, liberated from parents, cops, foster homes, and juvie, I'm getting a job. I'll have my own money, girls, and lots of sex."

"Davey," I asked, "how are you going to get a job if you have no education? My dad says the quickest way to become a loser is no school, no diploma, no training. That sounds like you, Davey."

"Yeah, Pete, people say that shit to me all the time. But let me ask you a question. Did Louis Armstrong go to high school? Was Henry Ford a college graduate? Absolutely not. They were smart and found a way to make it on their own. What I know—what I learned in jail, juvenile hall, and hustling on the streets—is that men will pay a lot of money for dirty magazines, dirty pictures, and sex with women. You're too young, but sex—you don't even know what that is, do you? Well, sex *always* sells. I'm going to figure out how to give guys what they want. You watch. I'm going to make it big. You can tell your dad to stick school up his ass."

Davey was right. I didn't know what he was talking about. He sounded wrong, dangerous, and weird. If the Pirates heard Davey's B.S. they would be rolling on the ground laughing their asses off at this sissy who made no sense.

Davey continued. "Pete, I'll see you about ten. I hope you're ready for a good time."

I spied the Pirates over at our meet-up. I got to my feet. "Sure, I'll see you in a little while. But you sounded strange a minute ago. I'm not interested in any of your job plans—comics and baloney sandwiches are great. No more sex talk, okay?"

I followed the broken sidewalk over to the Plaza. I noted the weeds in the cracks and around the borders slowly overtaking the slabs of the cement path. Just as I got to our hiding place, Jerry Kaye and the gang were getting ready to leave.

"Hey, Pete we're all out of here in a second," she said. "We had a good orientation yesterday. It's too bad you couldn't make it. But no harm done—soon enough we'll all be together in class anyways."

Jerry Kaye looks towards her four plex. Her mom was standing there next to Mike's, and looking at her watch. "Now it's time to shop for school supplies. Our moms are on our backs to get it over with today. We talked all of them into taking us shopping at the same time so we could get home and have Pirate time later. You want to come along? I know it'd be cool with my mom if you came with us."

I was relieved to have something else on the docket today. Not because I didn't want to go along with my friends, but because if my mom found out I went on a school shopping expedition with all my pals and their parents, her non-invitation would go over like a lead balloon.

Bill spoke up. "Hey, who's the guy you were talking to over on your steps? He sure looks a lot older than us."

"Sorry, guys. I can't go. My mom and I are meeting with Mrs. Bear in a little while, so I must stick around. And yeah, that guy on the steps is a lot older than us. His name is Davey. He's okay. He has a great new comic book collection he's invited me to come and see. I'm going over to his Aunt Peaches' this morning to check it out. If it looks good, I think all of us could have a reading party with Davey."

I offered this last part, perhaps a bit too hopefully. No one said anything. I could tell the Pirates were not impressed with my brilliant Davey idea. Mike announced it was time for the Pirates to rendezvous with their moms for pencils, pads, and notebooks. Three moms stood by, chatting and eager to get on with the dance of consumption. They looked like they were going to enjoy this even more than their kids. They waved to me. My friends drifted towards their parents and I was left with my reflections.

It was around 9:30. I decided to go to Davey's a little early. I knew it was okay, because I'd just seen Davey's Aunt Peaches head to work. I turned right and took the sidewalk leading to her house. The weeds were thicker there. Before I got very far, I heard, "Hey Pete— wait up!"

It was Benny Tail-Feather. I stopped and Benny came over and stood beside me. "Pete, I know you've had a tough few days. I just wanted you to know all of us Pirates are with you all the way. We're so sorry about what your mom did to you. My God, what an awful thing. We're going to play B-47 again next weekend. Jerry Kaye and I want a chance to get even and you need to be there. After all, you're our ace Flight Derby set-up guy and we need you to get a new course ready to go for a big tournament in a couple of weeks."

Flight Derby was a simple game within B-47 involving home-made ramps that, when hit at the right angle and at the right speed, launched bike and rider into the air. The one who jumped the farthest, won. I was usually in charge of designing and setting up the track on a patch of asphalt we swept clean. It was pretty straightforward to get organized; we had ramps that we repurposed every summer. I enjoyed the flight from the purpose-built plywood inclines, but not so much the injuries that went along with the landings (when the rubber meets the road, so to speak).

Benny turned and glanced behind him. "I gotta go for now, though. My mom's waiting, but I wanted to talk privately before we hit the stores with the others."

"Sounds great, Benny. Setting up a new course is always a blast. How about we do it together?"

Over his shoulder, Benny yelled as he walked away, "Okay, Pete. Pirates will see you this afternoon."

What Benny didn't know was that I lied, which was against Pirate code. A Pirate should never lie to a fellow Pirate. But I could never play B-47 again. The memories of my irresponsible shout of, "They're crashing!", the planes on fire, the bodies in the field, and my mom's resulting lye attack preyed on me from a place that was dark and deeply-etched.

***

My overwhelming, negative reaction to these memories was a common phenomenon of those who had experienced horrific events in their lives. This dramatic trauma is often recalled in precise and vivid detail, and these heavy remembrances can persist throughout a lifetime. At work are the levels of a few powerful neurotransmitters, namely norepinephrine and epinephrine, in the brain. When activated, these hormones key the fight-or-flight response and encode memories into the hippocampus and amygdalae, the important memory and learning structures that reside within the brain's limbic system. The limbic system is sometimes referred to as the emotional brain, and is unique to mammals, distinguishing them from other cerebral lifeforms.

Sometimes, during a particularly catastrophic event, these stress hormones serve to lock in the experience. The incidental details of the surrounding circumstances quickly decay, like the trivial details of day-to-day life that are here today, murky tomorrow. The traumatic episode remains in all its unadulterated glory. For the victims of trauma, tomorrow never comes. There is no escape. Life is continuously harrowed by the bad experiences.

Little did I know then, that my already lit-up midbrain, my emotional hard drive, was going to become overloaded with the data of what was about to take place.

***

I continued my walk to Davey's house. I was no longer excited by the thought of his comic book party. Instead I felt sad and alone, and had a sense of foreboding. I climbed the stairs leading to the front porch, then knocked on the door. It popped open slightly.

"Hey Pete, is that you?" a squeaky voice called from upstairs. It was Davey. I hadn't noticed until now how weak his voice was. "I'm running a little late—still getting dressed."

"Yeah, Davey, it's me. Want me to come back later?"

"No, don't you think about it. Come on in and shut the door behind you. I'll be ready in a minute."

"Okay, Davey. I'll wait in the kitchen." I grabbed a chair at the kitchen table. I had not been in Davey's Aunt Peaches' house before. Once I looked around, I was blown away. Peaches' home was laid out exactly like ours, and as far as I could tell, it had the same configuration of furnace room, kitchen, and living room on the first floor, with the bedrooms and bath on the second. But the floorplan was where the similarities ended—it was no basic, utilitarian set-up like my house. The colour on the walls was the same: a beautiful, warm, light yellow. The kitchen appliances were a shiny black lacquer and stainless-steel pots and pans hung neatly from the ceiling. The couches in the living room were white leather, and wooden Midwest antiques finished off the décor. There were interesting, nicely-framed photographs of family and friends on the walls. I'd never been in such a warm and inviting place. For a moment, I was put at ease.

Davey's voice interrupted my surveillance. "Pete, come up to my bedroom. I'm all dressed now and have the comics laid out so you can take a quick gander and decide which ones you want to read."

"Great, Davey. On my way." I hustled up the stairs. "Man, I can't believe how spectacular your Aunt Peaches' house is. It must be amazing to live in such a beautiful home."

As I got closer to Davey's room, I started to question what the hell I was doing. I didn't know Davey from Adam. He was six years older than me, and to say he was a bit weird would be an understatement. If my mom was aware of what I was up to, alone with Davey, to do who knows what, she would've blown a gasket.

Davey greeted me in the hallway right in front of his bedroom door. I immediately noticed something was strange. Davey was not dressed in the usual teenage garb of jeans, polo, sneakers. Instead he was wearing red plaid pyjamas, a black T-shirt, a ratty burgundy robe, and wool-lined slippers. I stared at him. I was convinced I didn't belong there.

"Pete, what's wrong? You're looking at me funny. Probably because I still have my PJs on. I decided since we'd be playing inside today, I would get really comfy and wear my most relaxing stuff, maybe take a bath in a little while. And yeah, if we decide to play together another time, you could bring your pyjamas along so you and I are in the same flow. Whaddaya think?"

"Pyjamas? *Taking a bath?* What are you, *crazy*, Davey?" I grasped for something to say. I wanted to leave, but all that came out was, "How about we stick to comics for today?" I felt like it was my only viable option—I was too flabbergasted and incredulous to navigate down a flight of steps.

Davey smiled and said, "Hey, no problem, Pete." He stood aside and waved me into his room.

He was set up in one of the bedrooms. It was nicely furnished like the main floor, but there was some evidence of its new, younger tenant, even though he hadn't really been there long enough make a substantial mark. A half-finished plate of food on the highboy dresser against the wall, and a few items of clothing hanging in the closet and on the back of a chair were his most glaring contributions. Besides, of course, the one I was there for. All sorts of brightly coloured comics were arranged atop his bed so they resembled the tail of a peacock. What a collection. He had all the big publishers, *Archie, Atlas, DC, Dell, Harvey*. And most of them were still in their plastic sleeves. If I'd had all these, I would have had a hard time resisting tearing them open.

"Wow, Davey, this is great!" I couldn't help myself. I climbed onto the bed.

I tried to lose myself in a *Wild Western* for the next half hour and put the pyjamas and bath debacle out of my mind. I glanced over at Davey from time to time. He was on the bed across from me and reading a copy of something I hadn't seen before, but I chalked it up to my vision not being so great out of the corners of my eyes. I was pretty well-versed with comics. Once I was finished catching up with *Kid Colt* and the *Black Rider*, I reached into the fan splayed out on the bedspread and drew a copy of *Strange Tales*. It turned out to be too gory for my taste, so I settled into a *Laugh* for some Jughead instead. As I searched the pile for my next comic escape, I was going to ask Davey what he was reading, but the cover looked even stranger close-up and I could tell it was not a title my mom would buy for me. In fact, I didn't think it was a comic book at all. It was a magazine. But there was something *off* about it. I began to feel a little funny again. This time, though, I thought I had the courage to leave.

"Hey, Davey? I think I hear my mom calling. I better cut our comic book session short and head home."

"Peter, I was looking out my bedroom window just before you got here and I saw your mom leaving with your sister. It looked like they were going shopping. Probably not back yet. If you're worried about what your mom will say about us playing together, I'll be glad to get dressed and as soon as she's home I'll go and have a chat with her—explain everything. She'll be cool when she hears from me."

I panicked. If Davey caught up with my mom and started to explain, in his high-pitched voice, about comic fun and games, he and I alone in Peaches' house, I'd be dead meat. More soap torture for me was a high probability and calling the cops on Davey, a certainty.

"Davey, don't you dare talk to my mom. If you do, it's curtains for me, and you will be in real trouble. You don't know what my mom's capable of."

"Let her try, Pete. There's nothing she can do to me that others haven't already. And by the way, after I talk to her, everything's going to be *cool*. Pete, I know you're a little shy, so for now, you'd better go home. Comics can wait. But come back tomorrow morning at nine. If you do, I'll keep my mouth shut. But if you don't show, I will spill the beans to your mom, and we'll see what that gets you."

I was terrified. I ran from Davey's room, down the stairs, and out the door. It was noon, and as I emerged back to the Plaza, I saw Benny, Jerry, Mike, and Bill, back from school supply shopping. Jerry yelled over to me. "Pete, my mom bought strawberry and chocolate ice cream cups from the Good Humor Man, and we've been waiting to lick some spoons together. Can your mouth handle it? It's soft ice cream. It should be okay."

I couldn't focus on what Jerry was saying. My thoughts of Davey, the creep, were crowding out everything going on around me. I was afraid and could barely respond. "Ice cream spoons would be great, but I have to get going. My mom and I are meeting with Mrs. Bear in just a little while."

Mike said, "Pete, you're going to really like Mrs. Bear. She's very nice and seems like she's going to be a good teacher."

"Hey Pete, even I, who hates school most of the time, liked Mrs. Bear," Benny added. "I think we're going to have great time in fifth grade with her."

"Sounds great, guys," I said. "I'll see you tomorrow."

I headed for my house. I needed some time to process all that happened. I saw my mom had parked her car in front of the coal bin again, something the residents didn't appreciate. As I got nearer to our four plex, the front door opened and out stepped my mom with . . . *Davey*! No pyjamas this time. Jeans, a T-shirt, and white sneakers were front and centre.

Oh my God, I thought. He's talking to her. He's told her everything about our weird party. My goose is cooked. I squatted near the edge of the porch, out of sight.

But my mom was not freaking out. To my surprise, she was *laughing*. "Davey, I don't know why, but I like and trust you," I heard her say. "I'm telling you, though, there is to be no *monkey business*. If you screw up, I'll have your head. Understood?"

Davey chuckled. "Mrs. Gregg, Peter's a good kid. We'll have a good time with the comics, and you know Mrs. G, Peter hanging out with me is a positive thing. I'll teach him about growing up and being a good person, just like in Cub Scouts. And besides, I know you need a break for yourself every now and then, so when Pete's with me, it's time for you."

My mom waved Davey off and as she turned to go back inside, she must have caught a glimpse of my bright red polo. "Oh Pete, you're here. Let's get ready for our meeting with Mrs. Bear. We have to go soon. Davey filled me in on the great time you guys had checking out his comics collection. Pete, I like this guy. I think it's okay if you spend time with him every so often. It's about time you had a good male role model in your life."

CHAPTER 9: GOODBYE, MRS. BEAR

My mom had the funny habit of giving her cars names. A Carla, Rita, and Dolores sat in our parking spots over the years. But the most eccentric name belonged to her current vehicle. An old, bright-red sedan she called, Porsche. Initially, I don't think she knew anything about the famous German sports car. She must have come across the name on its own in some magazine. Once she realized her car had the same name as the prestigious German sports car, she loved asking parking attendants to bring up her Porsche (on the rare occasion we happened to be somewhere with a valet service—usually a department store). She delighted in the mixed reactions of the staff, when all they could locate in the stall indicated on the ticket stub was an aged Ford.

"Pete! Hurry up. We're late. Go ahead and get into Porsche. I'll be there in just a few minutes."

Being late was nothing new for my mom. Her tardiness was such a predictable thing that I would tell her we need to be wherever we were going at least twenty minutes before the real start time. And surprise, surprise, even with the time fudge she was usually lagging behind, the deadline shaved to the thinnest margin. That day we had a certain time set by the school, I couldn't play my fudge game. We were five minutes away from the start of our meeting and we hadn't even left yet.

My mom never seemed concerned about the inconvenience and disrespect she showed others through her disregard for time commitments. When I was involved in her time theft, I became anxious. When I grew older, I still wasn't able to abide being late. I lose respect for those who waste my time with broken promises and nonchalance with their word. In fact, my personal operating mantra became: Tell the Truth, Keep Your Word, and Be On Time. I realized this was a very prescriptive code, but for difficult times and decision making, it served as my brightest lodestar.

My mom finally jumped into the car, which was still parked in front of the coal bin. We headed out of The Project's parking lot and turned onto the narrow two-lane road that wound its way for two miles to the school. As we made our trip to see Mrs. Bear, Mom decided to talk to me about the power of a good education.

She turned down the jazz playing on the radio and launched into her story.

"Peter, I would have given anything to go to school. I didn't have the chance. My dad died of a massive heart attack when I was twelve, and my mother had no commercial skills so she couldn't get a job. This meant I had to find work to help our family. I had two sisters and brothers still at home. So, I took on two full-time jobs—mornings and evenings, plus a part-time gig here and there to make sure my siblings continued their education. I had no choice: I was the oldest.

"But I was envious. Every time I saw my sisters or brothers packing their lunches and heading to school, I would be stuck getting myself ready to work three jobs from eight a.m. to midnight. Until I met your dad, I worked cleaning hotels, packing meat, waitressing, and tending bar. It was rough and we barely survived. I don't feel sorry for myself, but man-oh-man, I would have loved a real education.

"I will work my tail off making sure you have the opportunity to go to school and achieve all you can. Your job is to study hard, get good grades, and become a *really good man*. If you hit the books, you can escape The Project and never again have to live the way we do now."

I sunk low into my seat. I felt like I'd been straight-shooting for a life of hell recently. not one of any kind of upstanding person. I had to pull myself up by my bootstraps.

We arrived at the school parking lot. It was blisteringly hot and humid. My shirt was already sticking to my back, and I saw sweat forming on my mom's upper lip and brow. Huge white, billowing clouds drifted by, coupled with a gentle breeze, lightly fluffing our hair. It smelled like rain was coming.

We climbed out of Porsche and headed for the school. The building was one of those marvels of World War II construction—a flat roof supported by grey cinder block. Sturdy, serious, and full of purpose. A large athletic field, still bright green, signaled summer was not quite ready to surrender to autumn. The pitch gave way to a coarse cement walkway which led up to massive steps that took you to two large front doors. A pair of domineering flag poles - one flying the national flag, and the other, the state's - stood at attention to the right of the entrance. The only disruption to this no-nonsense picture of a school of stern pedigree was the bright teal trim on the windows and doors. All in all, the school shouted, "You're here to learn, grow, and change. *No frivolity allowed!*"

We were late. We sprinted past the field, up the steps, and emerged through the heavy entrance doors to a dimly lit hallway. The floor was covered in greenish-grey industrial carpet. The walls were painted in a muted, off-white colour. There was nothing on the them except a framed copy of the Declaration of Independence. Most impactful was the smell; a dank, musty, sour odour permeated the place.

We stopped the first person we saw. She was a young woman, dressed neatly in a black dress with matching stockings and shoes. She appeared to be quite upset. Tears ran down her cheeks and she had a handkerchief twisted around her fingers, covered in her smudged makeup.

"Sorry to intrude," my mom said, curiously. "We're here to see Mrs. Bear. Could you direct us to where we might find her? Although, this must not be a good time for you. Should we find someone else for directions?"

"Oh no, that's quite all right," she said as she tried to hide her handkerchief. "There's a very difficult situation going on at the school today. We're all quite involved in it–it's very serious. As you can see, I'm pretty upset. I'm sorry, but may I ask a question? Are you Mrs. Gregg and is this Peter?"

"Yes." My mother appeared confused.

The woman brightened for a moment. "Ms. Schaffer would like to see you and Peter in her office. I'll show you the way."

We followed our guide down the hallway, past several empty classrooms with desks stacked against the walls. Janitorial staff scurried about putting the final touches on upgrades for next week's opening. Some people, who looked like they might be teachers, loitered in one of the classrooms. Most seemed to be in the same mood as the woman leading us. Finally, we arrived at a large office with a sign above the door that read: Ms. Schaffer, Principal.

We entered a cavernous, brightly lit room. The walls here were painted in a calming peach colour. There were plants everywhere, and a substantial oak desk with a CEO chair sat in front of a large window. Around the desk in a semicircle were four black, vinyl tub seats, and across the office on a large sidewall was an informal meeting area with a couch, coffee table, and two easy-chairs.

"Dorthy, this is Louise Gregg and her son, Peter. Guys, this is our amazing school principal, Dorthy Schaffer."

Principal Schaffer was a tall, elegant woman who looked to be somewhat older than my mom. She had long, dark hair and a serious, but kind, face. Her long fingers were shaped like a ballet dancer's, and I noted she wasn't married because she had no rings at all. A short span of pearls set off her beautifully tailored green-beige business suit. This was a person I'd listen to.

Ms. Schaffer stood from her chair and moved from behind her desk to greet us. "Mrs. Gregg. Can I call you Louise?"

"Of course. Okay if it's Louise and Dorthy?" My mom was in cordial mode. They shook hands.

"Sure, that sounds great. I think we're off to a good start. Before we chat, just let me say goodbye to Sandra so she can get back to work." The principal nodded and smiled to our guide. "Thanks, Sandra. And by the way, Louise, Peter, this is Sandra Brooks and she's going to be Pete's teacher for next year."

"Great to finally meet you guys," Mrs. Brooks said. "Peter, I'm so looking forwards to you joining our sixth-grade class. I know you might feel a bit afraid, but if we work together, we will make sure sixth grade is a great learning experience and a blast for you."

She turned from me to my mother. "Mrs. Gregg, it was very nice meeting you, too. After school starts, if you have any questions or concerns related to Pete, please feel free to give me a call." She addressed the principal, who had made her way back behind the giant desk. "Thanks again, Dorthy. I hope the next time we're together it will be under happier circumstances. We'll talk soon."

Mrs. Brooks shuffled out the door and closed it behind her. I looked up at my mom. She knew I was bewildered.

She licked her lips haltingly, and said, "Dorthy, there must be a mistake. Mrs. Brooks kept referring to sixth grade. Pete is going into fifth grade and Mrs. Bear is going to be Pete's teacher. Has something happened to change this decision? Unfortunately, we weren't able to make it to yesterday's orientation, but when I talked to Mrs. Bear, she had no problem rescheduling and understood our situation with Pete's lips—hot sauce and all. Did missing orientation cause you to replace Pete with another student and assign him to Mrs. Brooks' class?"

"No, no, Louise, I assure you, changing Pete's teacher had nothing to do with missing orientation. Someday I want to talk about what happened to Pete's lips, but not now. It's much more serious than that. Usually I would be reluctant to have a student in the room for a discussion like this, but the situation and its resolution involve Pete so much that I think it's important he hear everything straight from the horse's mouth."

I sunk as low as possible in my tub chair. My paranoiac thinking had started to take over. Things seemed grim. I was sure we were going to have a *lye soap torture discussion* and talk about how Mrs. Bear didn't want to deal with my mom or me. Or worse, somehow, they'd found out about Davey and the comic book party. I was probably headed to juvie for being such a bad kid. My Uncle Jimmy had warned me about this. He had said that if I didn't behave myself, I could end up behind bars and never see my mom, dad, or sister again. He was in juvie when he was younger. He told a gruesome tale describing how he had been taken away from his family and shoved in a jail cell with four other kids. He said the guards made Scrooge from, *A Christmas Carol,* look sympathetic. And he had only stolen corn and chickens from a neighbour to help feed his family. I felt like what I had done was so much worse. I was sweating and scared beyond belief. I expected the cops to barge through the doors at any moment.

"I don't know how to say this any other way, but just to say it." Dorthy Schaffer started. She took a deep breath. So did I. "At about two o'clock this morning, Mrs. Bear had a massive heart attack and died in her sleep. We're all in shock. I'm numb. But school starts next week, and we need to be ready. No matter how sad we all are, we must . . . move on."

I grabbed the arms of my chair. Dead! My new teacher was dead before I'd even had the chance to meet her! I had never known anybody that passed away, except for my Aunt Rose's piano teacher. Now my world was being turned upside-down again, and when considered against all my other woes, I was absolutely swirling in a state of fear and uncertainty.

My mom's voice broke into my anxiety-fueled dread. "This is awful. I'm so sorry, what can we do? Her poor family." My mom genetically, and through socialization, had the temperament of an attack dog. But there were times when a situation managed to pull at her heartstrings and she suddenly became a caring, empathic person.

Ms. Schaffer began to cry. "I'm so sorry, Louise and Peter. I'm very upset, as you can see. Please give me a moment and we will keep on."

She spun around in her chair to compose herself. There were a few muffled honks into a tissue. After several moments, the principal was back to us.

"Louise, Pete. I know this is a shock, and everyone here at the school is devastated, but we have to figure out what we're going to do about fifth grade. As you know, school starts next Monday. We had only enough students for one fifth grade class. There's not another fifth grade we can jam Mrs. Bear's students into. We have no full-time substitute or replacement teachers for her class, and because the school district is short of funds, they will not let us bus fifth grade students across town where they might have space. In a nutshell, we have to solve this unfortunate problem on our own." She paused and took a deep breath.

"So, here's what we are going to do. We are taking most of Mrs. Bear's students and holding them back for a super version of fourth grade. We have the resources to take this step, and in most cases this is a good decision because kids that are held back gain all the benefits of in-depth, repetitive learning. In addition, the self-confidence that can stem from being older, bigger, and more emotionally secure (than the novice students entering the grade for the first time), is considerable. Mrs. Bear's class was a diverse cocktail of age, gender, test scores, physical and emotional maturity, economic status, and such. She was such a gifted educator that we were sure she could handle it, and she was on-board for and enthusiastic about this mix, herself. Unfortunately, we don't have another teacher to match her amazing skills, so we must offer some last-minute alternatives." I waited for her to go on. Was I going to go back to fourth grade?

"For the few kids that we don't think a fourth-grade repeat is a good option, we are going to skip them forward to sixth grade. Peter is one of those we want to move on to sixth. If we kept Pete back, we feel it would be a waste of his time. So, on Monday, Pete will report to Mrs. Brook's sixth grade class where we know he will excel and flourish."

My mom looked unconvinced. "Dorthy, are you sure this is a good idea? Look at Pete. He's small for his age. Because his birthday is in September, we had a choice of starting him in kindergarten when he was four or waiting a year until he was a late five. We chose four. So, if he goes into sixth grade now, he will be two years younger than the other kids in his class and will graduate from high school when he's fifteen. I'm not sure this is such a great idea. What do you think, Peter?"

I coughed. I wasn't expecting my mother to ask for my opinion. "Uh, I don't know. Sixth grade sounds really scary. Are Benny Tail-Feather, Jerry Kaye, Bill Thompson, or Mike Anderson going with me to sixth grade?"

Ms. Schaffer blinked. "Are those your friends, Pete?"

I answered confidently. "Yes, they are my *best* friends. We're all in a club we started called, The Pirates. We do everything together. We live in the same project, so we walk to and from school together. When we are in school, we eat lunch together, we study together, and best of all, we have a blast playing together."

She looked concerned. "Pete, I hate to tell you this, but none of your friends are in the sixth-grade skip group. I'm sorry. You will make new friends, and besides, you can still walk to and from school and play with your Pirate pals. Remember, we have no other real options. But we will all make sure this works really well for you." She gave my mother a hopeful smile.

"Guys, I have about ten other students and their families to talk to this afternoon and evening, so I had better go. This is not the way any of us wanted to start a new year. We will miss Mrs. Bear so much. She was a gifted teacher and an inspirational mentor to our younger faculty." Ms. Schaffer stood and moved towards the door.

"Okay, Pete, time to go," my mom said. "Thank you for your time, Ms. Schaffer. We are so sorry about the passing of Mrs. Bear. I want to talk to Pete a little more about fourth grade versus sixth grade. And I need to confer with my husband. I'm sure that will be all right, won't it, Dorothy? I hope you will be a little flexible on this next step. I'm not sure Pete can handle the kids in sixth grade."

The principal opened the door, hinting that it was time to go. "Louise, I understand your concern, but there is no wiggle room on this decision. If I made an exception for Pete, I would have to open negotiations with all involved parents and students. I can't do that, so

Louise, I'm afraid we're going to have to live with my decision. I'm sorry about this." There was real earnestness in her voice.

My mom compelled me up and out of the tub chair with a swift arm. We walked out of Ms. Schaffer's office and headed for the car. I could tell she was angry. As we hustled along, she began to chat about the looming decision of fourth versus sixth.

"I don't know what that woman's talking about. I'm a parent. I have the right to insist on what's best for you, Pete. *We* will decide if it's fourth or sixth!" She had worked herself up. "I'm going to give that woman a call tomorrow morning and give her a piece of my mind!"

Wow. Maybe she was on my side this time. The last thing I wanted was sixth grade. I needed to be around my friends. I didn't need the intimidation of the older (and much bigger) sixth grade boys, and anyways, I didn't do all that well in fourth grade. I was sure I'd drown in sixth grade studies. "Mom, I beg you, don't let them put me in sixth grade. I will be happy and learn a lot more if I can become a super fourth grader."

She adjusted the purse strap on her shoulder. "Pete, I'm not sure yet. Let's talk more when we get home."

She followed through on this recess for a few seconds before revving up again. "Now that I think about it, going into sixth grade early—yes—it might be great if you graduated from high school two years ahead of kids your age. It would give you a real leg-up on the world: an early start on your life."

I was losing her. "But Mom, I thought you were going to talk to Dad first? And besides, I'm getting pretty good at football and baseball. There's no way I can be on teams where the guys are a lot bigger and older than me. And if I can hang out with the Pirates a little more, I will do so much better in everything I do. *Please!* Fourth grade is a *must*."

"Pete, I'm tired of hearing about your damn Pirates. And I made up the story about having to speak with your father. I don't want Ms. Schaffer to think she can push me around. You see, Peter, you always want to be in the driver's seat with these types of people. And we both know your father would have nothing meaningful to add. Let's just get home for now and we'll hash this out there."

We made our way to the school's front doors. I knew my mother had drawn her line in the sand, so I did my best to keep quiet. I noticed the flags now stood at half-mast. I felt like one was for me, and the other, Mrs. Bear. The world outside had a slight haze of rain to it. As we neared Porsche, I felt sad again. I knew from the way my mom was just talking I would probably have no choice. I would be in sixth grade, drowning.

My mom tended to dig in her heels when she was confronted with an opinion or idea that was different from hers as she can't stand to lose. Her, *my way or the highway,* behaviour was one of her standby problem-solving techniques. I was concerned. I would potentially have to contend with sixth-grade bullies and my mother's resentment of Ms. Schaffer. She did not let go of grudges easily. I anticipated much humiliation due to my mother's obstructionist tendencies. I was certain she would inject herself into the PTA and various fundraising events just to make my principal miserable. I was constantly worried I'd have to answer for her battles fought in the weeds of hubris. Especially now, I had more than enough on my plate as it was.

Once we were on the road heading back to The Project, my mom turned on the radio. She fiddled with the dial a bit and landed on Kay Starr's, "The Wheel of Fortune." She cranked the volume to ear-splitting levels and lost herself in it for a moment. That song didn't reflect her usual taste in music. Once it was over, she switched back to her favourite station. She preferred a lot of swing and jazz, with the wonderful drum and brass sections. My dad and Uncle Jimmy called the genre *jungle* music. I didn't catch on until I was a bit older that this moniker arose because a lot of the artists were black, or associate with black people. It was a crude remark meant as a shot at my mom from my dad and uncle's high horses of country and bluegrass. Louis Armstrong, Duke Ellington, Frank Sinatra, Benny Goodman, Tommy Dorsey, Ella Fitzgerald . . . it would be one after the other at the same volume, nixing any chance for me to take one more shot at pleading my case.

We arrived at The Project just as the sky opened to a massive thunderstorm. Lightning dotted the black horizon and thunder rumbled in loud bursts. There was a torrent of rain coming down, which made the ground froth and spit. We jumped out of the car and sprinted for our front door. My mom quickly unlocked it and we hurried into the kitchen to take off our drenched clothes. We stashed them in a limp and soggy pile to slouch beside the hamper in the furnace room. Then we ran upstairs in our wet underwear and dashed into our respective bedrooms to change into dry stuff. My sister and her babysitter were in my mom's room. I heard my mom paying the babysitter and sending her on her way. Once dressed in dry chinos, a black polo, and her furry slippers, she grabbed my sister and headed back downstairs. I was not far behind. Just as I walked into the kitchen, I heard my mom twirling the dial on our rotary phone. Her call was quickly connected.

"Hello, this is Louise Gregg calling. May I speak to Ms. Dorthy Schaffer? It's important. Hi, Dorthy? Louise. Gregg here. I know you're very busy, thanks for taking my call . . . yes, I wanted to ask one more time about how smart it is to put Pete in sixth grade. Yes, I understand. No, I didn't think of that. I didn't know his test scores were so high. If his scores are so good, why hasn't he done better in school? Yes, I'm sure you're right—too much Pirates and our home life certainly contribute to Pete's distraction. Yes, I trust you. All right . . . yes, all right. Sixth it is!"

She hung up. My heart sank. Sixth grade bullies, very little Pirate time, more grade pressures, family war, and, oh yes, I couldn't forget my newest conundrum—Davey. All those things heralded a very dismal future.

CHAPTER 10: BRIDGES

The phone call to Ms. Schaffer sealed the deal. I was in sixth grade, no doubt about it. I decided to stop fighting and accept my fate.

We were still a little damp from the soaking we received during our sprint from Porsche to the house. I mimicked my mom, who vigorously rubbed a towel through her hair. Just as I tossed my used towel into the furnace room, I heard a knock on our front door. My mom beat me to it. There stood a drenched Davey.

"Davey, what the hell are you doing out on a night like this? You look like a drowned rat."

I was amazed my mom didn't ask Davey into our kitchen so he'd get out of the rain. Instead, she kept him standing outside.

"Davey, what can we help you with? Pete, do you want to come and say hello to your friend?"

"Hey, Davey. You look wet beyond belief."

He was holding a copy of *The Plain Dealer* aloft as a makeshift umbrella, but the newsprint had long lost any of the limited structural integrity it may have once held. It had not kept him dry. His T-shirt and flimsy, black nylon windbreaker stuck to him. His shorts had that same clinging appearance. He looked more like a shrivelled, overripe piece of fruit than a rat, to me. He was wearing his grimy sneakers without socks.

"Yeah, Pete. I wanted to make sure you and Mrs. G are okay. I just heard from Jerry Kaye about your teacher croaking in her sleep. Pete, are you going back into fourth grade like the rest of your friends?"

"No, Davey. I'm skipping to sixth grade. I don't know why, but I am. My mom and the school principal made the decision for me. It's going to be okay. It will all work out." I thought saying it out loud might make it true.

My mom broke back in. "Thanks for caring, Davey. Pete and I are fine. Say, are you busy tomorrow? Since you and Pete had such a great time at your comic book party earlier, how about another session tomorrow? It's supposed to remain stormy and I want to take Pete's sister over to see her aunt, so it would great if he could play with you."

I said nothing, because Davey was already pressuring me to show up the next day, even if he did already follow through on his ultimatum. Still, I felt offered up against my will.

I thought my mom was casual about my hang-outs with Davey because she saw him as a well-timed, unpaid babysitter. At nine, I was full of energy, I liked to take risks, and I tended to run against the grain, as my mom put it. She was busy with a new baby in the house and couldn't keep up with me. So, time with Davey was perceived, even under my mom's suspicious eye, as a relatively safe bet, compared to my being left to my own devices. Plus, it took me away from the shenanigans of my outdoor tribe. My mom strongly disliked my friends and their families and vocalized it regularly.

"I can't wait for your dad to get a decent job so we can move away from all the trailer trash that live here," she would say. And, "Pete, your friends come from loser families—I don't want any of that rubbing off on you." Sometimes she'd throw in a slight directed specifically at Benny and his family. She was convinced his mom, Bernie, has an especially low opinion of her parenting style. "If you're not careful, I expect you'll start pow-wowing just like your most despicable friend, that Tail-Feather boy. I'll never figure out how they escaped the reservation."

My mother thought she was better than anyone else living in The Project. Even though Davey seemed to have her convinced he was cut from some radiant cloth, my mom likely thought of him as the means to an end. Good enough to spend time with her son and keep him busy. To her it was a harmless, neutral way to soak up time when I was out of school, and to make sure I was away from any bad influences. She saw a convenient arrangement and overlooked his obviously strange demeanor.

My thoughts were broken by Davey's suave reply. "Great idea, Mrs. Gregg. Pete could come over about eleven. I think we can have a great time until around two. What do you say, Pete?"

"Okay, Davey." I tried to be polite, but was unable to muster any real enthusiasm. "The only thing is I'm seeing the Pirates in the morning. But yeah, I can probably make eleven."

"Davey, you should get home and sort yourself out—dry off. Pete will see you tomorrow."

My mom closed the door and both of us looked up at the large white-faced clock hanging above the entry to the furnace room. It was six p.m. and no sign of my dad: an omen he had launched into his weekend bender. From now until he reappeared, my mom would be brooding and bawling, so wired for conflict that in a few days she'd be primed to explode. I was sheltered in the eye of the Category 5 hurricane, but soon I'd be slung into the ferocity of its outer bands of chaos and anger. I did my best to stay out of her way during these weather events. Beneath my outward cool I was developing the makings of a rich PTSD stew. When I entered the kitchen for supper that night, it seemed suddenly cold, austere, and foreboding.

***

Later in my life as a behavioural scientist, I learned that Post Traumatic Stress Disorder (PTSD) in children is a response to situations where they are continually subjected to forces which cause extreme stress and anxiety. Dramatic experiences featuring the loss of life, prolonged physical and sexual assault, or continuous family conflict, either singularly, or in combination, sow the seeds for PTSD.

The symptoms of PTSD in children are complex and synergistic. A child with the disorder withdraws and becomes simultaneously numb and hyper-vigilant. They are constantly worried, and experience great shame and self-loathing, in addition to constant (and oftentimes unwarranted) fear. The child also suffers long states of expressed or hidden depression.

That dark and wet early September night I experienced many of its symptoms, but back then, no one knew about PTSD. I was just a kid with school problems, crazy parents, and a lust for running, catching, and escaping into imaginative play with my friends.

***

I ate a sad dinner with my mom and thankfully, oblivious sister. Mac and cheese and salad were on our plates. The food passed quickly from fork to mouth, and soon our plates were scraped clean. Just before we took our dishes to the sink, my mom slapped her hand down on the table.

"I'm so sorry you kids have to live through your drunken father's weekend benders. He's a criminal to treat us this way. Wasting our money on booze and his whores. It's no wonder we can't buy you guys new clothes or eat out once in a while. I'm not sure I can take much more of this. I'm going to call your Uncle Jimmy. I'm not sure what he can do, but at least he tries to talk some sense into your father. It hasn't worked yet, but it's nice to have someone to talk to about this hell I'm living in."

The rest of the evening oozed into a haze of crummy television shows and a little vanilla ice cream for diversion, while my mom attempted to unburden some of her anguish over the phone. I gave up the ghost at about nine p.m. and headed up to my room to escape the weeping of a poor woman.

My room was a nothing burger for the most part, but for a nine-year-old boy it was heaven. I had a comfy single bed with a garish blue-and-white Brooklyn Dodgers comforter which always kept me warm and happy, especially since I could look down at the face of one of my baseball heroes, Roy Campanella. My walls were covered with posters of more sports figures, and heroes from the comics. It was Superman meets Johnny Unitas. I had a little black desk and a swivel office chair we bought at a flea market shoved into a corner of my sanctuary. The chair served as a clothes rack for discarded T-shirts and jeans for another day's wearing, and the desk was a solid base for my new passion of reading and writing boy stories. Next to the desk was a tall, skinny bookcase. In it I had stacked some of my prized possessions—books, and athletic awards and trophies I won in the various sports competitions I got involved in. The floor was slippery oak hardwood, which made for a fabulous sock skating and sliding rink. Fortunately, for my sake, my parents didn't bother me here. When I was in my room with the door closed, it was my own private keep.

I woke up at around midnight from a sweaty and fitful dream. I fell out of bed still only half awake and stumbled to my desk where I had a glass of water ready for such moments of drought. I took a big swig, and as I had no desire to revisit sleep, I went and stood in front of my room's big dormer window. The window was wide open. The screen hopped with the last of the mosquitoes and other night bugs drawn to the light from my desk lamp. I took a deep breath and looked out onto the southern part of the Plaza and beyond, to the flashing lights of the massive communication towers and the smokestacks of the goliath oil refineries a few miles from our house.

I took another deep breath. The air was heavy with the oppressive humidity that drove me from slumber, one infused with the sweet smell of late summer lilac and garden phlox. Now that I was awake, the aroma was so overwhelming that I felt slightly dizzy. I looked to the dark horizon where lightning was dotting the sky. Thunder rumbled half-heartedly in the distance and clouds surfed by on the winds of an exhausted storm.

I walked over to my bookshelf. I spied the copy of Robert Louis Stevenson's, *Kidnapped,* that my Aunt Florence gave me for my birthday the previous year. It was a revelation. I had read it over and over again. It was about an orphan who was thrown into some trying circumstances and must get by on his wits, with a little help from an older and more-daring man he befriends with a similar drive for restitution. The protagonist's orphan-hood, and the sad liberation this circumstance incubates, caused me to ask what my life might be like if I were to shed the shackles of my parents.

This book primed me for a life of more books, bookstores and libraries. When it wasn't Pirate time, I would sneak to our little public library a half-mile walk from our house. I'd grown to love its oak reading tables, the hundreds of coloured spines to choose from, and the old people sitting on comfy chairs passing time perusing their favourite reading material. From that time forward, a library and its wondrous scent of bound pages, offered me a refuge in its sanctuary of words, thoughts, and grand deeds.

I passed my fingers over the other books I'd collected since. I was trying to decide which one to settle down with when I reattempted sleep. The stories here tended towards a common trend of protagonists who must overcome their natural temperaments and toughen up to become self-sufficient, resilient, and sturdy, either by necessity of circumstance or sheer will. The books were about what makes "a really good man", so I was keen to take it all in. Lessons on morality and redemption were borne out of challenges, well-met. I preferred these adventure stories, with their strong themes of loyalty and friendship, and I gravitated towards these topics when penning my own.

My newfound lust for reading had me tearing through the books most boys of a certain age, if they loved stories, had on their bookshelf. Over the past year, I'd lived life on the Mississippi with Tom and Huck as painted by Mark Twain. I'd fallen under the spell of Jules Verne, whose Captain Nemo and his submarine drove me to experience underwater worlds I had never fathomed. I devoured Jack London's, *The Call Of The Wild, White Fang,* and *The Sea-Wolf.* But the literary voyage that impressed me the most was a more obscure work of London's called, *The Star Rover.*

That book, my favourite yet, offered me great inspiration and philosophical clarity in my times of need. It was the story of a man held in prison on charges of murder. His captors tried to break his spirit by means of a device called "the jacket", an instrument of forced compliance that compressed the body of the wearer to an agonizing degree. The protagonist trained himself to withstand this torture by entering a kind of trance state by which he walked among the stars experiencing past lives of different ages and cultures. The bulk of the narrative takes place there.

I have read *The Star Rover* many times over throughout my life. London's prose and storytelling drew me in, time and time again. But at a deeper level, through this indulgence, I had gained a tool for survival, balance, and spiritual inquiry.

***

I remember when I had read *The Star Rover* for the first time. The power of its mysticism washed over me, but I knew waiting in the shadows of Sunday evening was the war between my mom and dad. Sure enough, it went off that night, for at least half an hour. Instead of cowering in the furnace room waiting for the dogs of war to finish up, I retreated to my room. I got comfortable on my bed and called to mind the rituals that London's protagonist used to guide his consciousness into a trance state.

I closed my eyes and breathed deeply. As I took each breath, I allowed myself to move deeper and deeper into a vision of a place of tranquility and peace. The more I employed this technique, the more environments my semi-waking dream conjured up for me. Whether the heather-clad hills of Scotland, the murky seascapes of the Nautilus, the white and wondrous wilderness of Jack London, or just a serene landscape I had seen in a National Geographic, I sank further into a magical inner climate of calm. In my world of beta-wave euphoria, my mom and dad's fighting disappeared, time stood still, and I emerged from my transcendental journey more relaxed and less anxious.

Later in life I would come to know the mechanics behind the power of transcendental meditation. When I lived in Washington, DC, I had the good fortune of being taught the technique by Buddhist monks. In graduate school, my peers and I experimented with psilocybin, hashish, and LSD, and the texture of the hallucinations they produced. These experiences, although much more powerful, mimicked the trance state I produced as a boy. A state which allowed me to survive my world and not tip over into a fuller expression of PTSD or even worse, stress-induced child psychosis.

***

Saturday morning broke with a thud. My book had fallen to the floor. I had chosen, *Kidnapped*, again for my midnight boil of self-discovery. I'd slept in. I looked out my window and found it was still hot and muggy. Rain had ebbed its way to a steady drizzle. The clouds lay close to the ground—a heavy grey blanket suffocating all life below their shroud. I got dressed and ran down to the kitchen. No one was there. I hadn't heard any stirrings from my mom's room, nor any noise from my sister. So, as far as I could tell, I had the place to myself. I grabbed a stale donut my mom bought on her grocery trip two days ago. It was chocolate. Not my favourite, but it would still the rumble in my stomach.

Donut in hand, I made a break out the front door into a soggy Saturday morning. I scoped out the Plaza to see if any Pirates had made the scene. Sure enough, they were all there clumped around our meet-up place. Despite the rain, it remained somewhat hidden by our clever pruning of the trees. Benny Tail-Feather signaled me to join the gang. I trotted over and finished half of my donut on the way. I threw the rest of the sugar and lard concoction into a rusty red trash bucket.

As I arrived, I heard Jerry Kaye's voice loud and animated. "I can't believe it. I have to repeat fourth grade again. I'm sorry, but it's not my fault Mrs. Bear died. I passed fourth grade fair and square. My Dad is so pissed at Ms. Schaffer for making me repeat, he says he's going to force the district to bus me across town so I can attend proper fifth grade. Until then, he's going to drive me. I won't be going to school with you guys again. And because I have to leave so early in the morning and don't get home until late at night," she started to sob fat, angry tears that stood out from the rain on her cheeks, "the only Pirate time I'll have is on the weekends. And to put the icing on the cake, he's saying just as soon as we can afford it, our family is going to move away from The Project to be closer to my new school. This really sucks!"

Jerry Kaye was so upset she hardly noticed the weather. She must have raced out the door in a flurry, leaving without her raincoat or hat. Her hair was plastered to her head and her clothes and face were dappled with raindrops. Her bedraggled, manic appearance suited the fire in her eyes. She turned to Benny. "Benny, what's going on with you?"

"Yeah," he said, "I'm repeating fourth grade, too. My mom heard that a few kids from our old class are going to skip fifth and go directly into sixth grade. Because I'm a little older and bigger than you guys, she asked if I could become a skipper. Ms. Schaffer said, no, because I wasn't academically capable of sixth grade work yet. As you can guess, my mom blew a cork, but finally accepted there's nothing we can do. Besides, you guys are going to be in fourth with me, so it won't be so bad. Jerry, I'm really going to miss you."

Bill chimed in. "This fourth-grade repeat is a bunch of shit. We didn't cause this. Let's get our parents together to go down to Ms. Schaffer's office and demand a proper fifth grade. She has to do it."

There was silence from all of us. We all knew there was no way our parents were going to march to the school to challenge Dorthy Schaffer on anything "en masse." Anyways, Jerry Kaye's dad had sealed her fate. She was leaving our school for a proper fifth grade across town. Case closed.

But Mike added one more question, putting me on the spot. "Hey Pete, you haven't said anything. How do you feel about fourth grade repeat?"

Everybody looked at me. I was cornered. I decide it's best to tell the truth. "I'm not going into fourth. My mom and Ms. Schaffer are making me skip to sixth. I don't want to do it. I want to stay with you guys in fourth, but they would have none of it." I felt like Pontius Pilate for what my friends must have thought was the utmost betrayal.

Benny was hurt. "Pete, you going into sixth doesn't mean you're better than us. It just means your mom sucked up to Ms. Schaffer and you got a better deal. I've had it. I'll see you guys later. Pirates are dead." Benny stomped off.

Jerry, Mike, and Bill said nothing about Benny's outburst. Instead, the three of them stood up to leave. Mike and Bill moved on their way, and only Jerry said goodbye.

"See ya, Pete. Don't worry about Benny. He's just upset and feels put down by the school saying he's too stupid for sixth grade and you're not. He'll get over it. We're going to have plenty of Pirate time on the weekends and vacations, and before you know it, summer will be here and then it's full-time Pirates, if we can get you to keep your nose out of those books you've started reading. Okay, Pete?"

"Thanks, Jerry Kaye." I gave her a weak smile.

She turned and left. I was alone with my thoughts. I felt like a water bug skimming along the surface of a much deeper reservoir of feelings. I got up, pulled some branches across the hideout's entryway, and headed for the house. I hadn't taken more than a couple of steps when I heard, "Hey, Pete."

It was Davey. He slid up in front of me and continued. "Glad I caught you. Your mom said you would be here. How about we start our comic book party at noon instead of eleven? My Aunt Peaches is going to be around until 11:30. So noon would be better. I'll have the comics, baloney sandwiches, chips, and Cokes ready for when you show up. We'll have a great time. Oh yeah, and I cleared the time change with your mom. She says it's okay. Just a reminder you might want to bring your PJs along—more comfortable."

"Okay, Davey. See you at noon tomorrow, it sounds like fun," I said, lying through my teeth. The last thing I wanted to do was pay the tuition of time with Weird Davey just so I could stuff my face with crap and read his comics. But I had to go because my mom was counting on Davey to look after me so she could have some R&R. I stood my ground and added, "By the way Davey, I won't be bringing pyjamas."

CHAPTER 11: HOOKED

Storms in the Midwest are bipolar in nature. One moment it's hot, humid, and cloudy, with heavy downpours more suited to a tropical jungle. Then, a few hours later, a cold front tears through, and the temperature drops dramatically. The rain is replaced with hail, booming thunder, and sulphuric lightning.

Sunday morning, the weather shifts were in full bloom. I went out to visit the Pirates hangout, but no one was there. As I was heading back to my house, the sky unzipped and dropped marbles of ice that plunked onto the sidewalk, faster and faster. Wind whipped the trees to tattered skeletons, leaving scant traces of the bright-green summer dresses they wore moments earlier. It was dark and ominous—perfect twister weather. I sprinted home, ran inside, and threw my clothes into the steadily growing pile of casualties in the furnace room. I headed upstairs. There was no sign of my mom or sister on the main floor. I went into my room. Someone had been in there recently as there was a piece of paper on my desk:

Peter,
Gone to Sue's for coffee. Left a bit early. Have fun with Davey. I'll see you this afternoon.
Love, Mom.
PS: If you have any problems with Davey, leave, and call me at Sue's
-M

Sue was Mom's youngest sister. She was the personality star of the family; warm, engaging, a great mom, and my favourite. On top of all her great traits, we shared the same birthday, so I felt a special affinity with her. I was rarely allowed to see my aunt, even though our house was only a few miles from her and my Uncle Sam's place. I didn't know why. I'd ask to see her, but my mom always delivered the same perfunctory excuse of, "busy lives and busy times!" She didn't even attempt to get us together. So, when she went off to her sister's for a hen party, I felt left out.

I read a recently acquired library copy of, *The Last of the Mohicans,* for an hour or so. Then I decided it was time to head to Davey's. I pulled on some fresh clothes and went to the washroom to scrub my face and comb my hair. I didn't want any funny business from Davey this time, and I wanted to look like I meant it. I checked out my bedroom window for the weather. Another shift. It was totally clear outside. A bright blue sky heralded an early Indian Summer. I usually looked forward to these respites from the humidity. It was too bad I couldn't enjoy it. I had more sinister pressure systems to contend with for now.

I trotted over to Davey's. When I read my mom's note, I considered not going at all since she would not be there to enforce it, but she would definitely hear about my no-show later from Davey. I was not so keen to endure another bout of lye soap from my mom. My mouth, lips, and bottom were still not back to one-hundred percent.

The front door of Peaches' was ajar and I could vaguely make out Davey through the screen. "Hi! It's Pete. Ready for some good comic times?" I wanted to make my intentions clear. Good comic times are all I'm in the market for.

"Oh, Pete! Come on in. I'm just throwing some sandwiches together."

I pulled open the screen and found myself once more in Peaches' Shangri-La. All the dishes were done, and everything was clean and in its place. There wasn't a speck of dust or disorder. The only ruffle in this sea of tranquility was Davey. He was in the kitchen, slapping baloney and mayo onto slices of bread he'd laid out side by side.

"How many chips do you want?" He was in a mad whirl, pouring out a large packet of salted chips on his tiles of bread.

"Pile them on," I said. I was so hungry. Davey's smashed baloney delights looked like just what the doctor ordered.

"Let's get some lids on these kids." He methodically slapped a fresh slice on top of each sloppy square, and then punched it down until you heard the chips crush beneath. One by one, they submitted to his fist in a precise game of Whac-A-Mole.

Davey moved away from the kitchen counter with a plate stacked high with the sandwiches. It was the first time I'd seen his full outfit for today's party. He looked like some swinging bachelor I had seen in one of my mom's fashion magazines. Once again, Davey had on a robe, pyjamas, and slippers. But this day he'd really gussied up his act. Black silk pyjamas replaced the old, tattered ones I saw before, and to top it off he was wearing a beautiful teal velveteen robe.

Davey had added a daring touch to his ensemble. He had left his robe untied, and I noticed he hadn't fastened any of the buttons on his black silk shirt. His chest was exposed, which was nothing too disconcerting. But when I looked down, I noticed his bottoms were also gaping open where the seams were meant to be buttoned. I could easily see his penis. Davey noticed I was staring at him.

He laughed. "Hey Pete, you like my new stuff? Got it a couple of days ago. I can't believe how comfy it is. I don't like anything done up—makes everything too tight. How about I get you a matching set? We can keep your stuff here, out of your mom's sight. I know she would never understand how cool it is for two guys to hang out with each other in their lounge wear. Bachelor life, you know. Chicks don't get it."

I was so freaked out by Davey's state of undress and what he had just said. "Davey, I've told you I'm not wearing pyjamas at your house. It's weird. You know, I'm not hungry anymore. I think I'll just head home."

"No can do, Pete. I promised your mom I would take care of you this afternoon. I can't let you go home to run around the house and neighbourhood on your own. If I let you walk away, your mom would kill me. Right! Come on, Pete. Let's not repeat what happened last time when you just walked away in a huff. Let's go upstairs, relax, and have a good go at our favourite superheroes. And, oh, by the way, when I leave in a few weeks I'm going to give you all of my comics."

I couldn't believe how much I loved comics. Despite the family warfare to come in the evening, Sunday mornings were special to me. I would get up early, long before anyone else in the house, and make a beeline for the main floor where the paperboy had stuffed the Sunday edition between the front door and the screen. I opened the pages until I arrive at my gold mine—the weekly comic section. I would catch up on *Prince Valiant, Archie,* and, *Little Orphan Annie* who joined me for breakfast. I inhaled the pages of words, colours, and characters, between bites of whatever I'd been able to scrounge up. My Sunday morning ritual with my comic strip friends grounded me, acting as a protective balm against the harshness of the weekend.

***

Davey was a skilled manipulator and intuitively knew of my comic addiction. He played on it, and like any other dealer, hooked me by being my source for new product. There was no way I could amass on my own the volume or variety of titles he was offering. I needed my *Superman* fix, and Davey used comics to his advantage to ensnare me. They became my kryptonite.

My comic compulsion extended beyond the two-dimensional. I was equally dazzled by animated cartoons and feature films, but didn't get to engage with them as much as I would like (the movie theatre proved less accessible than my home-delivered and grocery-stand connections). *Tom & Jerry, Looney Tunes, Merrie Melodies,* these moving strips entranced me. My comic book compulsion, years later, incubated one of the most important life decisions I would ever make.

***

Just days after I shed my blue and gold graduation robe and mortar board with a degree in economics, I was lost. Several weeks before I received my diploma, I was declared 4-F. I was unfit for service in the draft for Vietnam due to a sports injury incurred during college football. Before I got this bad news, I had been preparing, along with two of my best friends, to go to war, even though I hated John F. Kennedy and Lyndon B. Johnson for getting us into the whole mess. I felt there was no evidence of any US interest beyond self-righteous egotism and nationalist arrogance that Communism must be contained at-any-cost rhetoric. Later, I would bristle, thinking of how this obstinate belief came at the expense of the lives of well over fifty-thousand American kids.

Even though I didn't agree with the conflict or want to get involved in what I viewed as the civil war of a country all the way in Southeast Asia, I was eager to serve my country and come home in one piece with my buddies. So, when I heard that I would not, in fact, be joining the US Army, I didn't know what to do with myself.

A few months after this letdown, I entertained a stint at being hired as a pilot for a large international airline. But while I was in training, I figured out I would die of boredom as a bus driver in the sky. I quit. I spent the next few months reading about the history of animation, checking on my merger stock holdings, and working out. The injuries sustained over my college career established that I was too small and fragile to play in the NFL, but I did consider a tryout offer from a Canadian Football League (CFL) team. Though I'd been prevented from joining my country's army or the NFL, there was a chance I'd be able to play the game I loved, north of the border.

During this time, I receive a call from Buck Taylor, the equipment manager at my alma mater. I could make out the familiar chaw of mouth tobacco he kept packed into his lower lip, an unmistakable quirk of his speech.

"Hey, Buck!" I said into the receiver. "Sure. Great hearing from you . . . no, I'm still living off some of the bonus money and seat ticket sales I made last year."

My student career in high-octane college football allowed me to collect a wage as paid talent, and I was reaping the rewards of the previous year's performance bonuses and the profits made selling off my share of the home game tickets allotted to each player which was two-hundred dollars per ticket, times twenty, times eight home games, amounted to a handsome under-the-table payoff. Buck called to relay a job offer that might provide a more secure financial future now that my golden goose had flown the coop.

Buck was a legendary figure who has served as the equipment manager for our football team for over twenty-five years. About ten years prior to the call, he'd become especially close to Bob Jones, an outstanding tight end at our university. After Bob graduated, he immediately married his college sweetheart, who was the daughter of the founder of The Magic World Theme Park and The International Film and Animation Studio. Marriage created a Vice President for Operations position for Bob. And so, as part of his role he was always on the lookout for new talent to blend into the growing demand for junior management needed to support the off-the-charts growth Magic World and the studio had experienced over the past five years. Bob preferred recruiting football players from our program, especially those with business and economic degrees. Buck was an inside source who helped fill Bob's talent pipeline.

"Really?" I said. "A lead ride operator, and then maybe something in the studio? Hell yes, I'm interested. When's the interview? Sure, I can make it. Wow, Buck. Thank you. No, I'm not very excited about the CFL . . . yeah, I'm pretty sure my football days are over. Ha ha, yes. Thanks again, Buck. We'll talk soon."

I got the job at the Magic World Theme Park, a dream come true. It was June by this time, and I was assigned one of the most coveted positions in the park: a Captain on The Rivers of Adventure "E" ride. I donned the name, Rangoon Pete, whenever I was behind the wheel of the pontoon boat I'd been assigned to skipper through an intercontinental waterscape. The ride meandered along seamless replica sets of notable rivers of the world and the veldts and jungles along their banks.

I made my way around the circuit through Africa, Asia, and South America spieling bright, bold, and complex descriptions of geography and natural history, all the while protecting my patrons from the crocodiles, great apes, pythons, hyenas, lions, and hippopotami. I enjoyed this role and the endearing exchanges I had with my smaller passengers. I made sure to take special care of the children in my charge during the ride. I wanted them to have fun and feel safe. I'd crack jokes and invite them to help me pilot the boat. This was not as dangerous as it might seem. The boat ran on rails submerged beneath water, kept artificially murky to conceal the mechanics and preserve the magic.

Before each shift, I gave myself plenty of time in the men's dressing room to properly transform. My casual duds were exchanged for the dashing attire of a Jungle Boat Captain: open toed hiking sandals heavily-starched khaki pants, a short-sleeved, button-up safari shirt, and a jaunty, wide brimmed bush hat. My accoutrements comprised a large black utility belt with a pouch for blank bullet storage, a holster, and the finishing touch of a Colt pistol which I'd use to keep some of the more ornery animatronic beasts at bay during the scripted roleplay. Using my best acting skills, I offered highly-animated and colourful descriptions of the rivers, foliage, and wildlife we encountered.

I spent the rest of the spring and summer managing this and other roles within the park's themed zones. I was also a sheriff for a while, and a spaceman. I had the fortune of meeting and chatting with the world-famous science-fiction writer Ray Bradbury at one point. He was there to witness what was billed as one of the greatest feats in the world at the time—a flying human being. Jet Pack Man nearly crashed and burned while I was busy regaling Mr. Bradbury with my love of his novel, *The Illustrated Man*.

Despite this great happenstance meeting, the Rivers of Adventure remained my favourite gig.

By the time summer was over and I had made my rounds through the various attractions of the theme park, the spark of an old dream for my life was reignited. My lingering comics addiction, now that football was probably over, might be a career after all.

Once the rush of summer slowed, the fervour in the park settled to a mild autumn buzz, and the atmosphere became more relaxed. One day, in mid-September, I was busy checking everything on the boat, making sure we were ship-shape for when the park opened. I would be the first boat in the convoy that morning so I was in charge of conducting a deadhead: a run with no passengers on board to make sure all of the animals were working, the flumes and waterfalls flowed consistently, blanks fired properly, and the timing signals coordinating all of the boats on the river sequenced as designed. Everything looked good. I slowed the boat to a crawl using my foot-driven accelerator pedal and it gently bounced along the guide rails serving as navigation pathways before it slowed to a halt. I was ready to head out on the first tour of about twenty I would do that day.

As I pulled alongside the dock to moor my boat, guests began to trickle in and line up. I welcomed two folks from London and three from Chicago into my boat, then held off on setting sail for about ten minutes so I could try to fill my cabin with a crew of eight or more. While I was getting everyone settled, I noticed our ride foreman off to the side of the dock. He was talking to a tall guy with a black crew cut hair, grey slacks, white shirt with a skinny dark blue tie, and black walking shoes.

"Pete!" he yelled. "Let Wade take the first party. Ron wants to talk to you."

It turned out that Ron Martinez, the park's vice president of operations, was the man who wanted to speak to me. I'd heard about him before. Rumour had it he only got his job at the park because his employment was a caveat his parents had written into the title to the land where the park now sat. The buyer had to agree to take on their son for the sale to go through. Unfortunately, this gossip discounted Ron's natural flair for business, great people skills, and highly-effective management IQ.

Ron said hello, offered a few pleasantries and then cut to the chase. "Pete, would you like to be considered for a more serious position at the studio? It would be an entry-level opportunity at first, but several of the guys running motion pictures saw you play football and think you would fit on their team. And maybe after a while, things are changing fast around here, you know, the sky could be the limit with your possibilities. What do you think?"

This was it. The break I'd been looking for. Comics into life. Damn right I was interested. The next thing I knew I was headed north on the freeway, dressed in the only suit I owned; white shirt, dark red tie, and some borrowed black shoes from my Rangoon Pete get-up. I arrived at my meeting with a studio interview committee who were screening me for the job Ron told me about. Once there, I spent two hours on the griddle answering questions about games lost and won during my football career, as opposed to the economic and management issues I expected. I was hoping to use my degree. There were no pauses to discuss the job offer, even briefly. But Ron got a message to me by my next shift. He told me to show up to work at the studio the next week. I had made the cut.

After six months of orientation and general introduction to the studio film production process I decide I wanted a different job. It wasn't that I didn't like the business of making movies, but the financial modelling needed to greenlight films was not of interest to me. Much of my orientation involved watching and learning about how cartoons and animated features were made. It was a painstaking process that involved seasoned animators drawing scenes onto cellulose acetate panels, or "cels". One scene may have twenty of these cels, which are layered one on top of the other in a large tower, and then photographed straight downward from a high perch in a high-ceilinged studio.

The men filming the stacked layers of hand-painted cels are called Long Lens Multi-Plane Animation Technicians. These folks did their job suspended high above the studio floor, lying on their stomachs on platforms supporting their cameras. The camera created the illusion of a flat scenery, combining the layered panels into one scape of texture, depth, and when the camera panned, motion. Each incremental snap of the shutter formed a tiny portion, a single moment, that would later be processed and sequenced into scenes. Depending on the complexity of the art that was required, the feature-length animated film resulting from those scenes could take as long as four or five years to make. This trade intrigued me. For whatever reason I loved what those people did. I want to become one of these LLMPA techs.

I aggressively attacked my new goal. I consulted with the chief animator, the head of the studio, and my disappointed sponsors, who gave me the studio job in the first place, asking what I needed to do to trade a sharp pencil and suit for a platform high in the sky creating great animation. But all I heard back was resistance. Just pure BS.

And then I ran into Stan Lockwood, the president of the Long Lens Multi-Plane Animation Technicians' Guild. I finally heard the truth.

"Pete, has your dad or mom, or an uncle or aunt, ever been a member of our guild?"

"No, of course not, Stan."

"Well, Pete, I'm sorry, but there you have it. Our guild is closed, which means only sons and daughters, or nieces and nephews of members can join and become employed as a long lens, multi-plane, animation technician. Sorry, but you're dead in the water, kid. No matter how many strings you think you can pull, it will make no difference. Our guild is strong. No compromise."

I was devastated. I would go on to a promising career within the studio, but my heart would always be in the stories filmed many storeys in the sky.

***

Davey's offer of all his comic books enticed me. The idea of a stunning new comic book collection to fill out my existing stash (ever disintegrating from over-reading) called me upstairs to his bedroom.

Just as I considered the consequences of such a step, something happened that startled me. There was a change in the air. Something evil was loose. Peaches' apartment, otherwise open, light, and inviting, began to close-in around me. It was as if the devil himself took a brush and started painting the corners of my vision with the blackest ink. The whole room felt darker, like the kitchen at our house when my mom attacked me with her lye revenge. Pigments were more saturated, ominous. Things were grey, dark, still, and closed off. The borders were creeping in and crushing me, like the shrinking circle that ended my Road Runner cartoons. I'm wasn't sure I could escape Wile E. Coyote this time. So, instead of jumping up to run away (this feels reckless and indiscreet in the face of my present circumstance), I disregarded the safety flares exploding in my mind and opted for a suggestion.

"Davey? Let's eat downstairs. It will be easier, less messy, and with options for seconds an arm's length. Can you run upstairs to your bedroom, snag your copies of Superman and Batman, and bring 'em down here to the kitchen so we can check out the new stories here?" I couldn't imagine how black the world upstairs might be.

"Oh God, Peter. You're such a pain in the ass, but okay you little shit, I'll bring some reading material down. I hope that will satisfy you while we eat. But make no mistake, we're going upstairs to dive into the rest of my collection right after lunch."

He was back rather quickly. While he was gone, he had made sure the gaps in his black silk pyjamas were even more overt. I said nothing. We dove into our lunch. I was careful not to get any mayo on the covers of the comics I was reading, especially since they could become mine sometime soon.

As we finished, Davey made a surprising editorial comment. "Pete, I don't know about you, but I think Superman is a much tougher dude than The Flash. If I were in trouble, I'd want Superman on my side. I think ol' Batman would just run away really fast in that sissy lightning bolt shirt of his, never to be seen again. Come on, we're finished. Let's go upstairs and we can talk more about Superman versus Batman."

Davey put the dirty dishes in the sink and headed for the stairs going up to his bedroom. Without dwelling too much on the evil vibes polluting Peaches' house, I followed him upstairs. I couldn't afford to rock the boat. Both of us went into his room, me just behind him, even though he'd just confused the Flash with Batman. It wasn't a mistake anyone who knew even the basics of comics would make.

As we settled into Davey's space, I noticed there were two large piles of comics neatly stacked on his bed.

"Hey Pete, before we dive into these, I want to get a picture of you with my new Polaroid camera. You ever see one of these?" He handed the camera over for me to inspect. I had no idea what I was looking at. I turned the camera over in my hands and after making a few oohs and ahhs, I handed it back to Davey.

"Great, right? Pete, this is an instant camera. Develops the film right on the spot. I want to get a shot of you so that I can remember our times together after I leave here in a couple of months."

Davey posed me. He had me sit on the bed and placed my hand on top of one of the piles of titles.

"Look up at the camera and smile."

While the camera engaged in its automatic whir and clack, I looked down and saw that I had put my hand on a magazine, not a comic. It looked like one of the ones Davey was reading on Friday. *Fucked* was written on the masthead and below the title was a strange photograph of a nude young woman with large breasts erotically sucking on a cucumber.

I jumped off the bed and shook my hands as if I'd just burned them. "What the hell have you done, Davey? Gross! Tear that picture up right now. When I tell my mom about this, she is going to kill you."

Davey started laughing. "Petey Boy, I'm *not* tearing the picture up, and if you keep causing trouble in our little comic book parties, I will show your mom the picture and tell her how much fun you have looking at all of my dirty magazines."

"Shut up, Davey!" I screamed. As I let my fear out, Davey moved to the bedroom door and locked it. He came back to the bed and grabbed one of the filthy magazines from the second pile and opened to a page of pure perversion. He took his penis out of his pyjama bottoms and started to massage himself.

I was dumbfounded. I had never seen anything like this before. Davey's hand moved faster and his penis grew straight and erect.

"I want out of here right now!" I screamed. This felt wrong and bad and I didn't want to be there. I lunged for the bedroom door and fumbled frantically with the lock. By some miracle, I managed to unlock the door and vault down the stairs. Davey's voice carried after me as I reached the porch.

"Remember, Pete. I have the pictures. You're mine. I'll see you later this week for more fun."

I bolted home. Things continued to close in. The picture of me smiling with my hand on a pornographic magazine put me in a yoke of psychological imprisonment. I couldn't escape. I was trapped.

Guilt and humiliation washed over me as I rushed into the relative safety of my kitchen to be confronted with my mom sobbing hysterically.

She looked up at me and huffed. "Peter, your father is a criminal. He's a no-good drunk, who whores around every weekend leaving me to deal with the shit he pushes us into. I've had it! First thing Monday morning I'm calling your Uncle Jimmy and I'm going to ask if we can come live with him and your Aunt Florence for a few weeks. Just long enough for us to get our feet on the ground."

CHAPTER 12: SNAKE FIGHT

Making threats to leave my dad was not a new play for my mom. Her leaving fantasy was so prevalent, and she cried wolf so often, that I learned to just shrug it off. I'd give her a hug to comfort her and placate her wails with a now canned response that had been perfected with frequent use. "Dad's going to stop drinking and running around. You're the love of his life, and when he gets his great new job selling insurance, times will be good again. You'll see."

Besides, school would start the following week and I expected she'd recant her Uncle Jimmy rant as soon as she realized it was not the best time to just up and leave. But this time felt different. She was sadder, angrier, more desperate, and seemingly at her wit's end. She seemed more resolute. There was a possibility her rancor might be turned into action this time. Her substitution of retreat to my Uncle Jimmy's and Aunt Florence's (as opposed to the usual shelter of my Aunt Thelma's house) was also curious. This potential prospect of escape to their ranch put me on edge.

My aunt and uncle were rich, as I mentioned before. Money was no problem for them: the biggest challenge they had was how to spend it. They usually opted for neat, bright, shiny objects, and readily invested in whatever grabbed their interest. More land was always on the docket for purchase: my uncle made it clear he had his sights set on becoming the Sultan of Dorset. They bankrolled the breeding of championship quarter horses, raised cattle and hogs for market, and owned several restaurants and a nightclub. Their most profitable ventures, though, were the numerous active oil-and-gas discoveries on several parcels of their land. Their drilling granted a steady profit.

In addition to being a part of my uncle's circus, my Aunt Florence had her own duties as a ringmaster elsewhere. She was principal of the rural school that served Dorset's students. My sister and I didn't see much of her when we visited in the summers as her position as an educator provided her with a hard-won ticket to sanity during those months. She spent most of her Junes, Julys, and Augusts at Big Sky University, an institution nestled in the dazzling Rocky Mountains, where she studied the subjects of R&R, hiking, fly fishing, and great rustic mountain cooking with her teaching colleagues.

When my aunt was away, my uncle's natural tendencies came even further out of the shadows. He lived large, in the grey zone. Rules were for other, less important people—there was no indulgence too outlandish that it should be avoided. New cars and pickups were a given. Sometimes he'd get overzealous and buy an airplane. Usually, he'd have an attractive female assistant to accompany him on business trips. He was full of life and willing to try just about anything. His was a carnal life lived to the hilt. There was no emergency brake.

***

A few years later, when I was about thirteen, my uncle took me along to haul premium yearling steers to the largest regional cattle auction in the country. It was exciting. Auctioneers would call out price and purchaser in an upbeat, rambling cadence, while cattle shuffled into the auction arena stirring up small tornadoes of dust with their hooves. Cowboys in the stands were dressed in their finest ten-gallon hats and neckerchiefs. The energy of the place got me all riled up with a giddy fever.

In the end, a conglomerate of exclusive Midwest eateries represented at the auction, bought up all our prize steers. Though, I had a pretty limited understanding of business and revenue at that age, I could easily grasp that the quarter-million dollar check my uncle collected from the auction bursar was a lot of money. After nabbing the spoils from the sale of our animals, we navigated our way to the auction house's entertainment zone. There were tents and kiosks that served up a gumbo of fast food, great meat and sausage plates, and an endless array of pinball machines, skee ball, and foosball tables. My uncle and I both grabbed a burger. It was one of the best I'd ever had, made with prime beef not available in any grocery store where I was from.

Once finished, we wiped the mustard from our mouths and trotted over to an oil drum that was set up as a trash can to throw away our paper wrappers. A gorgeous, young blonde woman loitered beside it. She was dressed in a sheer black halter top and shorts, with black nylons strapped up to lacy garters that complemented her high heels.

"Well hi there, fellas," she cooed. "Is one of you cuties Jimmy?"

"Why yes, sweetheart. And who are you?" My uncle responded with a greasy affect. I didn't think it was from the burger.

"I'm Nancy. Your friend Vince sent me to join you for the private party you've booked. Am I right? Are you the Jimmy I'm looking for?"

"Absolutely, Nancy! I'm your man." My uncle winked at me. "And by the way, this is my partner, Pete. He won't be partying with us today. He's got his own shake-up he's jumping into. Don't you, Pete?"

I stayed silent. My uncle called me aside, just out of earshot of his new friend, and slipped me a hundred-dollar bill. "Pete, just between you me, okay?" he whispered. "I'll be back in about four hours. Go have some fun and we'll head home just as soon as Nancy and I have raised a little hell and partied ourselves out."

I spend the rest of the afternoon eating more junk and playing all sorts of games— games that I knew nothing about, but easy-going cowboys were more than willing to tutor me. I tried my hand at some pool, shuffleboard, and pinball. At about five in the afternoon, my uncle reappeared. Nancy was no longer with him, and he was a mess. He was drunk, his eyes bloodshot, and his clothes were noticeably distressed. His once proud, white straw cowboy hat sat off-kilter on his head, the brim bent and torn a little.

"C'mon Petey, let's head home," he slurred. "By the way— you're driving."

What was he on about? Me, driving? Sure, I'd torn up a number of pastures on the ranch tractor, and I'd even taken one of the old cars out so my grandma could see her friends and do a little light shopping in Dorset. But grabbing the wheel of a big stock truck and navigating a four-lane highway for who knows how many miles sounded a bit more advanced. Insane, really (to say nothing of breaking the law or likelihood of a killer crash).

We wove our way through the vendors to the huge truck barn. We had driven over in my uncle's GM diesel monster.

"Don't worry, Pete. I'm going to get us out of the city and then you can take over. I'm pretty tired. That Nancy was a little too much for this old cowboy."

We headed out. I was fully focused on every shift, every acceleration, and every nuanced instruction my uncle made as he captained the truck to the intended changeover point of Helen's Roadside Diner. Helen's was twenty miles out of town. I had to learn fast. I gritted my teeth the whole way. My palms were sweating and my heart pounded out of my chest. We made it to Helen's in one piece, but there was no rest for my nerves. My uncle ripped open his door and shimmied around the truck to my passenger side window.

"Okay, Petey. You're up."

I clambered down the running board and walked around the vehicle, making leery note of the dually wheels on the rear axle. "Please don't crash. Please don't crash." Somehow, I found myself in the driver's seat. I bunched up my jacket and stuffed it under me so I could see over the dash. I took a deep breath. The gears ground furiously as they struggled to heed me, their new, reluctant master. With much determination, I managed to merge my way into the slowest lane of traffic. I looked over at my uncle for some reassurance, but he'd fallen asleep. He woke up every so often to do a quick check on our progress. He'd press on one of the arms of his sunglasses behind his ears so that the lenses would tilt above his eyebrows. He did a quick survey to see if we were on the right track and then made an onward sign with his hand in a lazy, chop motion. The glasses fell back to his nose, and he dropped off to sleep again. I was left alone to try to influence the odds in favour of our survival. I was not keen on filling in as my uncle's chauffeur, but I did surprise myself with my competent driving, despite the circumstances. On we rolled. Miraculously, we arrived safely. I kept the truck on the road, and us in one piece, for what turned out to be two-hundred miles of our journey.

This trip to the auction house with my uncle was not unique. His repertoire of scallywag behaviours permeated most areas of his life. But perhaps even more concerning was his malignant narcissism. He had a dark side with a frightening capacity for human ruin without remorse. If my mom, sister, and I were to suddenly show up at his doorstep seeking refuge from my father's antics, we wouldn't know which Uncle Jimmy we would be holed up with.

Every year, until I turned fourteen, my sister and I spent summers at the ranch. Since we were temporary children sitting in for the kids my aunt and uncle never had, we were spoiled rotten. We had special cowboy and cowgirl outfits, with the Roy Rogers and Dale Evans looks. We were full-on, with cowboy boots and 10X beaver cowboy hats. My uncle arranged for each of us to have our own horse, hand-picked by his ranch foreman to be size and temperament appropriate. Our horses were ours to ride for fun, but we were also expected to work. We used them to herd cattle and to sequester yearlings for branding, dehorning, and castration. It wasn't unusual for us to spend eight, ten, or even twelve hours a day, yahooing cattle.

Horse work was great. Because I was much older than my sister, I became a midget ranch-hand while my sister spent most of her time with our grandmother and friends she had made over the many summers here. In addition to my enjoyable duties working with the animals, I had to do things that I just hated. Riding and hooking cattle for culling, eight hot and humid hours a day, did not appeal to me so much, nor did my chores on the hay baler. Pulling large, dusty bricks of plant material from the bale sled could at times reveal some poor, dead animal that was caught inside the knit of the block.

The worst task of all, and the most difficult, was leveling oats. The oats were combined in the fields: the straw left cut and raked behind the tractor in a long wake to be picked up later by the baler (this would be used in the livestock's pens in the barn). The stuff we were after was the oat grains which were combined from the tips and funneled into the back of the tractor. They had been left to dry in the fields and were now ready for harvest and storage. The grains were then transferred into a large wagon and transported to an old US Rail boxcar. The boxcar was situated on huge wooden railroad ties piled criss-cross on top of one another to about four feet high. Though the foundation smelled of burnt tar, and had seen better days, this second-hand storage solution served as a very reliable oat receptacle. My uncle didn't see any reason to put in a silo when he could find these boxcars readily at auction, and for a song. The grain we loaded into these cars fed the cattle, pigs, and horses over the winter.

An auger was attached to a chute in the bottom of the wagon and the payload was gobbled into this large, steel tube and elevated up through a corkscrew conveyor inside it. The oats poured into the retired boxcar through a four-foot-by-four-foot opening we called the witch's door. Because I was so much smaller than the other ranch hands, and strong for my size, it was my job to climb into the boxcar through this door. Once the oats spilled in after me, I spread them using a large twenty-five- gallon aluminum scoop.

Oat-spreading was hot, dusty work. The chaff from each little oat kernel stuck to sweaty skin and could cause rashes that got easily infected. The farmhands called these airborne hulls, bee's wings, and they stung as well as their namesakes. As oats flooded in, space and oxygen at the top of the boxcar became scarce and compressed. Clean air was limited as the atmosphere in the boxcar became dry and congested quickly, so it was hard to breathe. Instead of standing, I had to lie on my stomach to achieve a spread that took advantage of every nook and cranny up to the boxcar's ceiling. Each car had around a 4,100-bushel capacity, and as the designated spreader, I had to make sure it got filled to the brim.

That day was especially hot and humid—another one of those where you can wring your clothes of sweat every few minutes. Menacing, steel-grey clouds were closing in, and the wind was totally still. The stench of animal manure and urine lay over the boxcar and its pad in a bubble of eternal decay.

I was on my stomach shoveling like mad. The only thing I wore was a T-shirt with the sleeves rolled up, dirty stained cut-off jeans, and grey and brown sneakers that were once white. Sweat streamed from me like a cosmic faucet and my soggy state was acting as an industrial-grade adhesive, inviting the billowing dust to cling to me. Carl, the ranch hand, scooped oats into the centre sump of the wagon below so that they'd be taken up by the auger at a steady clip. He said it was probably a good twenty degrees hotter in the boxcar than the tropical soup everyone was stewing in outside.

And then, I saw it. Coiled in the far left corner of the boxcar was a large snake. Its head moved from side to side, and I could make out a red, darting tongue, which contrasted strikingly with the serpent's beautiful brown-and-gold diamond markings. By the size of the snake's wrappings, it looked to be huge. Not quite a python, but bigger than any snake I'd ever seen. I thought I knew what kind of snake I was against as it strongly resembled the one I chose to research for a school project a while ago. For my assignment, Animals That Scare You, I wrote all about the Copperhead.

***

Snakes are hated in the ranch lands where my aunt and uncle lived. No one ever acknowledged the good snakes do through their predatory cleanup and population control of rodents, rabbits, and the like. Unfortunately, my uncle and all of his ranch hands, friends, and fellow agriculturalists lived by the axiom: "The only good snake is a dead snake."

I can't say how many times I'd been in a pickup or car where the driver had put passengers' lives at risk by swerving through ditches at high speed, all in attempt to murder a snake. And snake killing didn't stop with these vehicular high-speed chases. There were many instances of ranch hands driving a snake from a tree just to hack it to death for the sheer joy of killing it.

Dorset's Killer Snake Roundup (KSR) was the culmination of this lethal snake lust. Copperheads and Timber Rattlesnakes were extremely dangerous, and found in large numbers in the brushy, rocky, and timber-dense lands of the rural Midwest. Each year, a few people were killed by one of these slithering devils—a lot of them, children. To even the score between snakes and the human element they'd tangled with, the little berg close to where my Aunt and Uncle lived, held a contest once a year. Dorset gained a bit of notoriety from these shenanigans and some curious folks came out from the neighbouring townships to have a go. Here was how the KSR worked.

Almost all the ranchers and farmers in the area left the confines of their tillage of land to become ruthless and courageous snake hunters for one day in summer. The start gun went off in the morning, signaling to all in attendance (whether participating in the hunt or hootin' and a-hollerin' from a safe distance), that it was time to "git some snake bags filled!" There was a party to set the thing off right. Multi-coloured balloons dotted the sky around whatever barn was hosting the KST that year. Lemonade stands were cobbled together and plastered with politicians' signs, and Future Farmers of America enrolment announcements were passed around. Several bands came out to provide music for the festivities, and of course, like at any good hootenanny worth a damn, there was plenty of liquor. Off in the back of an outbuilding, a bar would serve Snake Hunter's Punch which was a big pour of fine Kentucky bourbon, doused with a splash of sweetened lemon juice.

Each snake hunter was assigned a large burlap sack and a snake catcher wand: a long, grabbing tool with pincers on the end. This wand allowed the hunter to secure the head of the snake so he could drop the rest of its dangling body into his catch bag without fear of a deadly strike.

The snake hunters, from the eight in the morning start, to the close of hunting at four in the afternoon, scoured the woods, banks, roads, and fields—anywhere one of the coveted serpents might hide. My uncle was a zealous snake hunter and always made sure I tagged along with him on this over-the-top, out-of-control spree of animal catch-and-kill. As I watched him bag snakes, I was both terrified and transfixed by the sight of the creature's slithering majesty.

Hunters filled their bags with Copperheads and Rattlers, and at the end of the day, returned to the barn to calculate the weight of their haul. It was a real show. Each snake cowboy emptied his entire catch onto a large platform that served as a scale. Snakes that were not Copperheads or Rattlers were discarded and killed immediately. Their meat was fed to hogs owned by several of the hunters. What remained was the trophy catch of each KSR participant. These hissing, rattling, striking vipers were appraised, and the heaviest haul won. My uncle never got a trophy in the Killer Snake Roundup, but I didn't leave empty-handed. My tagging along had the mysterious effect of recalling some ancestral memory of the inherent dangers of snakes. Just a glimpse of one of these beasts conjured up a tangible, primitive fear I'd never be able to shake.

***

"Carl! SNAKE!" I reared back and hit my head on the roof of the boxcar.

"What'd ya say, Pete? Something about a snake? Shut up and keep shoveling, so when your uncle shows up with the truck we can get the hell out of here."

I screamed, "Carl, I shit you not—there's a huge Copperhead up here and it's coming for me. I'm out the witch's door right now." I was certain of my snake identification. I kept my shovel between me and my adversary.

To escape the snake, I'd have to borrow a page from its book. I carefully backed out towards the witch's door by slithering backwards on my belly. I reached my portal of salvation, to be confronted by Carl on the ground outside, a few feet below me. "No snake could survive being augured with the oats up into the boxcar, let alone the reel of the combine," he announced skeptically. "It would have to survive two sets of spinning blades so sharp they would turn any snake, let alone a big one, into little sausage bites."

I crawled out the door in a frantic mess of jumbled limbs. I slid down the boxcar ladder, my feet never touching a step, and crashed onto the ground in front of Carl. I looked up at him and shouted, "Carl, if you don't believe me, go up and check it out for yourself!"

Carl was about twenty-four or twenty-five, a high school dropout who worked as a ranch hand for my uncle for at least three years. He was long and lanky, with hair to match that was always in need of shampoo. He changed his clothes about once a week: always dark blue Wranglers, and one of two fake pearl button, western long-sleeved shirts. He wore a baseball hat that said, Diesel Cat Rules, that I suspect was permanently glued to his head. (I'd never seen him take it off). He's the picture of a prototypical white, uneducated, redneck.

Carl pushed me out of the way, and very smugly climbed the ladder leading up to the witch's door. On the way up, he paused to yell over his shoulder. "Pete, I can't wait to show you the piece of rope you thought was hissing its way to bite you on the neck." He laughed, and now at the witch's door, stuck his head into the boxcar's murky light.

There's a long pause and then Carl spit it out. "Oh my God, Pete! You're right. That sonofabitch is poised and ready to bite our asses off. Get me the hatchet that's in the tool box just under the seat of the tractor." Things did not augur well for this snake after all.

I ran over to the tractor. It was an old green John Deere, whose big work days were over, but was still great serving as a secondary transporter and light-duty vehicle. I found the toolbox jammed under the driver's seat and rummaged through it, finally locating the hatchet in and amongst the spider webs, dead bugs, and dirt, sharing space with a few sparsely used tools.

I sprinted back to the ladder, hatchet in hand, and climbed up to where Carl was perched just inside the witch's door. I handed the small axe to Carl.

"Pete, what took you so long? I couldn't breathe until you got back. You're right it's a Copperhead, and the damned thing uncoiled and slithered over to the darkest corner on the left side. I can barely see it now, it's so dark. Grab my flashlight from my belt and hand it over."

I unclipped Carl's flashlight and handed it to him. Carl aimed the beam where he last saw the snake and edged in farther. "Shit, Pete! It moved. Where the hell did it go?" Carl put the torch in his mouth and got on his belly. He made breaststrokes to gain some ground in the serpent's lair. I swam in directly after so I could spot him and follow the flashlight's beam in search of the snake.

"Carl! There it is. Over there. Move your light to the right." Carl took the flashlight from his mouth and adjusted the beam in the direction I indicated. The Copperhead was obviously stressed and slithered on top of the oats. I'd seen pictures of snakes surfing like this along sand dunes of the Middle East in my National Geographic's. The snake had an exotic allure, its body moving to some rhythmic mambo I couldn't hear. It was intimidating. I couldn't help but yelp, "Carl! Here he comes. That snake has it out for me."

"Hand me the hatchet, Pete. I'm going after it. Grab the light from me and keep the beam on that venomous bastard." I took the flashlight from him, like some baton secured in a relay race. But he was the one up for the challenge. I noticed how sweaty his hand was. He didn't say it, but he was scared. I located the snake and fastened the beam on it. In the small amount of time we took to make our flashlight and hatchet transfer, the Copperhead had recoiled with its head partially hidden under the first wrap of its body.

Carl moved in. He paused for a moment to take a spit of his mouth tobacco. Carl is one of those young old-school cowboys who gets his chew not from a sissy can of snuff, but rather an unlit Roi-

Tan cigar that he'll slowly macerate into a pulverized glop of tobacco and saliva to keep stacked inside his mouth, packed up against his cheek.

Carl swam closer to the snake. I was right behind him, focused on my task of illuminating our scaly antagonist. Suddenly, the snake uncoiled and shot to our right. "Go for it, Carl! It's loose again. And look!" I yelled. "It's coming right at us!"

"God damn it, Pete, what do you think I'm doing?" Carl had his arms straight out in front of him and wielded the hatchet like a baseball bat. For a moment he looked like Joltin' Joe DiMaggio as he pulled the hatchet up and back as far as he could to take a mighty swing at the Copperhead. He missed. The snake headed for Carl's face. This time Carl rose as high as he could onto his knees and . . . connected! It wasn't a direct hit, but it was a serious nick. A trickle of blood seeped into the oats.

"You got him. Whack him again right now and you can do him in for good."

"Shut up, Pete! I can't think . . ."

The Copperhead was bleeding from a wound in the middle of its long body. It danced to a different rhythm now, flopping madly and twirling around and around. He looked done for, but Carl couldn't wait to see what would happen next. He rose again, and with all the force he could muster within the confines of the boxcar, sent the blade of his axe deep into the snake's neck, separating the head from the body.

"You've killed it, Carl," I gasped. "It's over. I can't believe we survived."

During the half hour that we had stalked the Copperhead, the heat, humidity, and rancid smells of the boxcar and yard had dissipated. Riding on the coattails of death, every sensual element was back in spades. My adrenaline-stoked fear receded and in its place I found a sadness building as the result of killing an animal that probably, if managed correctly, could have been saved to live another day in the wilds, bushes, boulders, and forests of its primal home. His only motivation was survival and freedom. In the wild, if a someone was careless enough to step on it, animal law would prevail, and the Copperhead would have dominion to bite or maybe even kill its clumsy foe. I felt we had no right to blindly eliminate one of God's creatures simply to put salve on our primitive and irrational fears.

"Pete, go back down and empty the swill from the drinking jar. Bring it up here and we'll stuff the snake inside of it. That way, we'll be able to show him to your uncle, aunt, grandma, and the other ranch hands."

I found the mud-caked jar on the hood of the tractor, pried off the lid and tossed what was left of our morning lemonade. Normally, a few gentle taps from a hammer or some hot water were needed to loosen the lid from its candy crust and get at the bounty inside. My aunt's recipe employed excessive sugar that acted as a cementing agent around the threads at the tops of the mason jars. I must have had some traces of adrenaline coursing through my system to have made such short work of the lid with little effort.

I scooted back up the ladder with the jar to help Carl prepare the Copperhead for viewing. Carl had put on his yellow calfskin work gloves and stuffed the snake's lacerated body into the jar. Then he scooped up the head, catching some oats along with it. He closed the lid on the improvised mausoleum.

Just as we started down the ladder, my uncle rolled up in his pearlescent white Chevy pickup. He'd changed out of his familiar working rancher duds. I was used to seeing him in old blue jeans, a Cumbria work shirt, scuffed, ancient ostrich leather boots, gigantic cowboy hat, and custom leather, hand-tooled chaps. Instead, he was in his fancy city cowboy get-up, and the only piece I recognized was his huge silver rodeo belt buckle emblazoned with, "State Champion / Steer Roping / 1945" below a relief of a bucking horse and cowboy. He came by to check on my and Carl's progress.

"Looks like you guys are almost done. Hey, little man, this is some serious work and you've done great. Filling a boxcar with oats will make a real cowboy out of you. Guys, I have to go into town to buy a new water pump for the old D28. It's seen better days, but we have to use it to finish up baling over on the Cox quarter. I'll be back in a couple of hours."

Carl and I dropped down from the ladder's lowest steps onto the hard-packed clay foundation pad below. I felt shaken and proud at the same time. Shaken by the ordeal Carl and I had been through, and by the ambivalence I felt about murdering an animal for no good reason. I was proud, because to the folks living near my uncle's ranch, the story of an eleven-year-old boy stalking and killing a Copperhead would be a big deal. I knew my uncle would be over the moon with excitement over this courageous and manly deed, and he'd want everybody to know of his brave nephew's exploits. I was certain he wouldn't be able to contain himself. Friends, neighbours, ranch hands, the Dorset Evening News, and most importantly, our family, would hear what went down that morning.

"Hey, what the hell are you guys doing down here? Why isn't the auger feeding oats anymore? God damn it, Carl, I'm not paying you top ranch hand wages to stand around shooting the shit with Pete! I can't do anything about him, he's just a boy, but you had better get after it. I want to button up the boxcar this afternoon. Make sure everything is squared away for winter."

Carl didn't respond to my uncle's diatribe ridiculing his work ethic. Instead, he handed him the mud-caked drinking jar. "Here, Jimmy. Before you head off, take a look at what's inside. Be prepared to be surprised." He handed my uncle the container.

"Oh God, Carl, what are you going to show me? A spider or a rat? I don't want to see the mangled carcass of some unsuspecting critter we inadvertently pulled from the field. Just leave 'em to dissolve. Extra nutrition for the stock, you know." He winked, then shifted on his feet as he mulled it over. "But now you've got me curious. Let's see what you've got."

He started to unscrew the jar's lid. His hands were getting dirty from the mud that covered the outside. I shouted, "Uncle Jimmy, there are no bugs or rats in our jar. What is there is going to blow your mind."

Uncle Jimmy stopped his lid release and looked directly at me with a twinkle in his eye and asked, "So Pete, let me guess, you guys found oodles of old Spanish gold coins. I bet they're worth a fortune."

Carl jumped in, "Jimmy, go ahead and open the jar. It's not gold coins, but what's in there—what Pete and I fought and killed—is probably even more exciting."

Once the lid was off, my uncle stooped to set the snake jar on the ground in front of him so he could look directly downwards for a better view. Because of the snake's size, Carl had to cram its body and severed head into the jar with a great deal of force. The time it took my uncle to put the jar on the ground was just enough for the Copperhead's lifeless head to shoot out of the jar landing near my uncle's right boot. The deployment of the head was followed by the slow ooze of a portion of the serpent's slashed body out of the jar. Half of the beautiful pattern of the Copperhead's body was still inside, while the other was slopping sadly over the rim and folding on the ground.

"What the fuck is this?" my uncle yelled. He jumped back. We'd heard tales of men getting bitten, even after the snake was decapitated. "Was that thing up at the top, Pete, where you were levelling oats? Did it get close to you? Oh my God, Pete, were you bitten? Carl, where the hell were you when all of this was going down?"

I looked over at Carl. I could see he was upset. His stature was slumped, and his head hung low. He couldn't look my uncle in the eyes. My uncle's accusation and their underlying premise that Carl somehow shirked his duty to protect me, had hurt him. "Carl," my uncle prodded, "who killed the snake?"

I decided to answer my uncle's questions. "Uncle Jimmy, I saw the snake when I was on one of my last shovels before taking a break. I screamed for Carl's help, but he was raking oats from the wagon into the auger so he couldn't hear me. I kept my shovel between me and the snake and made a fast exit out the witch's door where I told Carl about the monster. Then we got a hatchet from the tractor, went back up in through the witch's door, and Carl went after it like one of the good guys in my Tarzan comics. He chased the Copperhead around the boxcar until finally cornering it. And then he killed it."

Carl lifted his head. "Jimmy, I couldn't have killed it without Pete's help. He's going to be a dandy little cowboy someday."

I felt my face flush with embarrassment at Carl's praise. Many years later when I was undergoing intensive psychoanalysis for my

PhD program in Behavioural Sciences, I recounted this scene to Marv Edelman, my chief academic advisor. He concluded, "Pete, even at eleven you were exhibiting a crucial component of your personality structure—a Courageous Giver, never wanting to take from a friend or colleague or even an enemy, but all the while, willing to grab any risk that might advance your goal, cause, or just plain fun. There are many guys like you dead in a warrior's grave, a medal on their chests for heroic sacrifice coupled with no need for self-aggrandizement. If the takers don't destroy you first, you just may have an opportunity to bear a noble epitaph: 'He dared to live a life worth living'."

"Okay, guys," my uncle said a little too loudly. He seemed to have caught some of our adrenal fever, and was now also fuelled by the fear and excitement of the demise of another evil Copperhead. "Let's get back to the house. I want to show this sucker to your grandma and your Aunt Florence."

Carl carefully placed the Copperhead back into the jar. First, the half of the body that had spilled over the lid, and then, the head with its eyes and tongue that could no longer see or feel the world. It seemed Carl had to work harder to persuade our prey back into its coffin. His gloves resisted the push, but finally the head was in, the lid screwed on tight, and the three of us rumbled the mile and a half back to the ranch house in my uncle's pimp pickup.

I'm sure we were quite the sight, bumping along the wagon paths through the pasture in such a car. It was a good fifteen minutes of hard riding over rutted pasture pathways worn bare and bumpy from years of serving the wagons, tractors, trucks, and heavy farm machinery of the ranch.

The ranch house was a large, two-storey home with an inviting arbour gate covered in honeysuckle. It was painted a brilliant white that contrasted with the steep, red roof with two dormers on its northern and southern pitches. In addition to the ranch house, there were four other structures scattered about the main property that were designed and painted with the same country look. Immediately to the left of the short picket fence that surrounded the house and lawn was a large four-car garage for all of my uncle and aunt's vehicles. North of the garage was a massive agricultural machine repair shop with the capacity to solve most of the mechanical problems found on a ranch. In between the garage and the mechanical shop was the pride of my aunt's ranch life—a state-of-the-art chicken coop housing her prize Rhode Island Red rooster and hens. The coop was air conditioned, cleaned twice daily, and surrounded by a state-of-the-art fence and security system aimed at stopping the predation by an overwhelming pack of real wily coyotes that savaged small livestock, pets, and vermin. The last structure in the mix was the ranch hands' dorm, where some of the essential workers slept and ate until they found a mate or more permanent living conditions.

Surrounding what was known as the Gregg Compound, was a lush forest of apple, walnut, maple, and oak trees. In the summer, vibrant green grasses grew splendidly around the house and through to the trees in the fields. The shag carpet gave way to the soft dirt of the pastures surrounding three charming red barns right out of a Norman Rockwell painting. During the day, horses, calves, and pigs could be seen roaming around the three barnyards, and at night they surrendered to the protection the Big Reds offered.

Carl and I entered the cold porch room that led into the kitchen. My uncle was behind us, looking for Charlie, his pet banty rooster. Charlie was an incredible bird with rusty red feathers that covered his body, and a bold yellow comb donned his majestic head like some royal crown. For over five years, my uncle had intuitively used what psychologists refer to as, operant conditioning, to teach Charlie to crow on command, play dead, rollover, count (peck) to five, and sort corn kernels into piles for himself, and piles for his lesser compadres, the ducks.

Carl and I removed our muddy boots and left them in the cold room with the sleeping farm dogs. We made our way into the kitchen to be greeted by two iconic features of the ranch. One was my beautiful, tiny, sixty-five-year-old Irish grandmother. The other was a massive cast-iron, six-plate, four-oven behemoth called an AGA cooker. It had a black enamel and chrome finish and ran on oil, not gas. Both of these fixtures emanated a radiant warmth.

"Hi, Gram'. Whatcha cookin' for dinner? All right if Carl eats with us?"

"Of course, darlin'. We're having chicken and dumplings tonight and we would love Carl to join us."

My grandma spoke with a lovely Belfast brogue. She raised my uncle and dad by herself, as her husband, my grandfather, took off with another woman when they were young. The only thing that saved her from having to turn them over to foster care was the meagre income she got from welfare, taking on small mending and tailoring jobs, and the paltry but well-meaning contributions my dad and uncle were able to drum up from their jobs as junior farmhands.

The AGA was the centre of action in the kitchen. Over to the left was a row of windows overlooking the cold room. Below the windows was a prep counter with four metal sinks. One of the sinks was extra-large and had a bright blue water pump attached to it so that the spout spilled directly into the basin. This was a crucial piece of ranch house engineering because there was no running water available anywhere in the house. We bathed in a large tin tub filled with water drawn from an outside pump and then transferred to the AGA's hotplates for heating before we mixed it with the cold in the tub.

On the wall just behind the front door was a crank telephone. The number at the ranch was two longs and a short, and all calls were made and received on an eight-person party line. The party line, when secretly listened in on, was a never-ending source of cheap gossip, community comings and goings, and general dirt on the neighbours. Sometimes when I was bored, I'd lift the earpiece off its walnut case and tune in. Over the years I'd overheard many a soap opera, whether it be Mr. Floot relaying news of the neighbourhood delinquents trashing his watermelon field and "eating their hearts out," or Virgil Carn ranting to Sam Nelson about "that communist running the UFA."

Kerosene lanterns hung in each room of the ranch, as there was no electricity anywhere in the house, or the houses of our neighbours. This made for long, softly lit nights where reading close to a lantern was the premier of in-home entertainment. Most adults, like my uncle (but not my aunt), dealt with this paucity of living by engaging regularly in the bars, night clubs, and movies found in the nearby, electrified communities.

Uncle Jimmy strutted into the kitchen, Charlie at his heels, clucking up a storm. Carl gave my uncle the snake jar just before we headed into the house. Now he had the snake in both hands behind his back. Suddenly, terror struck me. I sensed something awful was about to happen. My grandmother was one of my uncle's prime targets for practical jokes, and I knew she was deathly afraid of snakes. She was one of the nicest, but most high-strung people I'd ever known. I began to get anxious.

"Hey, Mom . . ." my uncle proffered, "could you wash this dirty drink jar?" He handed the muddy container to my grandma. "We need it for Carl and Pete to use tomorrow."

"Of course," she said. She took the clouded jar and moved to the sink. I held my breath. My grandma slowly unscrewed the top. The lid flew open with a pop and out tumbled the snake's head followed by its long, soft body. The Copperhead had been so compromised by its claustrophobic environment that it no longer bore any likeness to the once regal animal it was a couple of hours earlier.

"Oh Mary, Mother of God!" Grandma wobbled a bit and fell to the floor.

My uncle's riotous laughter turned to an embarrassed stutter. "I . . . I thought she could take a joke."

I ran to her side and kneeled, barely beating my uncle there. Her face was pale and fresh sweat lingered above her brow and on her front lip. Her eyelids began to flutter, and she slowly moved her head and coughed lightly. She was awake. Carl brought a cool, wet washcloth, which he handed to me. I placed it on my grandma's forehead. As I did this, I looked my uncle squarely in the eyes. I could tell he didn't like my angry glare.

"What are you looking at, you little bastard?"

I snarled through clenched teeth. "Uncle Jimmy, you are a jerk. I hate you for what you did to your mother. That's my grandma, you know. You could have killed her."

I didn't get another word out because I was knocked back on my butt by the thunderous slap my uncle delivered to the side of my head. I jumped up. "I want to leave tomorrow. You're a mean man. I never want to see you again."

"Get out of here, Pete," he growled. "Go to your room. As soon as I've taken care of your grandmother, I'll come and see you, and you can bet I'll straighten you out."

Carl suddenly remembered he had somewhere to be, and I headed to my room. I'd never been so upset. I knew our relationship would never be the same. There was a soft knock on my door. It was my grandma. I was so relieved to see her up and walking.

"Grandma! Are you okay?"

"Oh, honey. I just lost my balance when I saw that awful old snake. Your uncle was really silly pulling that joke on me. I don't know why I would expect him to do anything differently. He's been like this since he was your age."

We talked a little longer, nothing of consequence. It appeared she was better. I was tired so once I'd done a quick sink-and-washcloth bath, I laid down and fell asleep almost immediately. A short time later, I heard another knock on the door. This time it was my Aunt Florence. I was surprised to see her—I thought she was away at her retreat.

"Pete, get your things together. I'm driving you home tonight. I've called your mom. She knows you're coming. Your uncle will get over this in a short time. You'll see. It will be okay in just a little while."

He couldn't even tell me himself. I packed, said goodbye to my grandma, and jumped in my aunt's car, even angrier now. "It was Uncle Jimmy who almost killed grandma with that sadistic prank. I only tried to help. See you later, Uncle Jimmy. You're a stupid and uncaring son and uncle!" I really hoped this man was not my real father. My aunt didn't say a word as we drove away from the ranch.

I slept all the way back to The Project. I was home, wiser and hurt at the same time. Wiser in coming to learn how susceptible I was to please the powerful people in my life, and hurt by how these same people could turn and blame me for their transgressions.

CHAPTER 13: GETTING IT ON WITH JESUS

It was a slow, lazy Saturday afternoon at The Project. As I looked out the kitchen window, I saw the morning drizzle forming small drops on the large leaves of plants just outside our door. The weather had changed again. The morning drizzle was supposed to give way to a cold autumn storm replete with frost this evening. The Pirates were nowhere to be found. I needed a trip to the library. I'd completed the last book I checked out two weeks ago. I thought about walking over and picking up a new stack.

I could hear my mom talking to someone downstairs. I crept out of my room and took a secret seat on the top step of the staircase so I could eavesdrop on what was being said. I listened carefully. My mom was talking to Davey's, Aunt Peaches.

"Look Peaches, I think it's a good idea. I wasn't aware of Davey's problems until our chat this morning. I don't think he'll hurt Peter, but I would be lying if I didn't say I was a little worried."

"Louise, even though I work a lot, let me assure you I will make certain everything is on the up-and-up. Pete and Davey's comic book parties are great for Davey. He's not alone all day, and Pete is such a good kid. I think he will rub off on Davey. And besides Louise, I know you can use a little free time for yourself. Just think of Davey as a free babysitter."

"Okay Peaches, let's make it happen. I'll see you and Davey really soon."

I heard Peaches leave the house, so I headed down the stairs. "Was that Davey's aunt I heard you talking to?"

"Yes, it was. She came over to talk about Davey and you playing together. She knew I was worried, and our little chat took away many of my concerns. Pete, how do you feel about Davey?"

My mind kicked into high gear. I didn't know what Peaches had told her so she could have been setting me up. If I wasn't careful, I'd put my foot right in my mouth and spill the beans about our escapades into pornography. I decided to play it safe and say nothing.

I smiled at my mom. "Davey's okay. A little weird, but he has a great comic book collection that I love reading."

"Well, Pete, I trust you, and I'm sure if anything ever happens when you're at Davey's, that's not on the up-and-up, you'll tell me. Right?"

I remained silent. I was on the winning side now. No talk was good talk when you were walking on a quicksand of perverted lies.

"Oh yeah, Peaches told me Davey wanted to hang out a bit this afternoon. I told her unless something came up that you would be over at about two. Besides, I could use a couple of hours to play with your sister and take her to your Aunt's for tea and cookies. Sound okay to you?"

I responded a little too quickly. "Oh sure, sounds great. Have you heard anything from Dad?"

I didn't know why, but every Saturday I asked about my dad, knowing my question would provoke wild name calling, threats and eventually alligator tears. But that afternoon . . . nothing.

"It's almost two now. You'd better hightail it to Davey's."

I grabbed my heavy jacket and headed out the door for my date with smut. Moments later, I knocked on Davey's aunt's front door. I heard Davey yell from upstairs. "Is that you, Pete? I'm glad my aunt got my message to you. Come on in. I'm in my room."

I opened the front door, entered the house and slung my coat across one of the dining room chairs. I took the steps two at a time to Davey's room. I was anxious to see if he had any new comics. I walked in and there he sat on his desk chair. He had nothing on except his robe. It was completely open, exposing everything.

"Have a seat anywhere on the bed, Pete. Did your mom say anything about what she and my aunt were talking about?"

"Nothing. Very mysterious. Something about how good it was you and I were playing together and then a mention about them getting together at another time. That was it as far as I could tell. Absolutely nothing about the secrets of our parties." I tried not to look at his open robe.

"Okay, okay. Sounds great. Let's take a look at some mags, shall we?"

I picked up a copy of the new Spider Man. Davey jerked it out of my hands. "Pete, put that kid's stuff down and check out the pictures in that magazine over there. Remember that one? It's called *Fucked*. I've tagged a couple of shots that are really interesting to me." I moved farther away from the offending magazine.

Davey opened it and flipped the pages to the first marked spot. I didn't want to look, but if I didn't, I thought he would hurt me. The page showed a montage of three pictures of a young couple. The girl was white and the guy was black. They were having intercourse in what looked to be gymnastic positions. I was so disgusted I tried to close the magazine completely. Davey jerked my hand away.

"No you don't, Petey boy. This is great stuff. Don't you dare try to stop us from looking at these beautiful pictures."

"I hate you, Davey," I spat out. He slapped me across the face, grabbed my head and forced it down on top of the second picture. He held my head in a vice grip, making it tough to see the second image. What I could make out from my distorted position was that it was a picture of a teenage boy having oral sex with a young boy about my age. Davey had written on the page. His name was next to the teenager. Mine was beside the young boy.

"See if you would only be cool, Pete, we could have fun like these two guys. I'm sure your balls haven't fallen down into your nut sack yet so you couldn't get off if I sucked you, but I'm certain you would have a great time if you put those scarred lips around my dick and whistled Dixie."

I couldn't stand it anymore, I wiggled free of his grip. "Davey, I told you I want nothing to do with your sex pictures. You're a pervert and for once and for all, I'm out of here. Don't talk to me again."

I started to leave. Davey shouted at me, "Pete you keep acting like a little kid and I will punish you beyond belief. Now sit down, I want to show you something."

I was really scared. What if he hit me in the face again? I was afraid of what came next, so I obediently climbed back on the bed.

"That's more like it, Pete. Relax and watch. Very soon you'll be able to have a great time beating off like I'm about to show you."

Davey started stroking his penis. In a few minutes, it was red and erect in his hand. Davey's hand moved faster and faster until his head tilted back. His eyes rolled upwards and flickered, half closed, half open. He started to moan.

That was it for me, while Davey was still doing his business, I ran down the stairs and grabbed my jacket from the chair. Before he knew I was gone, I was out the door on my way home.

My feet didn't seem to touch the sidewalk because I was running so fast. My mind was churning. I had to tell my mom and dad about what was going on. But then I realized I couldn't say anything. Davey had that photo, and if I spilled my guts, the news would be all over The Project in a matter of hours. It would mean the end of The Pirates, and my parents would be destroyed. Silence was my cell. I'd participated in evil. I felt that I deserved whatever I got.

I was home long before my mom and sister returned from tea and cookies. I grabbed a Coke from the refrigerator and some chips from the pantry hoping a good nosh would settle my shaking hands and slow down my sweating. I decided to eat in front of the TV in the hopes of catching a new episode of *Sky King*. Just as I got relaxed into our most comfy chair, someone knocked on the door. I padded over, unlocked the door, and opened it. It was Davey.

He made no attempt to come in. He hissed through his clenched teeth. "Look, you little asshole. Don't ever run out on me again. If you take off again, like you did today, I promise your little sister will never look the same after I'm done with her. Understand?"

I was shocked, scared, and double stressed. Davey spun on his heels and walked away. I said nothing to him. In a daze, I moved back to the comfy chair in front of the TV and sank into despair. I thought the only way out of this mess was to kill myself.

Some time later, my mom and sister arrived home, bursting through the front door, full of energy and low grade chatter. "Pete, how was comics at Davey's this afternoon? Did you read any Wonder Woman like I told you? You'll see, girl superheroes are going to rule one of these days."

I replied, "The comics were great. Only *Spider Man* today, no Wonder Woman. Maybe next time. How is Aunt Sheila and the kids? Is Uncle Ted's bar doing well?"

My mom, in a surprisingly relaxed fashion, responded, "We'll talk later. I want to get dinner on so we can eat at a decent hour."

That Saturday's atmosphere was so atypical of my mom's usual pre-Sunday family war mindset, which is built upon the demons of pitched battle and the total punishment of my dad. As she stood in our kitchen she even seemed, dare I say it, at peace with her surroundings.

"Mom, I don't feel like dinner. I just want to go to my room. I'm re-reading *Call Of The Wild* so I want to get a good start on it this evening."

"Are you sure, Pete. I'm making one of your favourites, pork chops in logon berry sauce. Last time we had it you licked your plate clean. But if that 'call of something' is better than my pork chops I won't be hurt. Before you go to bed, I want you to take a good bath and lay out your Easter suit. We're going someplace special in the morning. But don't ask me anything about where we're going right now. I want to surprise you."

"Okay, Mom," I said as I made my way up the stairs. I shut my bedroom door, climbed down to the far end of my bed, and propped myself up into seated position with my back against the wall and my legs spread out. This was my favourite place for reading and *Star*

Catcher deep breathing and meditation exercises. I was so stressed from my session with Davey that my breathing was shallow. When I touched my face, it felt hot and sweaty. I was clammy all over, and my thoughts were a jumble.

I relaxed back against the wall, closed my eyes and started counting my deep breaths. One: deep breath in through the nose. Two: deep breath out through the mouth. I continued this for about thirty minutes. When I was done, I felt calmer, more focused. I pulled out an old half-eaten Baby Ruth candy bar that I had hidden in my desk for situations just like the one I was facing that night. I was hungrier than I thought so the blend of chocolate, sugar, caramel and peanuts blunted the rumble in my belly. I fell asleep with the *Call Of The Wild* slipping from my chest.

"Pete, it's time to get up." I heard my mom say as she was shaking me awake. "Get your Easter suit on and get ready to go. Don't bother with tea and toast. Where we're going, there will be oodles of food."

The Easter suit was grey with black piping around the pockets, lapels, and button holes. Black was also the colour of the buttons and shoes I wore to accompany this finery. I finished my look with a white shirt and a grey pork pie hat that I would immediately take off as soon as I found a convenient landing spot because I hated wearing it. But the hat was a favourite of my mom's, so anywhere we were going that I had to wear the Easter suit, I had to start with it on. As soon as I could find a break, I would yank the pork pie hat off my head in the hopes that it would get lost and never be found again. Somehow, we always found it.

Once I was dressed, I rushed downstairs. "Mom, are we taking Porsche?" I yelled out. My mom was sitting at the kitchen table, dressed to the nines. My sister sat beside her in a frilly white dress and hair curled like Shirley Temple.

"Yes, Pete, we're all going in Porsche. And I'm standing right here so you don't have to yell. We're waiting for friends who are going to join us, they should be here in just a few minutes."

Friends? Who in The Project could she be talking about? Sure, she had lady acquaintances she gossiped with every now and then, but I had never seen her go anywhere outside The Project with anyone. I heard a knock on the door. I raced over, curious as to who would be on the other side. I unlocked and opened the door. There stood Davey, grinning at me. Behind him was his Aunt Peaches. I was shocked and a sudden terror of being found out gripped me.

Davey was dressed just like he climbed off the set of *Rebel Without A Cause*. He wore a white T-shirt, jeans, denim jacket, sneakers without socks, and his hair was uncombed and greasy. His Aunt Peaches on the other hand, looked beautiful in a dark blue skirt, light blue silk blouse, bright red high heels, and a button-up blue sweater that matched the colour of her blouse. Her blond hair was neatly brushed to one side. The look was topped off with bright red lipstick.

"Davey, what are you doing here?" I snarled.

"Hey, Petey boy, didn't your mom tell you we were all going to church together. Seems like your mom and my aunt think you and I are basically heathens in the need of God's salvation. And besides, my aunt said if I refuse to go I could find another place to sleep tonight. Too cold for the streets. So, here we are."

"Shut up, Davey." Aunt Peaches glared at my nemesis. "Louise, are you guys ready? The service starts in thirty minutes so we better hightail it. And by the way, Peter, you look so nice in your suit and all. I wish I could talk your rebellious friend into at least clean clothes and washing his hair."

"Thanks Aunt Peaches. I didn't know that Jesus had a fashion police." Davey smirked. "And besides, Pete looks like a little sissy in that stupid suit. You feel really stupid don't you, Pete? Tell the truth."

I said nothing, but my thoughts were forming a spinning clash of questions. Who organized this torture trip? Why didn't my mom tell me Davey and his Aunt Peaches were going to be involved in this spiritual excursion? She said it was going to be a wonderful surprise, this was not wonderful. And most of all, what was wrong with me that my mom felt I needed divine intervention? Did she know about Davey and me?

"That's enough, Davey," my mom said. "Everybody go get in Porsche, I'll be right there after I lock up."

"Mom, I don't want to go," I pleaded. "I'd rather stay home and read my books."

"Not another word Pete, if you know what's good for you, you will go get in the car asap and keep quiet until we get to the service."

I slunk to The Project's parking lot. Davey was right behind me. He whispered just loud enough so I could hear him. "Petey boy. Mouth shut. We'll get through this God stuff. It will get Peaches and your mom off our back and then it will be party as usual."

Peaches and my sister caught up to Davey and I. None of us said anything. My mom finally joined us and herded us to where Porsche lie in wait. We all climbed in.

"I saw pastor Tom earlier this week," my mom said. "He's going to conduct our service today. I was at my wits end with Pete's father and I had nowhere to turn. Then when I was driving to the Kroger's, I saw this huge tent with a sign hanging high above the tent's entrance. It was connected to two large telephone poles, painted with big red letters saying, "Pastor Tom and Jesus Christ Forgive You. Accept God and Let Your Troubles Wash Away.

"I don't know why, but I swerved off the road walked into the tent and asked to see Pastor Tom. Well, I would have never expected it, but his assistant who I had briefly talked to when I walked in, came back in a few minutes with Pastor Tom in tow. He invited me into his small office just off the main dirt floor that served as the stage for the Sunday services. Pastor Tom is an old-time evangelist that moved his holy tent from city to city. He's only going to be here this weekend and then he's off to Waco for the next stop in what he called Jesus' Gospel Hour of Power. I told him about my issues with Thomas. He listened closely, asked great questions, and then after about a half hour gave me some good advice on how to treat myself, Thomas, and the kids with more love by all of us opening our hearts to the embrace of Jesus Christ.

"I thought it was such a good idea I decided to talk Peaches and Davey into coming with us to Pastor Tom's Sunday Service. After all, what can a little love and truth do but help save our souls?"

We were well down the road when my mom finished her sermon. I couldn't believe what I'd heard. Our family had never gone to church once. There was no Bible in our house, and the word God or Jesus Christ was never spoken. I guess if you're desperate enough any bromide that promises hope and possibility might be worth considering. But I was not sold that this was the path for me. As for Davey, this was a false errand that only had to be endured.

We arrived at our destination. We could hear the gospel music blaring blocks away as we transited with many other cars to designated parking spots. Once we got out of Porsche, the music was at the eardrum-killing level. The family that parked next to us immediately jumped out of their vehicle, dropped to their knees, and start praying.

The father's baritone incanted, "Oh God! Thank you for having us at your tent of worship, just like our brothers and sisters of ancient times who crossed the desert on foot and who slept in tents to praise you. We do the same by joining Pastor Tom in this magnificent day of worship and giving us thanks. In Jesus' name, amen."

As we passed by, the father, mother, and two daughters jumped up from their kneeling prayer position. They adopted the stride of race walkers and were on a direct path, along with hundreds of other people, to the entrance of Pastor Tom's house of glory. We were not far behind the crowd that engulfed the praying family. We entered the tent and all my sensual buttons were pushed.

When I was younger, my mom and dad had taken me to a couple of three ring circuses that made their way to the large city we were close to. I had travelled to Kansas City once to take in a championship rodeo with my uncle. The spectacle of these events pushed every limit of awe a little kid could muster. The bombardment of religious rock bands, choirs, huge stage defining torches, food wagons, swirling green, blue, red, and yellow lights bouncing off the uneven warp of the top of the tent, flooded over me. There were people of all ages, gender, race and religious persuasion there. Some were dressed formally, others in ragged clothes, possibly the best they could afford. Then Pastor Tom's servants, dressed in religious costumes from the biblical ages, led goats and sheep to where actors played out the drama of Joseph and Mary. There was a fake baby Jesus in the barn yard of Bethlehem.

A loud speaker cut in, "Ten minutes until your life changes forever. Pastor Tom is on his way. Get to your seats now and don't forget to give as much as you can to the young ladies passing through the audience. A dollar for Pastor Tom is a dollar getting you closer to heaven. Come on in folks. Start clapping your hands. The Pastor Tom Crusade Gospel Band and Choir are ready to lift the roof off this tent. Let's get it going. Praise Jesus."

We entered the large stadium area covered by the tent. A big band with at least twenty players, all dressed alike in bright red suits with black bow ties, were belting out a song. According to the program we had, it was called, "Hallelujah Train." All around us people were swaying, keeping time with the music, others were lifting both arms into the air rolling their heads back and with eyes closed yelling at the top of their lungs, "Praise Jesus and Lord is our Master."

I noticed my mom join in the "Praise Jesus" chorus. My little sister sat in her chair tapping her foot to the rhythm of the band. Peaches stood with her eyes closed, sinking deep into the tribal soup of old-time religion. Davey was a mad man. His arms raised, he danced with wild abandon, screaming, "I love baby Jesus!" He was so loud that a stadium guard came down to check and see if he'd blown his cork. I just watched, wondering what the hell this was all about.

There were three separate choirs anchoring the stage, one on either side and the third directly behind the huge speaking riser that I guessed was Pastor Tom's island of performance. The choirs got into a raucous sing off with gospel music going round and round. No one was seated, and the singing drove the energy to orgasmic chants of, "Hallelujah, Praise the Lord, and Jesus is coming."

Just when I thought the tent would explode with religious fervor, the lights dimmed. A spotlight centred on the totem-like oak podium which sat squarely in the middle of the massive stage. A huge baritone voice commanded attention over the loudspeakers.

"Ladies and gentlemen, boys and girls, are you ready to change your life?" A stultifying "Yes!" in unison erupted from the crowd. "Are you ready to turn your life over to the love of Jesus Christ?" Another massive "Yes!" exploded from the still standing audience. "Well then, it's time for me to introduce God's messenger of love and peace. The one, the only, Pastor Tom!"

The place went nuts. The band was back on, and all three choirs were singing in unison, "When The Saints Come Marching In." Then, a leprechaun of a man dressed in a black tuxedo flew out onto the stage. His freshly coiffed long brown hair flew behind him as he madly danced and sang along with the band and choir. To my right, two seats down from Davey, an elderly man had climbed on top of his seat. He ripped his shirt off and with arms outstretched, eyes rolled to the back of his head, foam spittle dripping down the side of his mouth, and screamed at the top of his lungs in what sounded like some obscure ancient language. The security guard that had visited Davey earlier rushed to the man and helped him down from his perch, moving him gently to the aisle. Pastor Tom sprinted to the man's side and encouraged more ancient talk.

"Brother, we are with you. God of the Old Testament is talking through you with tongues signaling the time of judgement is near."

He placed a hand on the man's shoulder and then the guard helped the old man out of the stadium. Pastor Tom sprinted back to his gilded perch and delivered a sermon of fire and brimstone with such passion and rhetorical flare that even I, who up until then was simply a passenger on Pastor Tom's Praise Jesus express, was a little impressed and amazed at the power this man had over the psyche of hundreds of people.

The power of Pastor Tom stuck with me for years. That day under the big tent, the band and choirs, the man speaking in tongues, the explosion of colour, light, and tempo, the intoxication of group symmetry in the form of chant and leading message, plus the wild ride of Pastor Tom's conjuring the greats of religious oratory like Amy Simple McPierson or Elmer Gantry propelled me towards one overriding question that I have attempted to answer all my life. Here's what I keep asking: What social forces influence people to change their behaviour–change their lives–for good or for evil?

***

Years ago, when I was in university, I was engaged in answering my question related to behavioural change and social influence. For months, I'd been consumed by the process of choosing a doctoral dissertation topic that would shed light on the power of those tools that cultures, organization, politicians, and charismatic leaders use to ply people to adopt their points of view. As I poured over research paper after research paper looking for a worthy research subject, I kept coming back to my Sunday morning with Pastor Tom.

One afternoon, I read in the paper about this new age religious movement that was anchored with high voltage Jesus rock services under the lights of a big evangelical tent. It was staked in a field that usually was the home of the travelling circus, or the county fair. I decided right then and there I had to see this updated version of Pastor Tom with my own eyes.

At about 6:15 that same evening, I travelled the almost empty freeway east of the city. I passed by brown rolling hills, parched fields, and hundreds of little track houses painted in a rainbow of hues. Then I arrived at the tent of Calvary Chapel. This was the second time I'd been to a formal religious service in my life. The first was with Pastor Tom. The second, in this field of spiritual dreams. I parked, and made my way to the brown, mammoth edifice to man's hope for everlasting life. By then I knew I was a confirmed atheist, willing to share my views with anyone who asked, on what I felt was the utter blight that formal religion laid upon the world. As I moved farther into the tent of salvation, I felt unconformable. Even being there was such an act of hypocrisy on my part. However, as my visit was in the name of scientific inquiry, I relaxed a bit and found a seat.

The service was Pastor Tom on steroids. Multi-media dominated, religious rock bands explodes into sound and chant, dancers, choirs, and drummers raised the euphoric energy beyond Mach ten. Right then and there I decided an anthropological study of this new Jesus Freak phenomena was going to be my contribution, at this point in my academic career, to the understanding of social influence and behavioural change.

For the next two years I lived undercover down by the beach, in a two-storey, white stucco house located in a poor neighbourhood. This was the Jesus Freak commune of the Children of the Lord. The Children of the Lord were a radical Christian group. They were dedicated to fomenting a violent gun centric revolution of believers to the proposition that Christianity should be the ruling belief system of a new America. Building our cadre of commune members was a never-ending challenge. The recruits who came to join us were just about the same as those who left. I made trips to nightclubs, concerts, bars, and other associated places of poor lost kids. We looked especially for those young people who were living on the street, engaging in prostitution, drugs, criminality, and general social deviancy.

Myself and five other commune mates were the recruiting crew. Our job was to talk those lost souls into jettisoning the streets, climb onto the open bed of the large blue truck we showed up in. They were to join us at our home of spiritual love and peace for at a minimum of a warm safe bed, a hot shower, clean clothes, and a nutritious vegetarian meal. All the recruits had to do, as the leader of the commune Sister Anne said, was, "fall in love with Jesus."

Once in the commune, our recruits were subjected to the powerful processes of values stripping, grooming, and the influencing of targeted friendship, spiritual love, and constant reading and study of the Bible.

In the commune, I was a part of the education crew. Fortunately, before I slid underground, I had taken six months to study the Bible and other religious writings. I wouldn't say I was a religious scholar, but I knew more than most of the commune members and targets. So, every evening I would lead Bible study, which was always followed by Sister Anne, sitting on a large oak chair, dressed in a handmade red and white calico dress with a shotgun proudly displayed across her lap, all the while lashing out at liberal democrats, black radicals, and dirty Jews.

Each night, at two in the morning, I would get up from my dorm-style bed, which was in a sleeping porch that housed five other commune members, and sneak into a large closet. I had a miner's headlight on and I would record my notes chronicling the events of that day. Everything went fine for two years. I would spend three days a week at the commune, the other four at home and the university. The data I collected, from my vantage point, was profound and important. But one night that all changed.

I was lounging on top of my bed reading a *Superman* comic. I knew Sister Anne would think I was committing blasphemy but what she didn't know wouldn't hurt her. "Hey Pete, Sister Anne wants to see you," a commune member named Fred said.

"Fred, do know what she wants?"

"Not a clue, but she did say it was important and you should get downstairs as soon as possible. Hey where did you get the *Superman* comic? Can I see when you're finished?"

"Not a chance, Fred. Reading *Superman* might get you into a load of trouble around here. I guess I'd better get downstairs and see what's twisting Sister Anne's knickers."

I slowly got off my bed, went to the washroom, straightened my hair and ambled on down the stairs. Once on the stair landing, I looked around. From what I could see, not only was I in trouble, I thought my life might be in danger. All the overhead lights were off. Only candles and small table lamps provided illumination in the room. The male commune members were seated in a semi-circle, with Sister Anne perched on a chair directly in front of her acolytes. The shotgun lay on her lap and she called me over.

"Brother Pete, come and stand in front of me." I moved over and faced Anne, with the brothers seated behind me. "Pete, you are no longer a member of our brotherhood. We know you've been doing the devil's work each night making notes of our secrets, and our promises. Now listen very carefully. We are Old Testament Christians. We believe in an eye for an eye and a tooth for a tooth. You have thirty seconds to get out of here or you are a dead man. Praise the Lord."

I took a glance around. Those men were serious. I started to go back upstairs to grab my last batch of notes. Luckily, every day I mailed my notes to myself so I had very few loose pieces of paper to retrieve.

"Don't even think about it, you son of Satan. Get out of here right now." Sister Anne shouted as she stood and pointed the shotgun in my direction. I got the message and in stark fear I was out the door in a second and into my car, heading north to my home knowing a chapter in my life had closed.

It took another year of analysis and writing to finish my dissertation, *Getting It On With Jesus*. My risk-taking and hard work paid off with several national awards for excellence in social science research and eventually a contract to publish my dissertation from a major book distributor. I signed the contract but never went through the painful process of writing and rewriting. Instead, Pastor Tom and the two years with Children of the Lord formed the backbone of my ever-expanding research, teaching, and consultation life.

***

What happened the Sunday evening after Pastor Tom's lift off was a significant validation of social influence in action.

As I mentioned before, Sunday afternoons, filled with my mom's anguish and stress because of my dad's drunken weekends, would give way to family war on God's day of rest. But after our revival meeting with Pastor Tom, that Sunday evening was different. My dad staggered home at about six. Still drunk, he couldn't navigate a straight line through the kitchen. Instead he bounced from one appliance to another. I stiffened, waiting for my mom's physical and personal abuse against my dad.

Instead of screams I heard, "Thomas, I know you're not feeling well. Let's get you upstairs, out of your dirty clothes, and into bed. If you have to throw up, I'll help you. If you're hungry later on, Peter and I can get you some chicken soup to sip on. Remember Thomas, God loves you. Together we can work it out."

I had never heard my mom talk to my dad that way, with honest love in her voice. Pastor Tom's induced détente for my family didn't last longer than a couple of weeks. Soon my mom and dad were at each other's throats again. That Sunday signalled massive changes that would change my family's lives. Pastor Tom's brief chat with my mom and the rousing revival service were a precursor of changes that fifteen years later would blossom into a different, more loving, no alcohol, more accepting and giving way of life. Unfortunately, this dramatic transition occurred just after I left home, so I never ever really knew those Greggs and they were never a part of my life.

CHAPTER 14: DON'T BE A RAT

I woke with a Pastor Tom hangover. My hearing was fuzzy from all of the rousing music and singing. I experienced flashbacks of the man speaking in tongues, Pastor Tom's sermon, and a swirl of the exotic. I laid awake for a while, shocked out of the lingering images of yesterday by my mom's invitation back to the real world. "Pete, rise and shine. Hurrah, it's Monday and it's the first day of sixth grade. I bet you're very excited."

I'd heard my mom throughout the night helping my dad with his DTs, comforting him when he was wrenching his guts out and all the while sleeping in the same bed with him. She had never done that prior to Pastor Tom's readjustment of love and peace he had given her personally several days before the Sunday blast off.

I answered back. "It's too early. It's too cold. I want summer back. And I don't want to go to sixth grade."

"Come on, Pete, get going. I know your pals are waiting over at the Plaza to walk to school with you."

She was right. I was late, so I hustled to the washroom, did my business, wet my hands and scrubbed my face and hair with cold water. Once groomed, I rushed back to my bedroom and put on my newish jeans, red polo, white crew socks, and my old smelly sneakers. I grabbed my blue bike couriers book bag, slung it over my shoulder and ran for the door.

Then it hit me. Stark terror of the new. I'd be standing alone without my mates, who were condemned to repeat fourth grade. There were rumours of out-of-control sixth grade bully boys. On top of that was an academic insecurity like I had ever felt before. The combination really turned on the sweat stress faucet.

Once I was out the door, I saw Benny Tail-Feather, Bill and Mike running towards me. My fear started to subside. Mike was yelling, "Let's go, Gregg. Time to shake school up."

It was so great to see them. We'd been walking the two miles to school together since first grade. But it was different that day. Jerry Kaye was not there. She was never going to walk with us again. She was probably already heading across town, driven by her dad so she could attend a proper fifth grade.

We walked out of The Project's parking lot. For the first time I noticed the leaves that were just turning yellow and red last week, were now starting to fall to the ground, reminding us of the cycle of life. There was contrast in the air today, an early warm wind greeted us, not a cloud in the sky, birds flirting here and there, seemingly not in a hurry to head south. None of us felt any risk of being caught in bad weather today. Not one jacket draped any of our shoulders.

We started doing boy stuff: kicking rocks, laughing at Benny Tail-Feather's farts, slugging an arm, and laughing at our silly jokes. In the midst of our re-connection, we talked.

"Pete," Bill said, "why have you been spending so much time with that weird Davey kid? I even heard from my mom that you, your mom and sister, went to church yesterday with him and his Aunt Peaches. Pete you've never gone to church since I've known you. Then there are those strange comic book parties you go to at his house. You haven't done Pirate stuff in a bunch of days. It seems like Davey has you under his spell. And by the way, my mom forbids me hanging out with him. She says there's something very wrong with his behaviour. So, what's the deal, Lucille?"

They were on to me. Davey must have let the cat out of the bag. I didn't know who he told but man, I was in trouble. I decided that the only good defence is a good offence, so I said, "He's got an amazing comic book collection, twice the size of any of ours with lots of new stuff. I can clear it with Davey, and I'll make sure you guys come with me to the next party."

Benny looked at me and shook his head. "No way, José. My dad says Davey reminds him of one of those teenage perverts he's read about. The ones that stalk young guys like us for sex. Pete, you'd better watch your ass. You're treading on water that can drown you."

All the other guys shook their heads in agreement. I wished I could tell the Pirates what was going on in my wild kabuki dance with Davey, but I couldn't. I decided that silence was my only option. I hung my head and kept walking while Benny Tail-Feather, Mike and Bill laughed their asses off recounting the last session of B-47 which resulted, according to what was going to become an urban legend, the utter destruction of every bike the Pirates had thrown into battle. I was even sadder as I listened to my friends tell their stories of all-consuming boy joy, all the while I was stuck with Davey and his blighted sense of life.

In a few minutes, I was back laughing with the guys, all of us sharing our exaggerated negative fantasies of what the first day of school would be like. Soon, fantasy turned into reality as we found ourselves passing the big athletic field on our right. Then it was up the cracked sidewalk to the grey cement steps leading to the front doors which gave way to the classrooms. Benny, Bill, and Mike turned left and went through the door for kindergarten through fourth grade. I waved goodbye to the guys and yelled, "See you at three. We have a new stick ball game to plan!"

Mike flipped me the bird and yelled back, "Gregg, you suck at stick ball. I can't wait to paint home runs off you." As the diminished Pirates turned left, I headed right, taking me to Mrs. Brook's sixth grade classroom.

As I was about to walk through the right-hand door, I saw them. Five big boys heading down the hallway straight at me.

"Is this the one?" The largest kid yelled. I stopped immediately, not moving a muscle.

"Yeah, that's him," a smaller member of what was apparently the sixth-grade boy's posse answered. "I saw him as he was leaving Mrs. Brooks' room and she stopped me and told me that was Peter Gregg. The only boy from Mrs. Bear's class that's skipping into sixth to join us. She gave me a warning: 'No hazing, and keep you and your friend's hands off this kid.'"

The bigger kid yelled. "Then let's get him."

They came running at me full steam. I panicked, turned tail and ran as fast as I could back the way we had walked in. There was no escape. The five attackers caught me. They threw me to the ground. I fought back hitting, kicking, and screaming at the kids that were walking by to help me. Nobody stopped. They just passed on by, eyes straight ahead, hoping, I guess, for a no attention, no involvement verdict.

All five of my attackers punched and kicked me at will. They threw dirt all over me. Finally, they stopped my beating, pinned my arms and legs to the ground, and pried open my mouth. They forced me to swallow the most God-awful concoction of really hot stuff and putrid smelling vinegar like liquid. I puked.

The big guy, who was obviously the wolf pack's leader, gave me another slap on my face. "Look, asshole, you've just been initiated into sixth grade. Don't think you will ever be one of us. Don't talk to the girls, and if you rat us out, you are dead meat. Understand?"

The bell rang, signalling it was time be at your desk. The class would commence in ten minutes. My sixth-grade welcoming committee took off. As they headed through the door, I heard one of the goons say laughingly, "It felt so good teaching that little pussy his first sixth grade lesson. Don't mess with us. Our rules. Our school."

I got up not knowing quite what to do. My nose was bleeding. I had scrapes on my back and elbows. I could feel a big knot on my forehead. My almost new clothes were ripped, and I was covered in grime and dirt. Only a few kids were close to where I was standing. I took a gulp of air and steadied myself. I yelled over to a girl who was staring at me. "Where's the closest boys' washroom?"

"Go inside the right-hand doors and then just to your left is a large boys' facility. Do you want me to go tell someone what happened to you?"

I shook my head no and followed her instructions to the large washroom. There were at least ten urinals, five toilets, and five sinks inside. Everyone was in class, so I was totally alone to conduct an injury once over.

I ran a water-soaked paper towel over my face, neck and scalp. After a few minutes of blotting blood and removing dirt, I could see I was pretty much worse for the wear, but not even close to being dead. I limped over to take a pee and came back to the mirror. I didn't know what to do. I couldn't go to class looking like this, but I didn't want anyone calling my mother. I couldn't bear enduring her wrath.

Just then, the washroom door burst open. I heard a voice. It was the school principal, Ms. Shaffer. "Peter, are you in here alone?"

"Yes," I answered.

"I need to talk to you as soon as you're able. Wash up. If you need to use the facilities, do it quickly and come out so we can chat."

I took a few more minutes. I tried to get my polo positioned so that it closed the giant rip enough that I didn't look naked. I dabbed the cuts on my elbow and scalp to get them to stop bleeding. I stuck some toilet tissue up my nose to encourage coagulation. I limped out the swinging doors of the washroom and came directly face-to-face with Ms. Shaffer and Mrs. Brooks.

"Peter what happened to you?" Ms. Shaffer asked while she held my hand. "Some kids just came to my office and told me a group of older boys just beat you up. Looking at you right now, I can tell this must be true."

All I could think was, "don't be a rat, Pete!" If I spilled the beans on these guys, I was dead meat. But what was my story? Mrs. Brooks broke into my fabrication of a possible explanation.

"Peter, some of the girls I talked to said it was a group of sixth grade boys that jumped you. Right now, we are going down to the sixth-grade classroom and you're going to tell us who the kids are that attacked you."

I coughed and croaked out, "No one attacked me. I was running backwards, I tripped and fell. That's it. That's what happened."

"Pete, I know this is tough for you," Mrs. Shaffer said. "I don't think you're telling us the truth. I think you're afraid of what those guys will do to you beyond this beating. Pete, you need to know, by state law, I will have to report what happened today and there will be an investigation. I will find out who did this to you and there will be holy hell to pay. I am not going to let these kids get away with it."

"Please Ms. Shaffer, don't say or do anything. It was just an accident. I'm okay."

"Pete, also by law I have to call your mom and report what's happened. She can come and get you. Your first day in sixth grade can start tomorrow if you're up to it."

All of my wounds were now starting to throb to the beat of pure sadism. My bed and books were calling. I knew if I didn't show up in class today the bullies would win and there would be no end to the torture they would dish out into the future. I became determined. This day would be my first day of sixth grade.

***

Jessy, the school's physical education teacher showed up with a first aid kit and a red Raiders flag football jersey. Ms. Shaffer had asked Mrs. Brooks to send Jessy over to my washroom. Jessy was over six-feet tall, had short crew cut brown hair, and was dressed in khakis and a white polo, with black walking shoes. There was a massive keyring clipped to his black belt. Jessy not only coached all the school's athletic teams, he also served as father confessor to many of the boys who came to him with their angst, fears, and recriminations.

Today was the first time I'd had the opportunity to talk to Jessy. Once, in fourth grade, he had noticed how I won all the sprint races at the school, even the ones that included sixth grade boys. I remembered him saying something like, "Pete, you should try out for our football and baseball teams. You're small, but fast as hell. I think you would have a ball and who knows junior high and high school are calling and being a good ball player might be a plus for you."

I knew we didn't have money for equipment that parents had to buy their kids who participated in extracurricular sports, so I said nothing to Jessy and let a sleeping dog lie.

My thoughts were interrupted by Ms. Shaffer. "Jessy, if you could take Pete into the washroom, clean up his scrapes and cuts, get that torn shirt off him and give him the jersey to wear for now. I've called the district and they're sending an investigative team, including a nurse, to talk to Pete this morning."

"Sure Dorthy," Jessy said. "Come on, partner. Let's go inside and get you looking ship shape." I followed Jessy into the washroom. He helped me take off my torn shirt. Some kids tried to come in and he swished then away with a gruff, "Find another washroom, just for this morning."

"Okay, Coach," the intruders responded.

Jessy proceeded to wash my cuts and scrapes clean. He dabbed each one with iodine and covered them with Band-Aids for the smaller ones and several large bandages for the bigger cuts on my knee and elbow.

"So, Pete, who did this to you? I know you're a tough kid from The Project and you don't want to rat out a group of sixth grade bullies, because who knows what they will do to you next time, but I won't say anything. It would be our secret. I'll just make sure they get what's coming to them. What do you say, kiddo? A little truth might help."

As much as I wanted to fess up to Jessy, I knew nothing ever remained a secret at this school. My only real shot at surviving sixth grade was to keep my mouth shut. "Jessy, I just fell down, plain and simple."

"All right, Petey, have it your way. Remember, I'm always here for you."

Ms. Shaffer opened the door. "Are you guys about done? The district investigative team and nurse will be here in just a bit. Pete,

I've called your mom and she's rushing right over. When you finish, come and wait in my office."

Jessy and I walked out of the washroom and headed for Ms. Shaffer's office. For the first time I looked down at the number on the jersey Jessy has provided me. It was 82. I insisted, from that day forwards to junior high school, high school, and university that my football number would always be 82. It was a powerful reminder of courage in the face of the bullies in the world.

We walked into Ms. Shaffer's office. She motioned for me to sit down in one of the tub chairs facing her desk. She excused Jessy with a thank you that I also chimed in on. Then she turned her attention directly on me, looking me squarely in my eyes.

"Pete, I know you're lying about what happened to you today. It's important for you to know that if you lie to these investigators and they find out the truth you can be in real trouble to say nothing about what your mom will do if you lie to her. Pete, I know what happened to your mouth. Benny Tail-Feather's mom told me. I'm frightened for you–for us–because if I ever again find out your mother has abused you the way she did before you first came into my office, I will have to turn her into the authorities. So, your lying has great consequences for all of us. Please, just tell the truth."

"I will, Ms. Shaffer. I just fell. That's it. End of story."

Tears tried to escape from Ms. Shaffer's eyes. She shook her head as if to say no. She looked so sad and exasperated. But what was I to do? I was certain the truth would not set me free. Instead, it would get the crap beaten out of me. Just then, my mom rushed into Ms. Shaffer's office.

"Pete, are you okay? What the hell happened to you? Dorthy, I told you this sixth grade idea was stupid. Pete get up. We're getting out of here."

Ms. Shaffer tried to calm my mom down. "Louise, I understand you're upset, and we have a lot of talking to do so Peter can have a good school experience. In just a few minutes the district investigators will be arriving to interview Pete. They want to find out the truth and take appropriate action so this kind of situation does not take place again."

"Okay, okay, Dorthy. I'll keep my big mouth shut for now. I'll wait around until this investigation thing is done and then I'll take Pete home. That okay with you Pete?"

What could I say? All I wanted to do was go directly to my classroom, face my attackers, not listen to those that might laugh at me, and basically get it over with so I could start the next day with a clean slate. I could tell this was a pipe dream on my part. I was in the soup, waiting for all the adults to allow me the freedom to deal with my problems in a way that fitted my situation.

"No, Mom. I don't want to go home with you," I said. "I want to get this all over with. I want to go to my class and then walk home with the Pirates. Please don't wait for me. I'm okay. I just fell. Why can't you guys accept that? So, Mom, I'll see you this afternoon. If I have to be in sixth grade, then that's the plan. Mom, it's all right."

"God damn it, Pete! You're not calling the shots here. Because I know you're upset, I'm going to let your lies go for now. When you come home this afternoon, you and I are going to figure out the truth. And then tomorrow you will pick out the boys that did this to you and they will be punished." I didn't say a word. What was there to say?

She continued, "You should also remember a bunch of kids saw what these bastards did to you. Pete, you can't shade the truth when eyewitnesses will say just the opposite of your whopper. You better clear this up, and start by telling those rent-a-cops that Dorthy called about what really happened. I'll see you at home. Oh, and by the way, tell Benny Tail-Feather to tell his mom to mind her own business and stay out of our family's life."

My mom had lost her Pastor Tom afterglow and was back on the warpath. She stormed out of Ms. Shaffer's office. I didn't know what to do or say, so I sat silently. Ms. Shaffer broke into my thoughts of dread and deceit and asked, "Pete, are you hungry? I have some cut-up veggies we can share, plus I can get you a carton of milk to wash it down. What do you say?"

Ms. Shaffer's mention of food reminded me how hungry I was. Cut veggies are not on the top of my food list, but at that moment they sounded delicious. Ms. Shaffer walked to a little red refrigerator she had next to her desk. She opened it up and brought out a plastic bag full of carrots, celery, radishes, and peppers. She also grabbed two cartons of milk. She walked over to me, placed a napkin on my lap and dumped a few vegetables on it. She opened one of the small milk cartons and handed me a red and white coloured straw poking out the top. I grabbed a handful of vegetables and chewed them into a cellulose mush, washed down with a big swig of milk.

"Peter, look at how you're eating. You must be really hungry."

"Thank you, Ms. Shaffer. I am starved. A carrot never tasted so good."

Ms. Shaffer's phone rang and she picked it up. "They're here. Yes, send them down. No, she decided to go on home. Pete will be on his own."

Ms. Shaffer cradled the phone and looked at me. "Pete, the investigators and nurse are here. Just so you're aware of it, we are bringing the five boys that others identified as the ones who beat you into the office, so all stories are in the room at the same time. Peter, I'm going to make sure no one here at this school ever hurts you again. You must tell the truth."

I reluctantly surrendered my vegetable feast to the trash can just as Jessy marched in with the gang of five. I now had a much closer look at my attackers. All were dressed in clean, neatly pressed sixth grade duds: T-shirts, new dark blue jeans, and popular athletic sneakers. Three of the five guys were not much bigger than me, but the other two looked older and were giants when compared to my slight stature. Ms. Shaffer scooted me and my tub chair over to the side of her desk. She grabbed extra tubs and placed them in front of her desk so they were directly facing me.

"Pete," she said as she pointed to the largest thug, "This is Luke." She pointed to the next biggest of my attackers. "Next to him is Will." Then she pointed to the other three boys. "And this is Neal,

Larry and Dereck. Guys, this is Pete. He's the kid the other kids said you beat up." Nobody said a word.

As the chairs were positioned and the lineup of sixth grade bullies were being introduced, two sorta cops and a nurse joined the party. Ms. Shaffer stopped and acknowledged the new participants and introduced them to us. "Guys, this is Officer Jones and Officer Tong. They are designated District Seven safety officers. Joining us is Elise Field, the District Seven nurse."

The sorta cops were dressed in dark blue militaristic uniforms. They each wore a big black utility belt with handcuffs hooked on the left side of the belt and a cop's control baton connected to a D ring on the right. Elise, the nurse, was dressed in a white medical jumpsuit, and was carrying a dark brown satchel. Ms. Shaffer sat the authorities over to the opposite side of her desk where they would have a full view of what was about to happen.

Ms. Shaffer started. "I think everyone knows why we're here. I've had the chance in a phone call to brief the officers and our nurse on the facts of the case." She looked at the three authorities and they nodded in the affirmative. "Also, Pete, I want you to know you are safe here, no one is going to hurt you, so please tell us the truth. What'd you say, let's get started?"

I held my breath. "Peter, it's a simple question. What happened to you this morning? Why were your clothes torn and why did you have cuts and bruises all over your body?"

I realized I couldn't just keep saying I fell. I had to come up with a more believable story. "Okay, look, the guys all rushed up to me to say hello as I was climbing the steps into the school. We stopped, and I think it was Luke who pulled out a bouncy ball and we started to play. I missed a couple of kicks and the ball sailed out into the field. On my second miss the guys chased and tackled me on the cement that's right by the edge of the field. Once I was down, they gave me a tickle bath. You know what that is right? Kids grab one person, get them on the ground and then tickle them until they shout GIVE, or pee their pants. It's a lot of fun. I guess the guys were a little rougher than they usually were. Because I'm a bit smaller than most of them I ended up a little worse for wear. That's what happened. No one was beaten or bullied. It was just good fun."

I did not know where that story had come from, but looking at the faces of the sorta cops and the nurse it seemed like ambiguity rather than certainty was ruling their expressions. Then I got the icing on my cake.

"Luke, what happened? Did you guys beat up Pete to haze him into sixth grade?" Ms. Shaffer asked.

"It was just like this kid, Peter, says. We went up to him to say hello and welcome him into our class. We played a little bouncy ball and gave him a tickle bath. As he said, he's smaller than most of us so I guess we got a little too rough. We're sorry he got hurt. It was an accident. We didn't abuse anyone."

Luke then looked straight at me and carried on. "If we had wanted to beat anyone, they wouldn't be walking around right now." Luke's four friends found this last comment hilarious and all laughed out loud.

Ms. Shaffer angrily broke in. "This is not funny. I'm not sure I know exactly what happened here, but let me warn all five of you, if I find out what you've told me is not true, including you Peter, I will make sure you are punished up to and including suspension."

She looked over to the authorities. "Do any of you have questions?" Only the nurse responded.

"Before I leave, I will need to do quick exam of Pete's injuries, just making sure he doesn't need to see a doctor."

The sorta cops both said something like, "No, we're okay," but Officer Tong added, "It doesn't look like there's anything for us to report back to the district. But, Peter, if you change your mind, get back us. You have a year to reopen the case. I think that's it. We'll wait for Elise to do her exam and then we'll be on our way."

Nurse Elise walked me back to the boy's washroom where Jessy had done his best to clean me up. She had a janitor put a closed sign on the door and proceeded to do a quick poke, prod, and manipulate assessment of my injuries. "Looks okay, Pete. I think in a couple of days you'll feel much better. You can put your shirt back on and when you're ready, you can go back to Ms. Shaffer's office."

***

"Pete, the rest of the kids will be back from lunch in about ten minutes." Mrs. Brooks, my new sixth grade teacher said. "I've assigned you to Wolf pod. You're going to be sitting next to Gus. He's a great guy. I think you two can become good friends."

Mrs. Brooks divided our class into five pods. There was Wolf, Leopard, Elk, Lion, and Chita pods. Each pod had six kids sitting in a tight semi-circle where the focus was on the front of the room. It was also pinched so that each pod member could have close conversations with their pod mates. "Just have a seat. As soon as everyone gets back from lunch, we're going to start our first math block. After looking at your math scores from fourth grade, I think you'll fit right in."

I slouched into my desk as all the students returned from their brown paper sack lunches. A tall skinny black kid slid into the desk next to me. He held out his hand, then grabbed mine and shook it while saying, "You must be Pete. I'm Gus."

Gus wasn't just skinny, he was rail skinny, with bright brown pools for eyes, high cheekbones and tightly curled black hair. He had a deep voice for someone his age, and as I would soon find out, he had a loud booming laugh and loved lousy boy jokes. He was wearing a white T-shirt, khakis, and white sneakers.

"Hey man, I saw those creeps that sit right over there," he pointed to the far right of the classroom, "beat the hell out of you. I know you can't rat them out, but man oh man what they did to you was completely dirty."

Just as Gus finished his hello and statement of sympathy, Luke and his attack team sauntered in. There were not seated in the same pods. Luke was in Lion which was as far from Wolf as could be. But instead of going straight to his pod he slithered over to Wolf. He stopped, bent over and whispered just loud enough so both Gus and I could hear him.

"Good going, asshole. You had a good story. Keep it up and don't you dare rat us out. If you keep your nose clean, we won't bother you, but if you screw up," he paused for effect, "you're a dead man."

When Luke walked up to me my head dropped, straight down, without me willing it to do so. I literally could not look at Luke. In behavioural sciences we call this the, "duck reflex." The duck reflex is an unconscious reaction by a victim when they encounter their abuser. When the duck reflex is operational in the victim, it never goes away. There is no hope for trust ever being re-established in that relationship.

Gus snarled under his breath, "Luke and his tribe are pure trouble. Someday, someone is going to give him payback, big time."

Mrs. Brooks took all of us through three modules: math, geography, and reading for content. She was a great teacher and what was so amazing about our class was that the pods were set up so we could learn together at our own pace. Before I knew it, it was three in the afternoon. The bell rang and my first day of sixth grade is over. What a day!

"Hey, Pete," Gus hollered as I started for the door. "I think I live close to you. You want to walk home together?"

"Sure, Gus," I said. "But I walk home with three of my friends that are fourth grade holdovers. We all live in the same project. I'm sure they would dig it if we all walked together."

Gus and I headed out the front doors of the school. To our right was Benny, Bill, and Mike. They signalled for us to come over. As we were walking over to the guys, I explained a little bit to Gus about the Pirates.

When we joined the gang, Gus said, "So you guys just hang out with each other, have fun, play games, and drive your parents bonkers? Sounds cool."

"That's it. Fun and friendship," Benny said. "Who is this, Pete?"

"Guys, meet Gus, the coolest guy in sixth grade. Gus this is Benny Tail-Feather, Bill, and Mike." They all shook hands.

Mike was the first out of the gate. "Pete, why do you have that silly jersey on? Bill, Benny, and I heard that after we left you this morning some of the sixth-grade boys beat the shit out of you."

We started our walk home down the steps to the pathway leading all the way to The Project. A big formation of ducks and geese heading south flew over in their V- formations. It was chilly out, but I was hot, and my cuts and bruises were yelping for attention. "Yeah, that's right Mike." Then I told them everything about investigation, my anti-rat fabricated story, Luke and his henchmen's reaction, Ms. Shaffer's warnings, and how only a couple of girls were willing to tell Ms. Shaffer what happened. Gus chimed in and added more colour commentary, blow-by-blow descriptions. He also told several stories of how Luke bullied other kids in fifth grade and no one challenged him.

Benny stopped abruptly on the path, we all followed suit. "Pete, tell me exactly what these kids did to you."

"Benny, it's nothing," I said.

"God damn it. Don't bullshit us. It's a hell of a lot more than nothing. Look at you. Now tell me what went down," Benny added emphatically. "Gus, you seem like a good guy, but this is Pirate stuff, and unless you're thinking of joining us you should probably head home on your own as we have some confidential things to talk over with Pete. Things you shouldn't hear."

Gus looked right at Benny and then Bill, Mike and I. "I'm in. You're cool cats. I'm not sure what Pirates do, but compared to my boring life, a little adventure, games and fun with pals would be a blast. So, if you'll have me, consider me your first black Pirate." We all smiled. There was no need for further discussion. Gus was now one of us.

"Okay Gus, but if you bust any of us, let our secrets out of the bag, you'll be an ex-Pirate faster than you can blink," I said.

"Not to worry." Gus make a motion as if his lips were sealed. "You'll find out I'll become the Pirate with the lips that are closed tighter than anyone else's."

With that matter dealt with I went on and accounted for every cut, bruise, and tear. "When it comes right down to it, four of the guys seemed a little reluctant to kick my ass, but the big kid, Luke, enjoyed hitting me twice as much and twice as hard. When I tried to fight back, he had the other four pin me down even tighter so he could punch me without resistance."

I was out of gas, ready to move down the path and get home. "Okay guys, I've had enough. Let's get going." I made a step intended to get our crew moving. Before I could get any momentum out of the guys, Benny asks one more question.

"Is this Luke kid the same tall loudmouth that lives over by us at Forest Glen?"

Gus surprisingly jumped in. "Yeah, that's him. Where I live is close to Forest Glen, so I see Luke almost every day on the way to school. We take the same path, but I walk alone and he's always dragging some guys with him. Sometimes they try to harass me, but I just keep my distance and soon they find another kid to terrorize."

Benny's faced turned into a mask of anger. He looked scarier than I'd ever seen him. "I know this guy. Last summer I was playing Little League Baseball on an all-district team and we had a game with the Forest Glen Dodgers. I was pitching and accidentally hit Luke, who was playing on the other team when my wicked curve ball didn't curve. This guy Luke, after dusting off the dent I had caused in his uniform, picked up his bat and came running at me screaming, "I'm going to kill you, you no good piece of Indian trash!" He took one swing and missed, but what Luke the bully didn't know was that my dad, who's a black belt in karate, had me in karate lessons three days a week since I was five. I was ready for unprovoked aggression. I ducked under the bat going by and hit him hard with a karate punch to the throat. He went down like a sack of potatoes and I was on top of him in a second beating the living hell out of his face.

"I was kicked off my Little League team for the fight. My dad was going to make a stink about getting me reinstated, but I said no. Who would want to play on a team where the higher ups don't have your back? I never saw this Luke kid again after the baseball fight. I don't know how I missed him here at school, but I did." The look on Benny's face was one of pure determination.

"Pete, I want you to know this guy is never going to touch or hurt you, or any of us, ever again. My brothers and I are going to see to this."

"Benny, don't do anything," I pleaded. "It'll just make things worse. Let's just ignore what's happened and I'm sure nothing else is going to go down."

Gus jumped in again. "Pete, I'm with Benny here. If we try to hide from these pimps, then they'll try to make us their slaves for the rest of the year. Let's plan an ambush of some type on this Luke monster and crush him once and for all."

"Gus, you stay out of this. All of you stay out of this." Benny's words stopped us in our tracks. "I'm going to make sure our friend Luke knows the wrath of warrior and Pirate power. His ass has hurt the last kid that's smaller than him. Stay tuned."

I was totally exhausted. All I wanted to do was get home, get on my pyjamas, grab a book, some chips and a Coke, and pretend today didn't happen. We started down the path again, homeward bound. Our conversation, and Benny's war declaration, had sucked the energy from all of us. The best we could muster was a couple of corny jokes from Mike, and Bill telling us about how he had snuck up on his older sister and watched her make out with her new boyfriend, and then used this dirty sibling trick to extort his sister's next week allowance. I thought Bill sounded creepy recounting what he did to his sister, but I was too exhausted to say anything. Soon we were at Gus's corner. We all said goodbye while each of us welcomed him to the Pirate society. Before he moved away, we set a time to meet him the next morning. Benny stopped to tie his shoe and told us to go ahead, that he'd catch up.

"Wow, Gus is a really good guy," Mike said. We all concurred. He went on. "Do you think Jerry Kaye will have a problem having a black guy in our Pirate group?"

"If I know Jerry Kaye the way I think I do, she'll have no problem. In fact, when she gets to know Gus, she'll think it's a great thing that we asked Gus to join us." Then I added, "Mike do you have a problem with Gus because he's black?"

"No, hell no!" Mike exclaimed. "But you know how girls and their parents are. Protection at all costs."

We pushed the rest of the way home and for one of the first times in memory I was so glad to see The Projects parking lot, a signal that we had arrived. Then I noticed something. I looked over at

Bill. "Hey, do you see Benny? He said he'd catch up, but I haven't seen him since."

"Now that you mention it, Pete, I can't remember seeing Benny for the last five minutes," Bill said. "Oh well, probably took some secret way home to his house."

"Mike, you see Benny?" I asked.

"Nope. I bet he's home already."

Mike and Bill peeled off and headed to their houses which were across the Plaza from mine. I was on my own with my thoughts about my missing friend. I was hoping he wasn't doing anything stupid and putting himself in danger.

Just before I hit our front steps, Jerry Kaye came bounding up. She stopped, looked at my face and exclaimed, "Pete! What happened to you? Did your mom do this? My God, first lye soap in the mouth and now she beats you."

"No, no, Jerry Kaye, I just had an accident at school. I was running backwards ..." and then I stopped. "Jerry Kaye, that's not what really happened. Some sixth- grade boys kicked the shit out of me as part of their initiation. I look worse than I am. I'm okay, but I'm worried Benny has declared war on the kid that did most of the damage to me. If he follows through on his threat, he might get hurt, or he might even get in trouble."

"Oh my God, Pete. Will your bad luck ever stop? It's like the world has it out for you."

I was about to reassure Jerry Kaye that I didn't need her pity when my mom poked her head out our front door. "Pete, you should come in now. You can see Jerry Kaye tomorrow. Oh, Jerry Kaye, how was your first day of crosstown fifth grade?"

"It was okay, Mrs. Gregg. The ride is really long, and the school is large and seems a little stuck up compared to our little school here."

"Well, I'm sure you'll learn to enjoy it. Pete will see you tomorrow and you guys can compare war stories."

***

I was worried about Benny, so I went to the Plaza Pirate meet-up place early. I was out and about in time to wave at Jerry Kaye as she headed to her dad's car for her safari to cross-town school. Mike showed up. The first thing out of his mouth was, "Seen Benny?"

I shook my head. "Man, I hope he's okay." I murmured. Bill found us and asked the same question. Both Mike and I shook our heads. And then relief. Benny walked over to us like nothing had happened.

"Hey guys, sorry I'm a little late. I had a few things I had to do before I could hit the trail this morning." I noticed Benny had Band-Aids on two of the knuckles on his right hand, and there was a red mark just below his left eye.

"Benny, where did you go last night? You bent down to tie your shoe and then I didn't see you again. And what the hell happened to your hand and why do you have that red mark under your eye?"

Benny smiled. "Something for me to know and you'll never find out, Pete. Relax. It's a great day. And I should say Indian summer is here and her warriors are dancing for victory. Now come on, you lazy critters. Let's go get Gus, head to school and have some fun. We've been far too serious the last few weeks. It's Pirate time—time for the lost boys to fly and to remind those that might do evil things to us they had better watch their asses." And then Benny let loose the loudest and most exuberant war cry I have ever heard from him.

"Yawah: Mother of all mothers and father of the sun, your warriors have fought, and the enemy is vanquished Yawah!" Benny yelled.

Gus and I turned right and headed for sixth grade, while Benny, Mike and Bill went left to fourth. After a bit of kibitzing with other students, Gus and I settled into our desks in Wolf pod. It was funny, after Benny's war cry none of us said anything other than to talk primarily about sports. It was like something secret and too important to talk about had occurred and rather than being rebuffed by Benny, we all collectively decided to remain silent concerning the gorilla in the room—our man Luke.

I looked around to see if Luke and his band of beaters were at their desks yet. They were in class, but Luke was a wreck. There was a big bandage spanning the bridge of his nose, he had two black eyes, his left ear was scraped and there was a large bruise turning into a black and blue knot on his forehead. Gus saw what I'd been looking at. He whispered, "I guess we know what Benny was up to last night."

Oh my God, I thought as I saw Luke get up from his desk and limp in my direction. He was going to cream me right here in front of everyone. Mrs. Brooks said nothing concerning Luke's new look. Later, I found out that although she professed to hate violence, Mrs. Brooks was somewhat glad to see Luke got what was coming to him. Luke planted himself directly in front of me, bent over so we were nose to nose, and said, "Tell that rubbish Indian friend of yours that my mom and dad are going to the cops and he's going to jail."

"Luke, I have no idea what you're talking about," I said. "But if I were you, I'd be careful messing with Benny Tail-Feather and his family. The men of his tribe are blood warriors of their Indian nation. They live by a different code than you, or I or any other white man. If you mess with their kid as they say, "you will owe them a life."

Benny and his family never heard from Luke or his parents. Luke and his crew had nothing to do with us after that. They left me, and all the Pirates unmolested for the entire time I was in sixth grade. Sometimes Benny would drift over at lunch to our eating pavilion for a chat, and I noticed if Luke saw him, he made every effort to get as far away from Benny Tail-Feather as he could. Benny's last comment about Luke was, "bully's with black eyes never win–they run."

CHAPTER 15: SWITCHBLADE

A thin, bright crimson ribbon of blood trickled from my nose onto my upper lip where it coagulated in small droplets. Davey had just cut me with his new compliance device–a six-inch switchblade. The knife was like the ones in gangster movies. It had a shiny black plastic handle that was its home when not fully extended, and a stainless-steel blade with what was called a pig-sticker point. It was so sharp that it could penetrate the thick skin of a mature hog.

Davey had pulled the knife on me and rubbed the blade across my face. Then he made a small slice inside my nose because I had thwarted his efforts at masturbation demonstrations and faux anal sex.

***

Earlier that day, the Pirates and I had taken an amazing field trip on our bikes to a friend of Benny Tail-Feather's father, Joe Musgrave, a champion drag racer.

Our invitation from Joe was a dream come true for most boys our age. A full tour of Joe's dragster shop included a chance to do a little work on a new super-dooper machine. It was guaranteed to crush the quarter mile going at least two-hundred miles per hour. If that wasn't enough, we would each have a chance to sit in Joe's existing land rocket and get our picture taken with him. He told Benny Tail-Feather's father that he was going to have the pictures framed and sent to us as a lifetime memento.

I was so excited about our dragster safari that all my lingering hurts from Luke and his pals receded into the background. I could only think of the bright red needles of machines and the courageous drivers who piloted them down the track, throwing off grey plumes from burning rubber with the smell of exploding nitro filling the air, the deafening whine and roar of the massive engine, and flames flying out of the exhaust. Then a great red and white parachute ejected to slow the car's mad dash much to an audience of speed lover's delight.

Jerry Kaye had decided drag racing wasn't her cup of tea and so passed on our field trip. We stopped and picked up Gus at his corner. When I told him about the safari, he wasn't sure about drag racing but was so committed to Pirate time he couldn't wait for the trip. The Pirates and I rode to Joe's garage amid a din of our gossip. I especially loved hearing exactly what Benny Tail-Feather had done to

Luke. On top of our expressions of the pure joy and anticipation of our dragster outing, I remembered something. I had told Davey I was going to join him in a comic book session that morning. "Oh well," I thought as Uncle Jimmy said, "better to ask for forgiveness than beg for permission." Or something like that. Davey could deal with it when I got home. Later that afternoon, after our trip I would go over and see what Pastor Tom had taught Davey. I laughed under my breath knowing how crazy that sounded.

We arrived at Joe's. He and his family live about five miles from us so were all sweaty, thirsty, and hungry from the ride. Joe and his family live in a small white bungalow. All of the doors, window trim, and exterior molding were made out of gorgeous pecan wood that had been milled and varnished by the hand of an expert craftsman. Sitting close to the house, but twice the size, was a garage that served as the design and fabrication home of Joe's drag racing company–Mid West Championship Racing Inc. Joe had already won four state wide titles in fuel car racing and a fourth place national finish in funny cars. All that in collaboration with his adult son, Andy.

Joe and his wife Laura greeted us. Laura could see she had four famished and thirsty visitors on her hands, so she disappeared and soon returned with two pitchers of cold lemonade and a plate full of walnut, chocolate chip cookies. Laura offered up her bounty and we devoured everything in a matter of minutes. Joe made a sly remark. "Good thing I only had one of you eating machines. I'd be broke, if all of you were at my table on a regular basis."

We all laughed with Joe and he ushered us from the driveway where we had ditched our bikes over to the garage. He used a big electronic wand with buttons to open the garage door. The huge industrial door rolled open on its titanium rails. Inside was the Church of Speed, the Church of Joe, the Church of Sleek Offerings of machine, man, and destiny. We were stunned. None of us said anything. Inside was a dragster, a red sleek needle of a state champion. Finally, Bill, in a strained whisper, said, "I love this. Joe, I want to be you when I grow up." We all laughed, but secretly I think, we were all on the same wavelength as Bill. Joe showed us around the garage. Each poster was a tribute to Joe's racing triumphs and chronicled his state-wide wins. Over to the far right was pièce de résistance.

There sat the state champion dragster. We swooned over this piece of art, this piece of engineering, this piece of a speedster's fantasy and through our oohs and aahs, we drifted into heaven.

Joe put us to work. He showed us how to fine sand the frame wields on the new machine. He gave each of us our own weld and metal sanding paper and let us go at it for about a half an hour. Once we'd gotten a taste of the hard work that it takes to build a champion ride, Joe took us over to the red needle and let each of us sit in it and hold the steering wheel. He bent down next to each of us while Laura snapped our picture.

Two hours flew by. Joe signaled that he had other things to do and sent us on our way back to the doldrums of The Project. Just as we were leaving, not too far up the road, I got a brilliant idea. We could have drag races on our bikes on the way home. We would guesstimate what looked like a quarter mile on the street. Then two of us would blast the start, racing to the end of each course. Winners got one point and raced again against a new challenger. We would keep our racing rotation going until we got home. The champion was the Pirate with the most points.

We ended up doing six rotations before we called it quits with about a half mile left to go. I was the overall champion with four points. Gus was amazing. It was his first Pirate competition and he raced with abandon, winning one round but most importantly, he seemed to have a ball. Benny came in last with no points and complained.

"Us big guys can't keep up with the skinny midgets like Pete and Gus. The odds are stacked against me on this kind of game, but give me B-47 and I will crush you." We all laughed, and Bill yelled a salute to Benny. "All hail Benny, the big ass Pirate." We laughed again. That day created memories that would last a lifetime.

We said goodbye to Gus at his corner. "This was the best day I can remember in a long time," Gus exclaimed. We waved goodbye and then peddled on, sharing our drag racer fantasies.

When we finally pulled into The Project's parking lot, I couldn't believe my eyes. There was Davey, pacing back and forth. The moment he saw us, he rushed our bikes. He grabbed my handlebars and shook them violently until I fell to the ground with a thud. "Pete, you bastard! Where have you been? You told me we would do comic books this morning at nine. I've been waiting for you. You broke your word and now you're going to pay."

No sooner had he finished his threat I caught sight of Benny Tail-Feather charging full speed at Davey. He knocked Davey to the ground, climbed on top of him and began to pummel his face with well-placed punches. Davey's nose began to bleed. Benny landed one more thunderous right to Davey's temple before I could tear him off of Davey's chest.

"Stop! Benny, he's not worth it. Like the pussy he is, he's going to tell his aunt, your mom, and mine and get us in trouble for hurting this piece of shit. Let him go, Benny."

Benny let Davey up. Davey brushed his face with his hand, wiped his bloody nose on his sleeve and turned. He walked towards The Project's houses screaming, "Benny Tail-Feather, you're a piece of Indian crap! You need to go back to the reservation where you belong. As for you, Pete, you should tell your friends how much you love our comic book sessions. Especially when I teach you the tricks of being a man instead of the coward you are, hiding behind chief asshole's moccasins. Pete, you better be at my house at two or the pictures will fly. Get it!"

I was totally humiliated. I didn't know what my friends would think, but it couldn't be good. "Thanks Benny," I said. "Davey had it coming. I wish I was brave enough to make him pay like you did."

"Look, Pete," Benny said. "Part of my tribe's way of living is that the strong among us have a responsibility to those needing protection. You're my friend and I know when you can, you will do the same for me."

Then came a devastating question and observation from Mike. "Pete, why do you hang out with this guy? We all know he's strange and nobody but you likes him. Come on, man, comics are one thing, but they can't be important enough to screw up your reputation."

Mike was right, but I was in so deep I couldn't own my own self-disgust nor pay the price to extricate myself from Davey's decay. I said nothing.

I picked up my bike. "See you guys Monday. Benny tell your dad thanks for a great day." We all wheeled home, but as I left my friends I was overtaken with anger and resolve that this afternoon would be my last with Davey. It would also be the afternoon I resolved my shame.

Home. As I walked into the kitchen I saw my mom hard at work doing house chores. Sitting right next to the kitchen sink was the large new Sears power washer and wringer my uncle had bought my mom. This contraption was made up of a massive porcelain tub mounted on legs supported by black rubber wheels. Attached to the tub and sitting above it was a set of large mountings containing yellow-coloured power rollers. These rollers were the industrial strength kind. The ones usually employed in hotel laundry services. The rollers were used to extract rinse water from clothes that were fed through them. My mom continually warned me not to get my hands near these potential manglers of flesh. She said, "They will gobble you faster than you can blink an eye. Keep clear."

Before my uncle's amazing gift, my mom had to do our washing by hand. She used a scrub board for cleaning and a clothesline for drying. She said that what used to be a day's labour, with the new machine it was no more than three or four hours.

Mom fixed me a great mayo and fried spam sandwich on Wonder Bread.

"Thanks, Mom," I said between bites. "The Pirate's drag race trip blew my mind. We saw everything. We went to Joe's place, he's Benny's dad's best friend from work. We got to sit in his state champion drag racer's amazing car. He called it the Red Needle. It was so cool."

I devoured my sandwich, chugged a carton of milk along with it, and excused myself for a bath, and clean clothes.

Just before I hit the first step, my mom said, "Pete, I saw Davey running by a few minutes ago. He looked really upset. Do you know what might be wrong?"

I lied. "No, have no idea."

"I don't see him much, but from the few times we've chatted, he seems so much calmer and real. I think our Sunday with Pastor Tom made an important impression on him."

I just shrugged and headed upstairs. Before I got to the top step my mom called out again. "Pete, are you going to Davey's this afternoon? If you are, I thought I would take your sister for a day of window shopping downtown."

I answered back. "Yeah, I'm going to Davey's at two and should be home about four. Is that enough time for you?"

"That would be great," she said.

I finally made it to my room, disrobed and threw my sweaty and grimy clothes into the hamper. As I walked down the hallway for a much-needed bath, my legs were sore from all of the bike drag racing we'd done. A good sign of a good time.

I ran a hot bath. So hot that the steam completely enveloped the washroom. As I soaked away my body debris from the day's wild ride, I started to plan my strategy of liberation from Davey's vice like grip on my soul. It was simple. I would lure him in, play along, and find the right moment to coldcock him with a Coke bottle. Afterwards, he could talk all he wanted, show the pictures if he wanted, lie about me if he wanted. I didn't care. I would be done. No more hiding. No more shame. And if I couldn't pull off Operation True Spirit, then I had no other choice but a drastic remedy.

I knew my soak was over because I'd stayed in the water so long that it turned lukewarm. My skin resembled an old prune. I hobbled back to my bedroom full of courage and determination. I put on clean clothes, climbed onto my bed, and did a quick Star Catcher. When my meditation was over, it was time to head to Davey's.

I barely got one knock on Davey's door when it flew open. He grabbed my arm, yanking me forcefully into the kitchen. "Stop Davey," I shouted. "You're hurting me."

"Shut up and get in here," he snarled. "I can't believe you let your dirty Indian friend hurt me. Pete, you're going to pay for not being willing to stop that monster."

Davey was so worked up he could hardly get his words out. Spit was drying in the corners of his mouth. His face was sweaty and flushed. He looked scary, out of control. He slapped me in the face. I took a shot at slugging him in the stomach, but it didn't do any good. I looked for an empty coke bottle—there was none to be had. He shoved and pushed me upstairs. Then he threw me into his room and slammed me on the bed. With one hand, he pinned my throat to the mattress, so I couldn't move. With the other hand, he reached into the desk drawer closest to the bed and pulled out the switchblade. He pushed the blade concealment button and out flew the pig sticker. He rubbed the flat side of the blade over and around my face.

"Peter, the game has changed," he hissed. "I thought you would eventually play along and have fun, learn some things. But I misread you. You're a religious asshole, with no appreciation for what makes life great, especially for men." I tried not to move.

"You need to know why I'm living with my Aunt. You see, a year or so ago, I had another friend just about your age. We played the comic and sex game. He went along at first, but eventually, because of his silly bitch mom, he decided to turn me in. Well no, no none of that. I caught him in a dark alley. I was on my bike and I ran him over. I messed him up really good, hospital and all.

"His mom turned me into the cops. I was convicted and because I was a minor, I was sent to juvey for a few months. I'm out on probation now, in my aunt's care, because my parents don't want me. So, you see, if you mess with me, you are going to be sliced up like salami. I'm still a minor. There's not much they'll do to me if I get caught."

During his stressed-out soaked diatribe, Davey had been pressing harder and harder on my throat. When he finally shut up I thought I was about to die right then and there. I coughed. Davey climbed off of my chest. I tried to get up, but he pushed me back onto mattress. "Don't you dare move, Pete." He slid the pig sticker under my chin and pressed it just hard enough. Not enough to break the skin, but with enough pressure so that I could feel the finely sharpened edge and its potential for death. "I'm getting some toys and magazines for us to play with. No comics today, just the good stuff."

Davey left and almost immediately came back totally naked. He was carrying his pornography collection and a rubber something that looked like a man's penis. "Petey boy, now the fun begins. I get very excited, turned on, when I perform in front of you. Get up."

He signalled me to move to the desk chair and to sit down. "Before you get comfortable, take your clothes off. I want to see if you get as excited as I do." I slowly took everything off except my underwear. "I said everything. Now do it."

"I will not take off my shorts. This is the last straw. Kill me, go ahead, but I'm keeping my boxers on. You fucking pervert!"

"All right," he said. "I'll let it go today, but next time it's birthday suits all around. Put your arms up on the arm rest." He took out some shoe strings and tied each of my wrists to the chair. "We're going to start with jizzing sessions. You know, it's when I jack off until I come. The name of the game is to see how many jizzes I can produce in an hour. You're going to watch and I'm going to watch you watching me for a full turn on. When I'm finished with the last jizz, you're going to take a Polaroid of me in full ecstasy. You on board, scout?"

For the next forty-five minutes Davey engaged in exhibitionistic masturbation and used the rubber penis for anal self-stimulation. I kept my eyes shut doing mini-Star Catchers. In between orgasms, Davey screamed at me to look at him. I yelled back, "Fuck off!"

Then it was over, except for the final act. Davey ran the blade of his knife across my face and inserted the pig sticker inside my nose. Then he cut me. "Pete look at your blood. It's a trickle today. But if you cross me again, you'll be bleeding a gusher. Put your clothes on and get out of here. I'll see you in a couple of weeks. I have to go see my probation officer and my no-good parents. When I get back it will only be a few more weeks until I permanently leave for foster care and that's when, if you're cool, I'll give you my comic book collection. You just have to play along. Got it?"

Davey untied my wrists. No Polaroid. He disappeared into the washroom. I dressed and left. On my way home, utter despair collapsed on top of me. This life I was leading was futility laden with pain, shame, and a need for self-destruction. Only one question remained. Did I have the courage to take matters into my own hands and shut off the grey light of evil, never to suffer again?

CHAPTER 16: ON A ROLL

I had to do something. I had no plan as I stumbled into our kitchen, finally home from Davey's perversion. Luckily my mom and sister were not back from their shopping expedition, so I had no distractions.

I noticed my mom hadn't put the washing machine and rollers away from the morning clean up. I could see the contraption's two main electrical cords were still plugged into the wall, indicator lights on the front of the tub and the side of the rollers were blinking, ON.

I slung my jacket to the kitchen floor. Underneath, I was only wearing a short sleeve T-shirt, so my arms were totally bare. In the back of my mind I heard my mom's warning that if I got caught in the massive jaws of the washing machine it had the capacity to eat me alive. I pressed the ON button for the rollers of death. They began furiously turning against one another, making a loud humming sound, while emitting an electrical smell. I aggressively thrust my hips directly against the white tub for leverage. Then I shoved my right hand into the teeth of the predatory rollers. In a matter of seconds, the rolling monsters gobbled my arm from fingers to shoulder.

I was screaming in pain. I heard the bones in my fingers being crushed. I felt muscles compressed so massively that they sent small blood contrails out. Skin lesions forced from fluid volume contacted with such pressure that there was no evacuation save exploding out the skin. I heard the nauseating sound of the radius bone in my forearm snap. Just before I lost consciousness, I saw massive red and blue welts forming up and down my arm.

Bam! The rollers exploded open just as they started to ingest my shoulder. It was too big of a bite for their chewing capacity. I was totally out, unaware of what had happened. I slid from the snare of the rollers that had gobbled me alive, but didn't do their job, and crumpled to the floor. The next thing I remembered was my mom leaning over me and through her hysterical sobs, her shrill voice yelled, "Peter . . . Peter . . . wake up! I've called the police and they're sending an ambulance. They should be here in just a little while. Oh my God! Look at you."

I was so groggy, but I was tepidly aware of what was going on. My arm exploded in pain. I couldn't move any part of it from my right fingers to right shoulder. It was swollen to at least twice its size and was completely black and blue. I realized I was lying in small pools of blood from my exploding contusions. Then I saw it. Poking out my right forearm, in plain sight, was the jagged end of the complex fracture of my radius bone. As I lie on the kitchen floor, I didn't think about my injuries. Instead I thought about what a loser I was. I couldn't even try and kill myself and have it go right.

"Pete, I was told not to move you in any way." I knew my mom was nearby but I could barely hear her. I closed my eyes. I wished I wasn't there. I wished she would stop talking. The next thing I remembered was the scream of the ambulance siren as it came barreling over the Plaza's pathways, stopping right in front of our house. There was a loud knock on our front door.

"Regional EMT," an authoritative voice shouted. "Please let us in." My mom jumped up from my side where she'd been sobbing while holding my hand. She rushed to the front door, unlocked it and let the paramedics in.

"Where is he, ma'am?" a short, wiry, closely cropped, EMT asked.

"He's right here, over by the sink, on the kitchen floor." My mom pointed to me. Then a second paramedic appeared. He was more muscular, taller, and had curly black hair.

"Shall I bring the gurney in now or wait until vitals are completed?"

"Let's take a look first," the first EMT said. They both moved to where I was lying.

"Oh my God," the second EMT gasped. "This kid looks like some farm boy who's been chewed up in a hay bailer or something. We've gotta move fast. He's in shock and we need to get him to the hospital ASAP."

The paramedics started to work on me while I was still lying on the kitchen floor. One cut off my T-shirt, then cleaned and bound my exposed wounds. The other paramedic put a blood pressure cuff on my left arm.

"It's 100/80 and falling," he shouted. "We've got to get a move on. Let's get the gurney now and get him strapped in. Be careful of that compound fracture. It's much worse than it looks."

I heard my mom's voice coming from outside. "No, Benny, I don't think it's a good idea, and I don't think the paramedics would allow you to come along. No, I have no idea what happened. I wasn't here. Yes, I'll tell Pete."

The two paramedics carefully lifted me from the kitchen floor onto the gurney, strapped me in, rolled me to the front door, and then carried me down the steps and slid me into the blue and white ambulance. On the journey from kitchen to mobile gurney, when my mom wasn't in earshot, I heard one of the EMTs ask under his breath, "Do you think they'll be able to save his arm. I've transported several kids with crushed limbs, but this is one of the worst. What a shame, nine years old and only one arm."

"Let's hope we have a miracle here and this guy comes out of this just a little worse for the wear," the other EMT said.

I barely remembered a neighbour coming over and offering to look after my sister. Then one of the EMTs told my mom she could ride in the back of the ambulance with him.

"Mrs. Gregg, we're going to need to get statement from you on the way in."

"Do you think he's going to be okay?" my mom asked.

"I don't know, ma'am," he said. "He's hurt pretty bad. His right arm is severely crushed and contused. We have great doctors at our hospital and they'll do everything they can, but I don't really know."

The EMTs secured the ambulance, and the curly-haired EMT got into the back with us. Off we roared over the bumpy Plaza grounds and then onto the highway. Once were on the paved road the short-haired EMT floored it, turned on the siren and emergency flashing lights, and we screamed at max speed on our way to the altar of science and medicine with a patient who was not sure being saved was a better outcome than a peaceful ending.

"Mrs. Gregg, I have to ask you some questions before we get to the hospital," the curly black-haired EMT said. He pulled a clipboard onto his lap and clicked open a pen. "Mrs. Gregg, why do you think your son got his hand caught in those rollers?"

"I don't know," she said. "I wasn't home when it happened. Pete was supposed to be playing at a friend's house while his sister and I ran some errands. I came home, at what now looks like just in time, to find him unconscious on the floor. I assumed it was an accident. You know how boys are, Pete's age, always into something. I had warned him a thousand times about those rollers. He doesn't listen, you know. Stubborn just like his dad and uncle."

"Mrs. Gregg, I understand. I don't know if you know this or not, but those of us that are EMTs are still sworn police officers so acting in that capacity now I need to ask you one more question. Our records show you and your husband have been investigated several times in cases of family conflict, now I need the absolute truth from you. Did you or your husband cause your son's accident?"

"What are you talking about? That question is so insulting I'm going to turn you in to your boss and have your job. Do you hear me? I would never purposefully hurt my son."

"I'm sorry, Mrs. Gregg, but district child abuse standards force us to ask causality questions any time a child is injured severely enough that they have to be taken to the hospital. I know you'll understand."

I was in the hospital for two weeks. I had two surgeries to repair crushed fingers and a very complicated procedure aimed at setting, pinning and casting the compound fracture to my radius. Beyond the care needed for the numerous contusions and cuts, there was the most dangerous and tricky intervention needed to dissolve a large blood clot in my bicep. If not treated properly the clot could have initiated amputation or killed me by moving to my brain.

•••

Kids are killing themselves in North America more and more every day. In fact, childhood suicide has climbed dramatically. It is now the second leading cause of death among children. But why is this awful and destructive death of children at their own hands happening?

From my life experience of everything that led up to the rollers, I think kids live in a compressive caldron of social forces. There's depressive biology, bullying of all shapes and methods, parental neglect and abuse, social isolation, and usually no one in their life that loves them, just because.

These forces work in combination and press down upon these children so much that they lose hope. They have no optimism for the future and end in a state of utter despair. Sometimes things change. Situations get better, but in lots of cases children just give up and act in desperation. Sometimes it's a cry for help, sometimes an act of retribution. It is always a cry that says, "I'm worth nothing."

Almost three decades after my failed suicide, I was aware of the cauldron of forces that I experienced as a child. I took up a case assigned to me by the family court where I was living. The hospital room of this small mountain health care facility was bathed with a low-level yellow glow coming from recessed lighting buried deep inside the cornices of the room. I lived in this community for five years, supporting my son in his quest to become a world champion downhill ski racer. I commuted by air to my university teaching and consulting practice three days a week. The other four days I spent writing, researching and managing a small counseling service. I was the only behavioural scientist within two-hundred miles so I could fill my schedule as tightly as I wished.

Part of my problem was that I wanted to give as much as I could, pro bono, to those who couldn't get help because they couldn't afford it. Those who could pay sometimes lost out because I tried to act in favour of the less fortunate. Additionally, I think growing up in poverty and with abuse, coupled with my time in the rollers and with Davey, gave me a treatment perspective that my mentally healthy colleagues might not have. Experience is the mother of all great teaching.

There were four beds with four patients in this all female ward. Of the four women who were being treated, three were elderly and the other was for Mrs. Bear, a woman in her mid-thirties. It was her I'd been appointed to see. Because of my disastrous and failed attempt of roller-induced suicide, I had dedicated as much time as I could to assist in the intervention and initial treatment of children who had attempted to take their own lives. Typically, I didn't get involved in cases unless referred by the courts, physicians, social workers, and the like. This time I was to see Cathy because of a referral made by the regional family court.

I looked down on what only a few days ago was Cathy's beautiful face. That night, all I saw were two swollen shut eyes, black and blue cheeks, and a half missing ear. Her lips were so grotesquely battered that they'd lost all their shape. I read the admitting physicians report and it included descriptions of battering on her legs and arms, broken ribs, and cigarette burns to her nipples. When I looked at Cathy, it was all I could do not to throw up and drown myself in the tears and anger of my feelings of disgust and dismay at those who can do these monstrous things to others.

Instead of melting into nothingness, I tried to purchase a grip of detached professionalism and attempted to interview Cathy through lips that could hardly move, emanating a voice so desolate that she could barely be heard.

Cathy could only talk to me for twenty or thirty minutes at a time, so it took four days to complete my intake evaluation.

In between my Cathy sessions, I conferred with the authorities and learned about her circumstances. Cathy lived common-law with her partner Granger. She and Granger had been together for ten years. They had a ten-year-old son named, Ellis. Cathy was a bookkeeper for the largest oil and gas company in town. Granger was a certified electrician, a member of a local biker gang, and a raging coke addict. Ellis was in sixth grade, barely passing. He was considered to show signs of early childhood endogenous depression. They lived out of town on a sprawling acreage festooned with junk cars, motorcycles, and ancient farm equipment. From the road, you could see their two-storey Victorian house was badly in the need of paint. Weeds grew everywhere and feral cats ran in and out of an open porch leading to the front of the house.

In-depth discussions with the police painted a bleak picture. Cathy was an active member of Alcoholics Anonymous. She had been married twice before and at one time was charged with child abuse when Ellis was three. She'd been treated for depression with Elavil but stopped taking it two years ago. Granger regularly beat her, with four episodes turning into arrests. But when the time came, she never pressed charges. Like so many abused women, she was reluctant to do so and Granger walked free.

Granger was the oldest son of a family of nine. He grew up on the hard-scrabble of the high mountain prairies. He hated school and loved women, fighting, boozing, and riding motorcycles. He had brushes with the law for car theft, battery, selling narcotics, and being an active member of a criminal enterprise. In his early twenties, he settled down long enough to earn a journeyman's designation as an electrician. Electrical work put food on the table, but his real passion was the outlaw, antisocial culture of his biker gang. What he wanted more than anything else was to someday be the president of his chapter.

Granger met Cathy at a biker party she was attending with a girlfriend. Both were looking for a little action. She claimed he swept her off her feet. He insisted that if she was going to be his old lady, she had to adopt biker law instead of the tight-ass rules and regulations of the man. She loved it. Adventure, freedom, and living by Granger and his friends' strict code of morality, justice, and sexual norms was intoxicating. She told me Granger would do a lot of coke, drink JD, and then would shove her around. When she complained, he said that beating women was part of their biker culture and it was okay. Stealing cars and selling them for dope money was cool, and beating the shit out of those who defied them wasn't just happenstance, it was demanded.

Ellis came along after their first year together. Granger didn't want a kid and insisted she give Ellis up for adoption. On this subject, Cathy wouldn't give in and so Ellis became the biker kid. Cathy's abuse charges against Ellis came about because when Granger was coked out of his mind, he would goad her into toughening Ellis up a bit by having her punch him so hard in the stomach that he lost his breath. On two occasions, neighbours heard about little Ellis being abused by his mom. They turned Cathy in to the city police. Both cases failed because of lack of evidence and so, as Granger said, "Bikers Rule!"

I had several interviews with little Ellis on my road to structure a plan to keep him and Cathy safe, improve their mental health, and blunt the toxic impact Granger had on them. Ellis told me of his horrific childhood: the beatings, the neglect, no friends, school his only refuge. During these sessions, I couldn't help but think of my own nine-year-old life and secretly inquired if I might be considered as a guardian should Ellis ever be put into foster care.

While I was still in the process of developing a treatment/structural intervention, Frank Lavine the family law judge that had assigned me the Cathy/Granger case, called and asked for a meeting.

"Pete, have a seat. Want a drink. I have a good Knob Creek that might wet your whistle."

"No thanks, Frank. I'm driving and that Knob sour mash really knocks me on my ass. So, Frank, what's up?"

Frank Lavine was the senior district family court judge. He was highly respected by both the legal and mental health communities and had lived in that mountain community for over thirty years. He was wise and had major influence in the deliberation and remediation of family and child cases of abuse and criminality. So, when Frank asked for a meeting I was honoured, but at the same time curious as to what was driving his interests.

"Pete, I'm at my wit's end with this Cathy/Granger case. Granger has beat Cathy within an inch of her life three different times. We arrested him and put him in jail, but Cathy never presses charges. She always goes back to him, seemingly asking for more. Now both parents are taking sadistic action against their young son, Ellis. We're within an inch of taking him out of the home and placing him in foster care until we come up with a more permanent solution." He paused and poured himself a drink.

"Also, Granger is in the bullseye of the Feds related to various crimes associated with that criminal outlaw biker gang he's the leader of. I hope they will potentially solve our problem by putting him in the slammer for a long time. But I have two general question I want to ask you. My questions inform the law but are not legal. I've attended several court/psychology conferences, but none answered the questions I want to pose to you. Pete, what I want is your informed opinion as a behavioural scientist and my friend. In your professional assessment, is Granger a psychopath? And why does Cathy keep going back to be beaten again and again?"

Frank's question triggered my memory of Davey and the number of papers I wrote generally examining the behaviour of the psychopaths and their infiltration throughout society, be they in business, education, law enforcement, and such. Granger could be Davey as an adult.

"Frank, I can't tell you specifically if Granger is a psychopath, because professionals have not examined or tested him. What I can do is quickly tell you about psychopathy." Frank nodded and settled onto his chair.

"A psychopath is an individual with extreme narcissism, unable to feel anything for anybody but themselves. They have few friends and experience significant problems building long-term relationships. They are usually violent and have no conscience concerning their wrong doing. They enjoy hurting people and are cold detached parents. When wrong, the psychopath never takes responsibility. They blame others for their mistakes."

I continued, "On the other hand, they can be very charming and outgoing with people they want to exploit or manipulate. Often employers will hire psychopaths thinking they are charismatic leaders and sales people until it's too late. Several years ago, I was working with the owner of a large construction company helping screen, through psychological testing and behavioural interviewing, candidates for the company's chief operating officer's position. My client's top candidate was highly experienced, had great references, was charming and appeared to be a charismatic leader. The only problem was that my interviews and testing indicated that the candidate had a high psychopathic potential. After my consultation with my client, she decided to not heed my advice, to look further and went ahead and made a lucrative and long-term commitment to this candidate. Five years later the psychopathic COO was indicted for millions of dollars of theft and destructive business practices." Frank nodded and finished off his drink.

"Lastly," I continued, "Psychopathy is probably inherited and there are many more male psychopaths than female. Psychopaths are hard to treat. There has been very little therapeutic success, either through drugs, therapy, or incarceration."

"My God, Pete, that's amazing," Frank said. "So, what I'm hearing you say is that society is at risk from these bastards and thorough testing and investigation is a necessity when either sentencing, hiring, or marrying people."

"That's a little strong, Frank, but yes, psychopaths, paedophiles, criminals, leaders of nations, all can wreak havoc while hiding under the cover of their charming, charismatic, facades."

"Okay Pete, just one more question on this psychopathic stuff. I hear lots of people in the popular press, movies, national media, and just generally among the public use the term sociopath. Is a sociopath the same as a psychopath?"

"I know what you mean, Frank. I hear a lot of people accusing friends, associates, movie stars, and media criminals as being sociopaths. Let me quickly note, a sociopath is not the same as a psychopath. There are far more sociopaths in the population than psychopaths. Here's the difference. Sociopaths have a code of ethics and values that are held by socially deviant organizations but express blatant disregard for the norms and laws of a larger society. Biker gangs, white nationalists, mafia families, drug gangs, and other outlaw outfits have a strict code of conduct that they adhere to with great discipline, while stealing, offending, and killing, all with impunity."

"Is Granger a sociopath?" Frank asked.

"Probably," I said. "But there's enough data that might suggest he's a true psychopath, but as I said I can't say for sure."

"What about Cathy?" he asked. "Why does she keep going back?"

"Let me say most of us will do almost anything to keep the love we are afraid we might lose. We might even sacrifice our children, families, health, and life itself on the altar of acceptance by those that injure and even kill us. It's the damnedest thing, but hundreds of women will lose their lives trying to be loved and accepted."

Frank stood. "Pete, thank you so much. I'm sadder but much smarter after this chat. Don't you dare leave us for the big city. By the way, how's your son doing? I heard he was second at Aspen NorAms."

"Thanks, Frank. Yeah, Nick did well. I'm here as long as his skiing demands it, but it's getting harder to commute each trip."

We shook hands and I left his office.

A few days later, I arranged for Cathy and Ellis to move to a woman's shelter in a large city several hundred miles away. She refused and took Ellis back home to live with Granger, who had been released from jail after she, again, would not press charges. Two years later after Nick was severely injured in a freak ski fitting accident which forced him to end his racing career, I moved back to the city where I was teaching and consulting. One day I got a call from Frank.

"Pete," he said. "It's a sad day. I thought you should know that last night the police answered a distress call from Cathy. They found Ellis hanging by a lamp cord tied to a ceiling beam. Granger and Cathy left Ellis alone so they could go drinking at the biker gang clubhouse. They came home in the early morning hours and found him dead. He left a note, let me read it to you."

"Life sucks. I have no friends, my parents hate me, bullies beat me every day. I don't want to live like this one more day. I'm done."

"God Frank, I don't know what to say." We said our goodbyes and then I sat there, thinking.

I thought about what would have happened if I had been a bit more imaginative like Ellis. What if I'd found my own electrical cord instead of ineffective washing machine rollers. I might have become a dead nine-year-old.

***

I received excellent care during my hospital stay. But on the first day of the second week, things got serious. I was visited by a child psychologist, a clinical social worker, and a member of the family crimes unit of the district police. It seemed to these professionals my accident was suspicious. For two days, with my parents sitting in, I was asked what felt like thousands of questions starting with what led up to, and motivated, me to stick my hand in the rollers. They asked about my health and nutrition at our house, disciplinary practices, emotional states of mind, the conflict between my mom and dad. They wanted to know about the Pirates and how I felt about visiting the B-47's crash site, Mrs. Bear's death and so on. They gave me tests with strange questions, every time my mom or dad tried to jump in the conversation they were asked to remain in the background.

The afternoon of the second day of this investigation, all the professionals met privately with my parents. Once this meeting was over my parents came back to my room looking shaken. My dad asked a very strange question.

"Pete, did you try to hurt yourself by putting your hand into the rollers?" As he finished his question, he started to sob, but pushed on. "We've been really bad parents. Pete, I'm so sorry. Can you ever forgive us? Would you rather live with another mom and dad?"

"Mom, dad, you're my parents. I don't want to live with anyone else. I didn't try to hurt myself. I was just messing around and got my fingers too close and the rollers ate me up. I'm sorry. I can't wait to go home, see the Pirates, and yes I want to get back to school." I lied.

The rest of the week flew by. The dressings on the surgical repairs of my hands were changed and new casting was completed. A long pen anchoring the two broken pieces of my radius was removed and a smaller permanent set of screws were inserted and re-sutured. Cuts and bruises were healing nicely. The only thing missing in my healing process was the gaping psychic wound Davey had jammed inside of me through switchblade fear and blackmail. I concluded death was no longer an option. There was too much to lose and not enough gain. I would pick my time and expose Davey. Now I had to figure out how to bring him down.

Once home, I spent another week in bed licking my wounds. All of the Pirates, except Gus, came to visit. They gave me grief and stoked the fires of new games to play. At first, while still in bed, I wondered why I hadn't heard anything from Davey. Then I remembered he was on a visit to his parents and probation officer.

Finally, on day twenty-one of my convalescence, I was out of bed. I went downstairs to the kitchen and I overheard my mom on the phone. She was talking to Ms. Shaffer.

"Yes, Dorthy. I think Pete will be ready to return to school next Monday . . . you're absolutely right, missing that much school is a real problem . . . I don't know, Dorthy, I'm so frustrated with this kid.

What nine-year-old would get his hand caught in a powerful industrial clothes wringer? Yes, I can be there . . . yes, I think you're right, it would be better to discuss all of this without Pete being in the room. Thank you, Dorthy. See you at eight, Monday morning."

Oh no, here we go again. What new wrinkles did the school gods have in mind for me now. "Hey, Mom, what's going on with Ms. Shaffer? I heard you talking to her. Something about a meeting on Monday?"

"Yeah, Pete. I think you know you're scheduled to go back to school on Monday. Other than that, I really don't know anything other than Ms. Shaffer wants a chat with me."

"I know I'm back to school on Monday. I'm going to walk to class with the Pirates. It's my arm that's hurt, not my legs. I've been in the hospital, my bed, and this house to long. I want to get back to normal, whatever that is."

My mom fought my Pirate walk declaration, but I wore her down. Monday morning, I was on the path with the Pirates climbing the school steps to who knows what. Benny, Bill, and Mike turned left into fourth grade territory, and Gus and I headed right into sixth grade purgatory. As we walked in, heading for our pod, Mrs. Brooks came over and gave me a big hug. Then she signed my cast.

"Pete, we are so glad you're okay. Everybody in the class was worried about you. But before you get settled in, Ms. Shaffer wants to chat with both of us. Let's hightail it to her office and get back as soon as we can. You have a lot of great things to learn so you can catch up with your sixth-grade studies. I know Gus will help."

Mrs. Brooks and I took a seat just outside Ms. Shaffer's office. I could hear Ms. Shaffer and my mom talking. I couldn't make out what they were saying, but their voices were highly animated. After a few minutes, Ms. Shaffer came out into the hallway where Mrs. Brooks and I were sitting.

"Sandra why don't you and Pete come in so Pete's mom and I can bring you up-to-date on what we think is the best strategy for Pete's education."

Mrs. Brooks and I walked into Ms. Shaffer's office. We each took one of the tub chairs placed across from Ms. Shaffer's desk, next to where my mom was seated. My mom looked worried. She stood and gave me a hug and shook Mrs. Brooks' hand. Ms. Shaffer came over and hugged me, too.

"Pete, can I sign your cast," she asked. It looks like you're running out open space so I better get my John Henry down to be among the counted ones." She used a bright red permanent marker and wrote, "You Should See The Other Guy–Dorthy Schaffer."

Ms. Shaffer returned to her big CEO chair behind her desk. She cleared her throat.

"Peter, your mom and I have been discussing what Mrs. Brooks and I think was a terrible mistake. Looking at your difficulty handling sixth grade school work without fifth grade preparation, your schoolyard accident, and the lost time in class it caused, and now this other unfortunate incident resulting in greater lost time. The three of us want you to immediately move back to fourth grade. We'll assign you to Karen O'Neal's class. She's an excellent teacher and all your, what do you call them, Pirates, are in the same class. Also, I've heard through the rumour mill that Jerry Kaye and her mom didn't like her dad's decision to transport her across town to fifth grade and so there's a strong likelihood she'll also be returning. If she comes back, we will also put her in Karen O's class. "Louise, Sandra, did I get it right?"

Both my mom and Mrs. Brooks shook their heads in the affirmative.

Ms. Shaffer continued. "Pete, you did nothing wrong. We adults screwed up, and fate stepped in ending up with a situation we feel would have been a disaster for you and your education. But, most importantly, how do you feel? Will going back to fourth work?"

I couldn't believe what I was hearing. Fourth grade, Pirates, reunited with Jerry Kaye, school work I could handle. I was on cloud nine, except for one thing. Gus. He was now a great friend. He was a Pirate. He and I would have to work extra hard to hang together. Then I thought about it and realized the only time we would not be in each other's groove was during school in our pod, so everything being equal, we could work it out.

"Fourth grade sounds like the best idea I've ever heard. You're not kidding, are you?" I asked with a sly smile on my face. "Can I start today?"

Mrs. Brooks chimed in. "Peter, I will miss you very much. You're a hard worker, but the obstacles for successful sixth grade are just too much. I know being with Miss O'Neal will be great for your education, and banding again with your Pirate pals has to be music to your ears. One thing I would like to suggest is that the first day of Pete going back to fourth is not now, but tomorrow. It would be less disruptive and Pete, it will give you time to explain to Gus what's going on."

"You're absolutely right, Sandra," Ms. Shaffer said. "If fourth tomorrow sounds good to you and Pete, Louise let's make the change then."

My mom said, "The sooner the better." I decided to say nothing. I feared any comments from me would trigger them changing their minds.

"Pete, come and finish the day with me in our sixth-grade class," Mrs. Brooks said. "Don't say anything to anyone about leaving. You can talk to Gus on your walk home. That way you and the other Pirates will be there to make it easier. You're not abandoning him."

We all got up to leave. My mom still appeared quiet and serious. I think something other than my change from sixth to fourth was discussed between her and Ms. Shaffer. As for me, I felt as if a ton of bricks had been lifted from my shoulders.

As my mom walked out the door, she looked at me and said, "Pete, try to get home early tonight. Jack and Tracy are coming over for dinner. Tracy told me over the phone they have exciting and important news to share."

CHAPTER 17: IT'S ALL IN THE LANDING

Jack Williams and my dad called the same city home. They met when they were just boys, drafted into the US Army to liberate Europe. They fought shoulder to shoulder in some of World War II's most vicious fights, like the Battle of Bulge and the Liberation of Paris. My mom and Tracy, Jack's wife, lived next to each other in enlisted force housing on a large Army base in the southern part of the United States while their husbands were off fighting in the war. This experiential glue of two young couples bonded together in the common purpose of defeating Hitler's tyranny and bringing him to justice for the bloody murder of millions of Jews, resulted in a lifelong friendship between all four people.

When my dad and Jack were discharged from the army after their service, all four of them returned home to the city where we now lived. But coming back to this town is where the new realities of civilian life for the four of them ended. My mom and dad were married on the day he was shipped out to fight with Jack in Europe. I was born six months after my dad's departure, so he returned home to a family, no job, no education, and no direction. Public housing was all my mom and dad had to show for their service.

Jack and Tracy, on the other hand, had been married the year before Jack was drafted. They had no children, and both had grown up in large families on very lucrative farms. When Jack and Tracy returned home, at first Jack went to work as the general manager of his family's agricultural holdings. The family trust agreed to pay him a lucrative salary for his work and they moved into a lovely farmhouse on the family property. A home that Jack's dad had reserved especially for his war hero son.

But after a year of managing crop rotations, fertilizer loads, commodity yields and such, Jack was bored. He convinced his dad to support him while he used the GI Bill to go back to school for a degree in aeronautical engineering. His dad agreed. He graduated and got a job managing design engineering for a large civil aircraft manufacturing company in our town.

***

On the way back from school, I told the Pirates about tomorrow's repatriation of me back to fourth grade. Everyone was stoked except Gus. "Gus, it will be okay. You're still a Pirate. All of us will walk to and from school together, play on weekends, holidays, and summer with each other, so it's only class time we'll miss. That's not much, so everything's going to be cool. You all right, Gus."

"Yeah, Pete," Gus said. "The way you explained it, feels like everything will work out."

Mike chimed in with more news. "My mom spoke to Jerry Kaye's mom. Jerry hates crosstown fifth grade so much that she and Jerry Kaye's dad have agreed to let her come back to our school next week. That will be super cool. I miss her."

I added to Mike's surprise. "When I was talking to Ms. Shaffer about my transfer, she also said Jerry Kaye was going to come back." Then I shouted, "Pirates United! Sweet."

I could see the kitchen table was set with our best table cloth, silver service, crystal glass, and my mom's signature dish, pork crown roast, was in the oven. The smells were overwhelming and reminded me how famished I was.

My mom announced, "Pete, it's about time you got home. Jack and Tracy are going to be here in about half an hour so get yourself ready. No jeans and T-shirt. Wear your new kakis and white polo I got you from Sears." I started for the stairs, but she was still talking.

"Oh, by the way, with all the commotion at school this morning I forgot to tell you your Uncle Jimmy isn't coming next week. Your Aunt Florence called. It seems your crazy uncle, who's never flown a plane in his life, bought a Cessna from one of his buddies. He got a few lessons from the plane's owner and he and Ted, his ranch foreman, got drunk and decided, without telling anyone, to take the plane for a spin." I stopped dead in my tracks.

She continued. "They got it off the ground, into the air, then flew through a rain cloud which your aunt said your uncle told her really screwed them up. It tossed the plane almost upside down and then they decided to land. They overshot the pasture where they thought they would bring the bird in and instead dumped it onto a road. There was a fire. Your uncle broke his arm and Ted had minor burns. The plane was totally demolished. Just like your Uncle Jimmy. It's always about the landing, in every part of his life." I went upstairs to change and thought about my Uncle Jimmy and his plane.

Jack and Tracy arrived at about 6:30 p.m. Jack was over six-feet tall, thin, and had brown hair parted on the side. He was wearing grey slacks, a white shirt, and a blue blazer. Tracy was a petite woman with long bleached-blond hair. She wore a brightly coloured floral dress with a peach sweater draped over her shoulders. My mom and dad were equally decked out. My dad in kakis with a short sleeve black sport shirt and my mom in her favourite bright red dress.

My mom and dad didn't go out much. There wasn't enough money for a good time with other couples. Also, they were somewhat isolated, having made only a few acquaintances since returning from the war, so they kept to themselves. Jack and Tracy were their only friends. Most evenings when the four of them got together, they did so over drinks, dinner, cards and gossip. I was sure that was on the menu for that evening.

Jack and Tracy had another big feather in their cap from my parents that always provoked stories and conversations. It was the vacation the four of them took to California. It was a time when my dad's drinking had escalated to mind numbing proportions and my mom was reacting with a more violent descent into her physical and emotional attacks on him. My Uncle Jimmy had got wind of my parent's upheaval. My mom had even called asking him to help get my father's drinking under control. But this time it was Jack who phoned him, concerned.

In their conversation, my uncle found Jack and Tracy were going on a road trip vacation to California in the next few weeks. Out of the blue my uncle asked if my mom and dad might join them with the hope to create a break in the conflict. Time with friends might turn down the flame of their relationship war. He offered to pay for everyone's trip. Jack and Tracy jumped at the chance to help their friends and so off all four went to Los Angeles to follow their dreams of seeing the majestic Pacific for the first time, walking on Hollywood Boulevard, and soaking up the sun on the beaches of Santa Monica and Huntington Beach. All four travellers came home committed Californians, with my mom, Jack, and Tracy making plans to relocate as soon as possible. My dad was less sure, not wanting to leave his brother and mom in the Midwest.

Since the California road trip, my dad and mom kept fighting. Dad didn't slow down his embrace of the bottle one bit, but at these dinner parties, California dreaming was always topic number one. Jack would double sell the opportunities and the news of the exploding Southern California aerospace industry and what that might bring in terms of jobs for himself and my dad. Every one of the couples' dinner parties, after vicious games of bridge, always ended with a group pledge for California.

My mom thought tonight would be different. She said Tracy had called to book the dinner, she had said she and Jack had something very important to share. So important, they wanted to chat about their news early in the evening before drinks and cards so everyone would see how committed they were to their top-secret idea.

After small talk in the living room mixed with high balls like manhattans, gimlets, martinis, and the simplicity of straight whiskey over ice, my mom called me down from my room to dinner. The adults were already seated, my sister was in her high chair. I slid into my usual spot.

Since our day with Pastor Tom, my mom insisted we said grace before we ate. A strange ritual with no substance behind it. When grace was over, my dad carved the roast and Mom loaded our plates with rich crown pork, crispy on the outside and pink in the middle. It was surrounded with mash potatoes boated in gravy, fresh julienned green beans, and a separate plate filled with tossed salad, topped with store bought French dressing.

We began eating. No one said anything. Dead silent. And then my mom broke in. "Come on you guys, tell us what's going on. I was so excited to hear your news that I was about to pee my pants."

Everyone laughed. Jack cleared his throat. "Grab your seats. Here's what's happening. Tracy and I are moving to California in a month. I have a job in Long Beach, at Douglas Aircraft as a structural engineer. They're going to pay me a lot more than I was making at Smith Aircraft and I have a promise of a promotion in six months."

Tracy jumped in. "Louise, I've already talked to a realtor. I have appointments to see ten houses when we get there, with more to come. She sent pictures of the ten homes, they all look great, and are much less expensive than what we would pay for the same house here." Tracy jumped up and grabbed her purse. She pulled the house pictures out and handed them to my mom. I could see my mom melt into a pool of good wishes for her friend and envy for what she might never have.

Questions and answers ricocheted between the four and then Jack stopped the conversation by going silent. He cleared his throat and said, "Thomas and Louise, we want you move with us. I talked to my new boss at Douglas. He said he would be eager, Thomas, to help you find a job also at Douglas. Guys, it would a new life for all of us and I know Peter would flourish in California with year-round sports, beaches to surf at, and great schools. Don't say yes or no right now. Think about it. If you choose to come, it would mean the world to us."

I couldn't believe what I was hearing. A move to California in a month. I'd just got back into fourth grade with more hang out time with my Pirate friends. This was a disaster. I was never asked to contribute to the conversations between the couples but right now I wanted to scream, "Let's stay put. Dad, you stop drinking. Mom, you go back to school. We will eventually move out of The Project. Stability and peace should be our mandate. Let's not drag our psychological baggage to California, only to have all of our same family problems grow on the steroids of radical change in the sunshine." Instead, I said nothing and as soon as everyone got up from the table in preparation for doing dishes, heavy drinking, and competitive bridge began, I excused myself and headed upstairs. Halfway up the steps I stopped, caught my dad's eye, and asked, "Dad, we're not really moving to California, are we?"

He answered without saying anything to my mom. "No, Pete, we're not moving any time soon, but someday we might join Jack and Tracy in Los Angeles, just not now."

I went up to my room as I heard my mom say to my dad. "Is that right, Thomas? We're not moving? We haven't even talked. You don't speak for all us. So, shut up."

Everyone disregarded my mom's caustic attack on my dad. I made it to my room as I heard the clink of the ice cubes in drink glasses, cards being shuffled, and laughs and taunts of young adults enjoying being with each other even though, under the surface, lurked the power of interpersonal conflict eating my parents alive.

I climbed out of my clothes and decided to sleep in my boxers and T-shirt. I was too tired to consider changing into pyjamas. I fell into bed and dropped into a deep sleep while trying to read my new copy of *Boy's Life* that Mike had given me. In what seemed like only a few minutes, I woke up to shouts and bodies crashing against kitchen walls.

"Jack, you're a stuck-up son-of-a-bitch. You think you're so much better than Louise and me. You sucked a paid vacation from my brother when we went to California with you guys and you never thanked him or us for his generosity."

More crashing. This time into the furnace room. I jumped out of bed and ran to the top of the stairs where I could see and hear what was going on. Tracy and my mom were trying to pry Jack's death grip away from my dad's throat.

"Fuck you, Thomas. You're nothing but a rum hound loser and if you ever talk to my wife and yours the way you just did, I will kill you."

Jack pushed harder on my dad so that his torso was draped over the top of the furnace. His nose was bleeding. He had a cut over his brow, his shirt was tattered and hanging in pieces from his shoulder. There were blood spots on his pants. Jack was also worse for the wear. He had a deep scratch, and blood was running just below his left eye down to the bottom of his chin. Like my dad, Jack's shirt was ripped to pieces and his blue blazer lie crumpled on the floor of the furnace room.

Tracy finally pulled Jack off my dad. He staggered backwards into the kitchen yelling, "Tracy, get our stuff. We are out of here. We will never see these pigs again."

I looked at my dad. He was bent over at the waist with his hands over his eyes, embarrassed, and sobbing uncontrollably.

Jack and Tracy, their belongings in hand, headed for the door. My mom noticed I was spying and yelled for me to get back to my room. She jumped in front of Jack and Tracy, in an effort to block them from leaving.

"Guys, don't go. Let's have some coffee. We can't end our friendship like this." Jack aggressively pushed past my mom and steered Tracy out the door. My mom slumped to the floor. "Thomas, what have you done? They were our only friends and you drove them away. Oh my God, we can't go on this way."

I didn't sleep the rest of the night. I heard my dad wash up, change clothes, and leave the house. The only thing I heard from my mom were her sobs and her pleading to Tracy over the phone.

"Tracy, you and I can work this out . . . I know they're both stubborn. Yes, I'll meet you for lunch next Saturday. I'm so sorry. No, I don't know where Thomas is."

I got up in the morning, got dressed, and made my way down the stairs. My mom was doing her best to clean up the debris from last night's war of the soldiers. I asked her what happened.

"Why did Jack and dad get into a fight?"

She looked up. "Pete, don't ever ask me about this again. I'm sorry you stuck your nose into this awful stuff, experienced it, and had to see your father in such a disastrous light. But it's over now, and we will never see Jack and Tracy again."

CHAPTER 18: DEAD CAT-GONE

Benny, Mike, Bill, and I were on our way to school. We walked along the sidewalk connecting The Project with Johnson County Elementary. Soon we would connect with Gus who was waiting for us at the turnoff to his house. It was a cold and rainy day. Bleak was the dominant mood, except for me, as I was really excited. Even though I'd experienced the trauma of the fight between Jack and my dad, I was over the moon. Today was the first day of my new life. Fourth grade ruled.

"Have you heard about it, guys?" Benny Tail-Feather asked.

"About what?" I responded.

"A bunch of cats in The Project are missing. Mrs. Bee over on the east side found her cat dead, laying on her porch, strangled with a shoelace around its neck. My mom said the Albertsons were also missing their cat. They called the animal shelter, they sent out an investigator who talked to a number of neighbours, five of which have also not been able to find their cats. The cops are supposed to come out sometime this week to see if they can find out more about what's happening. My dad showed me today's paper and there's even a small article about the missing cats of the Government Project."

Everyone thought all five of the missing cats, and probably more, were killed on purpose, like Mrs. Bee's. There was going to be a search party on Saturday to see if we could find where these poor animals might be buried.

"I think we should have a Pirate search," Benny said. "We know The Project better than anyone and I bet you those cats are down by the willows and the creek. What do you say, Pete?"

I didn't say anything, just nodded. My mind was racing ahead. My first thought was that Davey killed the cats. But that couldn't be because he wasn't around for the last couple of weeks. I wondered who else could have done those awful acts. I loved animals and anyone who hurt them on purpose was a real asshole in my book.

As we picked up Gus at his corner, we filled him in on the dead cats and the Saturday Pirate search. He was all in, sharing his disgust like the rest of us.

Mike said what we were all thinking. "You know who did this, don't you?" We all stopped on the path and looked at Mike.

"It's Pete's friend, that pervert, Davey," Mike said. Benny and Bill agreed. Gus said nothing since he didn't know Davey. I had to burst everyone's bubble. "It can't be Davey. He's not home. He's been gone for at least three weeks visiting his parents."

Benny jumped in. "Are you crazy, Pete? I saw Davey with his Aunt Peaches a week ago when they were walking across the Plaza to the parking lot." I was a little shocked. I thought Davey was visiting his parents.

Mike added, "Oh yeah, I've talked to Davey a couple of times when he's been bringing stuff from his aunt's car to her house. He's here for sure. Haven't you seen him since you were in the hospital, Pete?"

"No," I replied. "I guess I've been too busy with all of the sixth to fourth grade shenanigans that have been going on."

Benny concluded, "So, it could be Davey who's been killing the cats. He's been here. If we find out it's him, I'm going to beat Davey within an inch of his life."

I wondered if this was it. Had something happened that Davey was not seeing me on purpose? Maybe I was free. Now that I knew he was home, I was not going to seek him out. I would let sleeping dogs lie and perhaps I would be able to steer clear of him until he left for good.

"Pete, it sounds like you're really lucky to get this guy out of your life." Gus said. "From what everybody says, this Davey jerk is a real bad dude."

Finally, we were at school. It started to rain and hail. We hustled for the warmth of the school's front door. I went left to fourth with the guys, for the first time that year, and now it was only Gus veering right to the confines of sixth grade. As Gus walked away, he looked lonely. I was going to make sure the Pirates never let him down.

The first day of fourth grade was a breeze. My new teacher, Ms. Wells, was amazing. She was short, a little overweight, with a personality and sense of humour that dazzled us. She was almost as good of a teacher as Mrs. Brooks. In fact, I thought our math lessons were on par or even a little better than Mrs. Brooks'. That day, Ms. Wells' blond hair was pulled back into a ponytail, and she was wearing extra-large tortoise shell glasses which gave her an aura of fun smartness.

Now that I was in fourth grade, I moved from last place in school work to first. I was big enough to take care of myself when compared to the other boys in my class, except for Benny Tail-Feather, so there was no bullying or taunting. In a nutshell, I couldn't have been happier with school.

The day flashed by in no time. The three o'clock bell shocked us out of the fun we were having with our geography lesson dealing with flags of the world. My flag workbook was brighter and more detailed than anyone else's. For the first time in a long time I felt pride in my school work.

Bill, Mike, Benny, and I headed out the front door. We stopped and waited as Gus joined us. Instead of going straight home, we agreed with Scott Lancaster, the volunteer football coach, that we would join him and about ten other boys from the fourth and sixth grades to come to a try out for the Johnson County Elementary flag football team.

Football was and is a religion in the Midwest of the US. There's an adage that if boys are old enough to ride a bike, they're old enough to catch, kick, and run a football. The younger you start, the better the chances you'd have for that most prized of all payoffs: a tuition free scholarship to a great university.

The five of us walked over to the athletic field. Summer was gone so the bright green grass that was here a few weeks ago had given way to brown stubble. There were ten boys milling around coach Lancaster. He blew his whistle and commanded, "Huddle up, men."

Scott Lancaster in his other life was a highly successful business broker who worked with clients all over North America. That day he'd traded his grey pinstripe suit for jeans, a white pullover sweater, wild looking basketball shoes, and a red ball cap. Around his neck was a bright, shiny silver whistle. He was holding a clipboard with what looked like football plays drawn on it.

Scott Lancaster became Coach Lancaster when his love of football drove him to find a way, even in midlife, to become active in the game he loved, even if it was as a part-timer. Coach Lancaster had been an outstanding Division II linebacker at a small college in New England. But when he graduated, because he was too small for the pros, his playing days were over. Unlike older guys in countries where soccer or hockey are the national sports, programs for all ages abounded so anyone of any age could continue to play well into old age. In contrast, American football is terminal with no opportunity for participation beyond what's offered through schools and for the elite, professional programs. So, Scott Lancaster found what he called the love of his life: coaching boy's football at Johnson County Elementary.

We clustered around Coach Lancaster, and like so many other football coaches I would have throughout my life, Coach Lancaster and those other great men were the same in many ways. They were part taskmaster, part father figure, part wise man, and part shoulder to cry on. For me, it wasn't an understatement to say that the first day of football, with the Pirates and Scott Lancaster, set me on a path that saved my life.

***

I excelled at playing the game of football. Starting at Johnson County Elementary and on through my university days, I was always one of the fastest players on the field and I had great hand-eye coordination. I could run pass routes and catch the football better than most. In addition, I was tough, although smaller than a lot of the guys. In every program I played in, I built a reputation as a vicious tackler and blocker.

The technical aspect of football was a minor part of the game that consumed me. What really stayed with me from the school of football, were the lessons of discipline, team loyalty, self-sacrifice, merit-based appraisal, and most of all, the unconditional love that a successful team must generate for each other. We all screwed up, but we still loved each other in the end. All those life lessons football gave me, in addition to the years of psychotherapy, created the positive forces that eventually defeated the decay of Davey's perversion and my family's relentless march to interpersonal destruction.

***

Before we knew it, practice was over. The Pirates started on the path home. We couldn't stop talking about our first football practice, Coach Lancaster, and what positions we were going to try out for.

Benny declared, "Everyone, even the pussies from sixth grade, knew I was the only one capable of being the quarterback. Sorry guys, but it's true. You all saw it. I can throw the football farther and straighter than any of us."

We all laughed at Benny's self-promotion. Secretly, all of us knew he was probably right. There was no doubt he was the best Pirate athlete and probably the best athlete in the entire school. It made sense that Benny would be the quarterback. I was faster and more sure-handed, but that's where comparisons ended. Benny was number one.

After Benny's assignment of himself as our football leader, the rest of us played a more speculative game.

"I think I'm a wide receiver," I said, not really knowing what a wide receiver did.

Gus threw his oar into the pond and asked, "Do you guys think I would be a good lineman?"

Everyone laughed and I said, "Gus, I don't think you're big enough to block guys to the ground, but you're so skinny that you might slice them with your body."

On it went. Mike and Bill settled on taking whatever position Coach Lancaster assigned them, obviously the smart play.

Then Mike changed the mood. "So, guys, what about the dead cats? Are we still doing a Pirate search on Saturday with the rest of our neighbours?" I felt awful about how quickly I had let football take over what was much more important, which was finding who was mutilating helpless creatures.

"I'm in," I shouted. Everyone else agreed.

Mike continued, "Great. Gus, can you meet us at the entry to The Project's Plaza. Bring your bike and a brown bag lunch."

***

Saturday morning arrived on the waves of clapping thunder and brilliant lightning bolts. It was not raining hard, but it was still raining. I threw on my Dodger's ball cap, bright red rain jacket, jeans, blue T-shirt, and my grimy sneakers. I wasn't sure if any other Pirates would show up for our cat search party, but I wanted to give it a shot. I had seen Jerry Kaye on Thursday evening, brought her up-to-date on how great fourth grade was and how much we wanted her to come back to Pirates at school. I told her about the oodles of fun we were having playing football and finally and sadly the case of the missing cats.

After my update, Jerry Kaye looked at me and slyly said, "So, Pete, how much money would you give me if I jumped back to fourth grade with you guys? If you're willing to part with a lot of dough, I might give it a thought." Then she laughed.

"I don't know Jerry, it might be you paying us to be a full-fledged Pirate again." I said with a grin on my face.

"Okay, okay, Pete. I'm coming back. I will be walking the school path with you guys bright and early Monday morning." Then she added, "Oh, I almost forgot about the cats. I want to be in on the search party on Saturday. I could rip anyone who is killing innocent animals. Has to be one really sick puppy pulling off this crazy stuff."

I replied, "It's great you're back. Everyone, especially Benny, is going to go bonkers when they hear the news." I knew Benny had a crush on Jerry Kaye so I thought I would put it, in a subtle way, on the table, as something to be discussed later. I put that thought aside and added. "The missing cats make me sick. I hoped we can find something on Saturday."

Jerry Kaye changed the subject. "Peter, have you seen Davey? I haven't laid eyes on him in the longest time."

"No, I haven't seen him for over four weeks, including my hospital stay."

"The day after you went to the hospital, he caught me walking home and asked about you. He suggested that when you were back on the streets that the three of us might get together for one of your comic book parties. I think it would be cool. If Davey is still up for it, I would love to do it."

A chill enveloped me. "Jerry Kaye, I'm not sure I can do Davey's comics book parties any longer. Football practice is going to eat up a lot of my time and besides, Davey's a strange kid and I'm not certain I want to see him anymore."

"Okay, Pete," she said. "I have to go. See you Saturday, and I hope you get another comic book party with Davey set up really soon so you and I can go together. I love comics, too, you know."

As I left Jerry Kaye, I remembered thinking there would be no way I was going to hunt Davey up for one of his bogus pornographic parties so he could molest Jerry Kaye and I together. No Davey was the best Davey.

I walked from our house over to the Pirates meet-up place on the Plaza. The rain had slacked off and the thunder and lightning had disappeared. What was left was a grey, soggy day, climatically tuned to an awful job of searching for our neighbours' missing cats. I arrived at our pruned entrance and didn't expect to see anyone. To my surprise, all the Pirates were there. Gus has found us, and Jerry Kaye was more than present, full of energy and ready to go.

We all said hello, confirmed how great it was to have Gus with us and Jerry Kaye back in the tribe.

"Okay, Mike, you're our leader," Benny said. "What do we do to get things rolling?"

"Here's the plan," he said. "We're going to go to the Plaza entrance where the adults' search party is gathering. We'll listen to what they have to say, get clued in on their strategy, and then I think we should take off on our own. I've been talking to Pete, and we bet that if these cats have been killed one after another, then Davey's the culprit." The others nodded in solemn agreement.

"If he created a mass grave, it's going to be down by the creek, maybe as far up as the badlands. Pete knows that Davey likes scary things. Down by the creek, the willows and the marsh look like something out of a horror movie. We think he might have buried them there. Is that right, Pete?"

"Yeah," I said. "Spot on, but let's get going. We don't want the adults to think we've jammed out just because were late."

"Hang on a minute," Jerry Kaye said in a very agitated voice. "You guys are being unfair to Davey. You don't know if he's done anything wrong, so take it easy. I bet you it's not him. He's just different and makes all of you uncomfortable. And Peter Gregg, I'm really surprised at how judgmental you are. You know you are not exactly a model of stability yourself. So, let's everybody give it a rest. We'll do our search, see what we find, and then maybe we will reach some conclusions." I stared at Jerry Kaye. If only she knew Davey like I did. I was glad she didn't.

"All right, all right, let's go," Mike shouted. And off we marched, led by Jerry Kaye, in single file, looking as much as we possibly could like Snow White and her seven dwarfs.

We arrived at the Plaza entrance. There were about ten folks, all decked out in some form of outdoor hiking gear. Don Bromley was the group's organizer. He was one of the first to report his cat missing. He was a burly meat packer with a deep baritone voice. He grew up in Alabama and still had a strong southern accent.

"Glad to see ya'll could make it," he said. "It's nice for the younger generation to bless their elders with their presence." There was a long pause, then Don let out the loudest laugh you could ever imagine. "Just kidd'n ya'll. Let's get go'n! There's a lot of folks here in a world of hurt, cause their love'n pet has been snatched. Us old folks are going to search up here on the Plaza, and then down into The Project. We'll look under the porches, down sewer drains, behind the trees and bushes. Generally, we're going to leave no stone unturned until we find out what's happened to our pets. So where do you think you're going to search?" he asked Mike.

"I'm not sure, Mr. Bromley," Mike replied. "The six of us will put our heads together and we'll make a plan. We won't search up here in The Project, or through the Plaza. We'll concentrate on the creek, the willows, the marsh, and maybe up to the badlands. How about we meet you guys back here at three? How's that sound?"

"Sounds fine. Mike, I'm going to give you young folks this here horn. If you find anything, let off a blast and we'll come a run'n. We have another horn and if we hit pay dirt, we'll sound off our horn for you guys. Okay, let's get go'n."

The adults left and we huddled to get our bearings. The first of us to make a comment was Gus. "Look guys, my dad's a cop. He's talked to me a lot about how you do these kinds of searches. It's called searching the grid. What you do is divide a search area into grids, like a chessboard, with each square representing one grid. You then take a group of searchers and form straight parallel lines of people walking at the same tempo. The lines move through the grid with each individual searcher carefully scanning what's in front of them looking for clues and evidence."

"God, Gus that sounds just right," Benny exclaimed. "Let's do a grid search first down by the creek, then the willows, followed by the marshes, and finally up to the badlands as a last resort. What we're looking for is mounded dirt that might indicate a burial site."

We jumped on our bikes, blasted off the top of the cliffs, and shot to our first grid which was the banks of the creek. We lined up and began our search. The creek bank was overgrown with tough, long stalk grass. There was trash strewn randomly right up to the running water of the creek. It took us two hours to finely comb all the area making up the creek grid. We didn't find anything. It was lunch time, so we decided to take a break, eat our sandwiches and get ready for the next grid search at the willows.

I can't believe how hard grid searching is," I exclaimed.

"It takes so much concentration that I got a headache," Bill said.

"I guess now I don't know what we're looking for," Jerry Kaye said.

Then Benny spoke up. "Look Pirates, Gus's dad's grid search is the right way to go. Don't be kids and throw in the towel too early. Let's show the poor adults who've lost their pets that we can do a good job. We have to be patient, stick to our guns, and at three we'll see where we are."

We all agreed with Benny. We got up from our picnic and got set up for our willows search. The willows area was different from the creek. It was an area that spilled away from the creek's banks and flattened into a small pasture like area with long grass, small bushes, and startling willow trees. They were so full of leaves and branches that they were hard to see through, providing secluded homes for birds, squirrels, and butterflies during the summer. We got lined up. The willows area was so wide we would have to do at least two passes to do just a cursory search. On Mike's count, we started our line through the intense inspection of the grid in front of us.

About half way through our first willows search, Gus let out a yell. "I have something!"

We broke formation and all rushed over to Gus. Jerry Kaye was next to Gus on his left, and I was on his right. We got the first look at what he'd discovered. As the others arrived, we could see, sure enough, that the ground in front of Gus had been heaped into a fresh five-foot by four-foot mound.

"Oh my God," Jerry Kaye blurted out. "It must be the cats."

I had packed a small fold-up shovel into my backpack especially for excavation, in case we found something. I took out the shovel, unfolded it, and began a very slow, methodical clearing away of the dirt on the visible grave site. It wasn't long before we found the first cat. It was a beautiful Siamese with a shoelace noose tied tightly around its neck. The cat's small tongue, grey from time in the ground, dangled from the side of its mouth and its fur was matted and decomposing.

We removed the first cat and placed it into a burlap bag I had brought along. We carefully continued our uncovering and found fifteen cats, all in different states of decomposition. All with shoelace nooses around their neck. We filled the burlap bag and Jerry Kaye blasted our horn.

We made our way up the cliffs to The Project. Don Bromley had heard our horn and was waiting with his crew of searchers. We reluctantly showed everyone the poor cats we'd discovered. There were gasps of recognition, tears of loss, and exclamations of, "If I find out who the sick person is that did this I will torture him as severely as he's hurt these poor animals."

All the Pirates glanced at each other. We knew who did this. It was Davey. If we were correct, he had another nail in his probable psychopathic profile.

Young psychopaths, very often, mutilate and kill animals for the sheer pleasure of initiating pain and death. The realization of Davey's sadistic potential swept over me. I realized that a switchblade nick to my nose was a mere drop in the bucket when I thought of what he was capable of. Steering clear of Davey was a must. I thought my life depended on it.

By Saturday night The Project was a blaze with dead cat news. The newspaper ran an article in the evening edition about finding the buried dead cats. The cops interviewed all of the Pirates. We kept our mouths shut regarding our suspicion concerning Davey. Benny was shaken to the point that he threatened to beat Davey until he got the truth out of him. We convinced Benny that attacking Davey was just sinking to his criminal level. It would serve no good and it would get Benny into real trouble.

Later that night, my mom asked me to go get some small cosmetic packages she forgotten in Porsche. It was still drizzling so I pulled my red raincoat back on and headed for the parking lot. As I walked along, I was saddened and frightened by the death of the cats and Davey's probable role in those horrendous acts. I turned to enter the parking lot and was scared out of my wits. Davey popped up behind the cement wall holding a large bucket of coal.

He was dressed in a white shirt, untucked, with a black hoodie over it. His pants were also white, and he was wearing black shiny boots. But his dress was nothing compared to his personal appearance. His hair was peroxided pure white. He was wearing bright red lipstick, and in the shadow cast by the parking lot lights, I could see he was wearing heavy eye shadow.

"Miss me, Petey boy? How do you like my new look? The hay seeds around here won't dig it but the cool cats like you are going to be out of their minds on how dazzling I look." I stepped back and looked around to see if anyone else was seeing what I saw.

"I did a great job on the cats, right? Looks like my shoestring artistry on the little furry critters really set the neighbours off. People are so stupid to fall in love with dumb animals, especially cats. They don't deserve the love I can bring them by exposing them to the delight of men and women really enjoying themselves." I looked around again, but I was still very much alone with Davey.

"So, Petey, I talked to Jerry Kaye just after you went into the hospital. I planted the idea that she might want to join us in one of our delicious comic book parties. You know what I mean? Tomorrow's Sunday, so what about Sunday afternoon? Before you answer, remember my little sharp friend that cut your nose will slice you and your friend Jerry Kaye up in a minute if you don't go along. I'll get Jerry Kaye over to my Aunt's house about two. How about you show up at one for a warm up?"

I was stunned. I didn't say anything. I spun on my heels and ran for my house. I heard Davey laughing. "I bet you think it's great that I'm back. See you tomorrow, Chump."

CHAPTER 19: SATAN'S IN THE HOUSE

The dead cats were topic number one at my house on Sunday morning. I didn't believe it, but my mom said she'd never heard about her neighbour's lost pets until I'd told her about the Pirates grizzled discovery. That morning, though, she added a new detail I wasn't aware of, and I knew wasn't true.

"Pete, they think they've found the creep who killed the cats. The cops have arrested this guy, a railroad bum, who killed cats several years ago. They found him lurking around The Project yesterday afternoon. They asked him lots of questions and his story didn't add up, so they took him in. I talked to Jerry Kaye's mom earlier this morning. She thinks this guy is the perpetrator. We can stop worrying about unknown criminals and what they might do to our kids. Cats today, children tomorrow."

I knew all the Pirates' parents must have heard the same story as Jerry Kaye's mom and had passed the news on to their kids. I suspected my friends had probably chucked their Davey suspicions. With the arrest of this suspect they were probably ready to move on, playing outside, without looking over their shoulder, or hiding their pets, protecting them from some deranged fool. The only problem was that I knew the truth. Davey told me he did it.

My mom seemed very different that Sunday morning compared to her usual angst ridden self. Today she seems more relaxed, dressed in her best dress, and even looking happy. As she boiled water in the kettle for tea, she asked, "Pete, I hope you're going to Davey's this afternoon. I've met a new friend. His name is Todd and he's your aunt's neighbour. He wants to take me to lunch today so I'm leaving your sister with your aunt and if you're with Davey I can have a relaxing afternoon."

This was a strange turn of events. I didn't know why, but it never crossed my mind that my mom might deal with my dad's anti-social behaviour by seeking out someone else who might provide her comfort.

"Yeah, Mom, I'm going to Davey's this afternoon. I'll probably will be home around five, but what about dad? What if there's an accident or something and someone needs to go to the hospital? He'll be alone."

"Peter, I've given the best years of my life to that man. No more!" she shouted. "I have to take care of us, you, me, and your sister. I deserve a little fun, so I'm having lunch with my new friend.

Your dad is going to have to take care of himself. From now on, as I said, I'm done."

It seemed the worm had turned. I didn't blame my mom for wanting more from her life, but what she was telling me spread a dark shroud of sadness and loss of hope over me. The fantasy of happily ever after, for our family, receded into the deep folds of my mind where remembered hurts and desolation lurked.

Just as the steam whistle on the tea kettle made itself known, there was a knock on the door. It was Jerry Kaye. "Hi Mrs. Gregg. How are you?" she asked.

"I'm great, Jerry Kaye," my mom said, a little too cheerfully. "Come on in. Can I get you a cup of tea. Pete is not civilized enough to drink the beverage of kings, but I bet you are, Jerry Kaye. Am I right?"

Jerry Kaye walked in, slugged me in the shoulder and said, "How you do'n Pete? Great news, hey? They got the cat killer. I was happy it was no one from The Project. I think everyone thought it was Davey, but obviously it wasn't. We all just jumped to a bushel of conclusions and almost convicted him without evidence. Right, Pete?" She slugged my shoulder again.

My mom prepared Jerry Kaye's tea and excused herself to go upstairs to complete getting gussied up for her lunch date.

"Amazing that they found the creep that killed the cats so quickly. Even though you were dead set against him not being involved, it wasn't Davey."

"Jerry Kaye," I hissed under my breath so my mom wouldn't here. "You don't know what you're talking about. I talked to Davey in the parking lot last night and he told me straight to my face that he killed the cats."

"Oh, shut up, Peter," she said. "You're just jealous of Davey because he's flashy and has a great comic book collection. Also, he's not a Pirate which makes him less in your eyes. You want me to buy this hog wash you're pushing so you can have Davey and his comics all to yourself. I'm so disappointed in you. By the way, I saw Davey this morning and he invited me to join in on the comic book party this afternoon."

I knew this might happen, but when the Pirates thought Davey was our man it seemed apparent that Jerry Kaye might drop her compulsion to declare his innocence. But now that there was a suspect in jail it was easy for Jerry Kaye to poke fun at my scepticism.

"Jerry Kaye, you're not going to Davey's this afternoon. I don't care what you say. He did it. He's dangerous. You can get hurt. I'm not going to let Davey touch you."

"Pete, will you stop this BS. I've had it." Then she stormed out of our house.

My mom came downstairs looking stunning. She entered the kitchen. "Did I hear you and Jerry Kaye arguing? That's not like you two. In fact, I've never heard you guys disagree about anything. So, what's up today? Remember Pete, in the end your family and your friends is all we have. If you lose a friend, it's far worse than losing gold."

"It's okay, Mom. Jerry Kaye and I were just discussing who's best, Sky King or Sergeant Preston. I'm a Preston man, and Jerry Kaye loves listening to Sky King. It was a fun argument, no one won and no one lost."

"All right, Pete." My mom picked up my sister. "It sounds like you and Jerry Kaye are okay. Just as soon as I get your sister organized, I'm heading to your aunt's. Have fun and I'll see you later this afternoon. If your dad beats me home, just get him to bed and I'll deal with him when I get back. Okay?" She picked up a bag of my sister's things and headed for the door. "I love you, Pete. Don't worry, things are better and someday, very soon, everything will be even better. See you later, darling."

Then she was gone and I had a big problem. How was I going to stop Jerry Kaye from going to Davey's? It was only ten, the football Pirates had agreed to toss and kick the ball around for an hour or so at eleven. Before I went outside for my pigskin rendezvous, I decided to do a quick Star catcher meditation and focus on the Jerry Kaye problem.

My alarm went off after twenty minutes of deep breathing and focused problem solving. I emerged from my trance state far more relaxed, but none the wiser when it came to keeping Davey's clutches off Jerry Kaye. I was supposed to be at Davey's at two, so I still had some time in between football and my meet-up with the devil to figure something out. The only thing percolating in my mind was a high-risk strategy of marching directly to Jerry Kaye's house, spilling the Davey beans to her parents, and then accepting the blowback. Playing out this scenario in my mind scared the bejesus out of me. I was not yet ready for self-induced destruction.

I grabbed my football, a pure leather one that my uncle had given me last Christmas, and then I put on my Los Angeles Rams jersey. The rams were my favourite NFL team and I really dug the ram horns that adorned their helmets and I loved their blue and gold colour combination. The year before I had mowed Project lawns and earned a lot of money and saved it just so I could buy my Ram's jersey. I'd grown since I'd bought my treasure last year, so the fit was a little snug. Regardless of size, my Ram's jersey was one of my prized possessions.

I bounced down the stairs and out the door and found Benny and Mike already tossing the ball around. I quickly joined in, creating a game of three-corner catch. Gus rolled up on his bike and Bill appeared, a little ragged from a cold he'd caught. We quickly added them to our toss around. Benny could throw the ball farther than me, but my spirals were tighter and more accurate. Gus was a great catch, but not a passer. And Mike and Bill were bred to be burly linemen. As we slung the ball from one to another the conversation turned to Davey and the dead cats.

Benny shouted to all of us, "Can you believe it. I would have sworn Davey was the cat killer. We all know he's strange enough to pull off something like this, but now that they have a suspect in the slammer, I guess we have to suck it up and treat Davey with some respect."

I coughed, and then said, "Let's not rush to conclusions. The cops could have the wrong man, leaving Davey to run loose and just maybe try to hurt one of us."

"Give me a break, Gregg," Mike said. "You're upset because the arrest of the railroad bum proved you were wrong accusing Davey of killing the cats."

Just then I heard another voice over my shoulder. It was Jerry Kaye. "See, Pete, I told you so. I'm right with Mike, what you need to do is to go over to Davey's and apologize to him for anything you said that might have hurt his feelings."

"Give me a break, Jerry Kaye," I shot back. "Like I told you before, you don't know what you're talking about. So just shut up and I'll tell you right now there won't be an apology. The only people saying they're sorry is going to be you guys when you finally figure out who the real Davey is. Give him respect? Over my dead body."

My outburst ended our toss around. I stared angrily at Jerry Kaye. She stuck her tongue out at me and said, "Too bad you're so pig-headed, Pete. I guess you won't be joining Davey and me at his afternoon Comic party. Too bad!"

Benny walked over to me and put his arm over my shoulder and said, "Look, Pete, there's a part of me that wants to believe you. I think Davey's an asshole, capable of doing all sorts of evil shit, but probably this time you and I were wrong. The cops have their man, so you and I just have to let it go. Let Jerry Kaye figure Davey out on her own and all of us should get back to Pirate stuff. What do you say, Pete? Sounds right, doesn't it?" On that note, Benny turned and headed for his house. He called back over his shoulder. "See you Monday morning, Pete. Football practice will be great."

I was upset and embarrassed. I hoped I hadn't harmed my relationship with my best friends. As I walked back to my house, I concluded that my intervention with Jerry Kaye's parents was now out of the question. I would be second guessed and questioned about my motives, and I'd been seen as nothing more than a jealous friend. The only option I had was to go to Davey's place, wait for Jerry Kaye to show up and try to keep her safe. It wouldn't take long for Davey to show her how evil he was. If it wasn't too late, she could make a break for it and go tell her parents. Then Davey's cover would be blown and hopefully this nightmare would be over.

My walk to Davey's house was slow. I was filled with dread wondering how the afternoon would turn out, which translated into my molasses-like gait. Finally, I was at Davey's front door. I knocked. Nothing. I knocked again.

I heard Davey's voice from upstairs. "Is that you weasel, Pete Gregg?"

I didn't say a word.

"Come on in, asshole," Davey shouted.

When I entered, two baloney sandwiches, chips, and two Cokes sat on the kitchen table.

Davey came down the stairs. I couldn't believe my eyes. If last night's garb was flaming exhibitionist, this afternoon it was beyond the pale. He had on black, shiny pyjamas and black sequined slippers. It was all covered over with a plumb-coloured robe. His white-bleached hair was a strong contrast against the ebony black of his pyjamas. In addition to his outrageous costume, he wore overstated eyeliner and shadow and bright red lipstick. His face was powdered white and contrasted with pink rouge. My mom had shown me movie magazine pictures of old-time film stars and Davey, looked like the male actors in the desert sheik films.

At the kitchen table, replete with the baloney sandwiches, Davey said, "I thought it might be good to kick off our afternoon comic party with a peace offering. Our favourite: baloney sandwiches, chips, and Cokes. But before we dig in, Pete, I have to tell you how pissed off I was with you telling everyone about our little secret concerning who killed the cats. If people find out it was my death play that the cats starred in, I will be in deep trouble. In fact, I probably would go to jail if my probation officer got wind of my cat murder rituals. So, you keep your mouth shut. If you don't, here's what will happen to you." Davey drew his thumb across his throat. There was no translation needed. I was struck speechless.

"Eat up, Petey boy," Davey said. "We won't start our play until Jerry Kaye shows up. We want her here for curtains up on our little afternoon performance."

I finally found my voice. "Davey, you're not going to hurt Jerry Kaye. You'll have to kill me first before I let anything bad happen to her."

Davey let out a huge cackle. "Oh, there he is again, brave Pete. Listen punk, I've told you before, if you try to screw up my play it won't be Jerry Kaye that's hurt, it will be you, or your family, or your friends. So, watch your ass and go along. Have some fun and no one will get hurt. I assure you, this is the last scene of my production. It's going to be great, you watch. Now, let's eat."

"Davey, are you going to fix Jerry a sandwich?" I asked. "I'll bet she'll be hungry, and it would be good if we chow down together, maybe even read a couple of new comics while we're at it."

I dreamt up the Jerry Kaye sandwich ploy as a possible way to burn time, to put us closer to dinner, so much so that Jerry Kaye's parents might keep her home to be with the family instead of comics with a strange kid and me. But no dice. Davey saw through my attempted deception.

"It's getting late. If we wait much longer, Jerry Kaye's parents won't let her come. She'll have to stay home for their early Sunday dinner, so let's eat. When we finish, if you do the dishes Pete, I'll go upstairs and get the stage set for our play. When Jerry Kaye gets here, we'll be ready to go."

Despite my fear, the sandwich tasted good. I didn't realize how hungry I was. We finished eating in just a few minutes. I wanted to ask Davey why he killed the cats, but decided not to, fearing my questions might rile him up even more than he already was.

Davey left the table and headed upstairs. I started on the dishes, as the fear of what my captor was capable of gripped me. Just as I got the plates, silverware, and drinking glasses ready to wash there was a knock on the front door. My heart skipped a beat.

Davey yelled down. "Pete, can you get the door. It must be our dear little friend."

I went to the door. It was Jerry Kaye. She was dressed differently than the way she usually dressed. She looked like a little lady in her frilly floral dress, hair straight and slightly curled, and black patent leather dress shoes.

"Wow, Jerry Kaye you look different," I said, unable to hide my surprise. "I've never seen you so dressed up."

"Yeah, it's different," she said. "Davey said that we might do a little role-play from the comics and suggested I dress up so I can fit into some of the scenarios. I feel really strange. It looks weird doesn't it, Pete?"

Before I could say anything, Davey came rolling down the stairs. "Wow, look at you Jerry Kaye. You look stunning."

Jerry Kaye couldn't hide her shock at his appearance. "Davey what the hell have you done to yourself? My God, you look like one of those drag queens my mom's always showing me in her women's magazines. Davey, you look really strange."

"Jerry, come in. Sit down," Davey said. "We're going to have a lot of fun, and my costume is a must for the scenes of my play we are going to do."

Jerry Kaye was obviously stunned by Davey's presentation. "Davey, is your aunt here? What does she think of your costume? I bet she thinks you're a sick puppy. You know what, I think I'm going to take a pass on comics today." She turned away from Davey. "Pete, I'll see you on the path to school Monday morning." Jerry Kaye made a move for the door. "Peter, why don't you come with me? I'm sure Davey would like some alone time to scope out his play as he calls it."

Good move Jerry Kaye, I shouted to myself. "I think you're right, Jerry Kaye," I said. "Let me get my jacket and we can shove off."

Davey grabbed my arm and threw me against the long kitchen wall. I hit with a loud crash. Jerry Kaye screamed and jumped for the door. Davey grabbed her and pushed her down into a kitchen chair.

"Let's get this straight," Davey yelled. He pulled the switchblade out from his robe pocket. "The two of you no longer can make any decisions. You will do what I say, or you will get this in double spades." He grabbed my left hand, took my middle finger and literally cut off the tip. Blood gushed from my wound.

"Davey!" I shouted. "You asshole! You cut my finger. I'm going to kill you!" I grabbed an empty Coke bottle, jumped up, with blood splattering all over the floor, and took a swing at his head. I missed. Davey knocked me down and kicked me in the gut. He turned to Jerry Kaye and spoke slowly and clearly.

"Jerry Kaye, you see what happened to Pete? If you mess with me, you're going to look like sliced salami. Get up, go upstairs, walk into the washroom, and look in the medicine cabinet. There should be some gauze and Band Aids. Bring them down and we will take care of your little coward boyfriend."

Jerry Kaye didn't move. She just stood there and tried to stare Davey down. Finally, she spoke. "Davey, Peter was right. You killed the cats, didn't you? Oh Peter, I'm so sorry I didn't believe you. Davey, I hope you burn in hell for all that you've done to us. Killing those helpless animals by putting a noose around their neck and strangling them to death, that's going to land you a special place in Satan's house. You're despicable!"

Davey hauled off and slapped Jerry Kaye across the face. "Shut up you little bitch! Go upstairs, get the bandages, and come back here! Then you can fix this little coward's finger. And yeah, I killed the cats in a beautiful satanic ritual. Think of the noose as the stranglehold normal society has over the creative and dark forces of his holiness—the devil. Strangling the cats signals cosmic liberation of the natural, sexual forces needing liberation. The dark side is emerging. I'm a knight serving the Prince of Darkness. Now get upstairs."

Jerry ran up the stairs. Davey grabbed a chair across from where I was still lying on the floor. My finger was bleeding profusely, so I go up, grabbed a dish towel, and wrapped it around the wound. It wasn't long before my blood seeped through my makeshift dressing. In just a minute or two Jerry Kaye was back with bandage material. She had three older brothers, so she'd seen her mom fix up the myriad of scrapes, cuts, and bruises young boys accumulated on their way to becoming teenagers. I watched as she wound my finger with a combination of Band Aids and strong adhesive tape.

Her handiwork stemmed the bleeding. Davey stood and ordered us up the stairs and into his bedroom. Jerry led the three of us in a deadly procession up to Davey's den of perversion. All three of us went into his bedroom. He locked the door and announced, "Now my lovelies, the fun begins. The first thing I'm going to do is to teach you, Jerry Kaye, how to take Polaroid photographs. Several of the scenes in our play involve Pete and I in some very interesting situations. Not only will I enjoy these pictures long into the future after I'm out of this dump, but I will also be able to sell them to beautiful curious men who will love seeing the record of our play."

Davey grabbed the Polaroid camera off his desk and thrust it into Jerry Kaye's hands. He slowly walked her through how to take pictures with the camera. His lesson culminated with Jerry Kaye on her own, taking a picture of me on the bed.

"Great Jerry Kaye, you got it. Now let's have some fun. First Pete, you and Jerry Kaye take off your clothes."

"I'm not taking off my clothes for anyone," Jerry Kaye yelled. "Especially you Davey, you pervert."

Davey jerked the switchblade off the desk where he had stashed it when we came into his room. He flicked the blade out and grabbed Jerry Kaye by the hair, forcing her head backwards and exposing her throat. He laid the blade flat across her neck. He began rubbing it back and forth. Jerry Kaye's carotid arteries were now bulging, and the stress on her bowed throat was causing her neck to turn a bright crimson red.

"Jerry Kaye, you're going to do exactly what I say or . . ." He brought the blade to the cutting angle and slightly nicked Jerry Kaye's throat. A small trickle of blood flowed from just below her jaw where Davey had made his incision on her neck ". . . OR I WILL KILL YOU!"

Davey released Jerry Kaye's hair. Her neck folded forwards and she started screaming.

"Help me! Help me! Help me!"

Davey slapped her across the face. He walked over to where I was laying and picked up my hand with the cut finger. I tried to yank my way out of his grip, but Davey twisted my wrist backwards and I screamed in pain and gave up. He grabbed Jerry Kaye's head again and made her stare at my cut.

"Both of you listen to me and listen really well. Up until now I've just been playing around. From here on out, if you guys mess with me, then just as I said, you're dead."

Jerry Kaye sobbed hysterically and slumped to the floor. I jumped up and started to take off my clothes.

"See, Davey, I'm doing as you say." I was hoping I could save Jerry Kaye. "How about I get naked and you and I will have some fun, but before I do let's let Jerry Kaye go home. She can't handle our rough games and we'll do a lot better without her here. I'm sure she'd give you a promise of silence, which I assure you, I will make sure she keeps."

"Fuck off, Pete," Davey snarled. "Finish getting undressed. As for you Miss Jerry Kaye, get up, stop acting like a baby, and get into your birthday suit. I'm going to the washroom to freshen up my look and I'll be back in a few minutes. You guys better be naked when I return. You have no choice."

Davey walked out of his bedroom and locked the door behind him. I helped Jerry Kaye wipe the dried blood from her throat. "Jerry Kaye, we can't fight him anymore. I've been around him enough to recognize when he's reached his limit. It's now. I'm afraid if we push any more, he will indeed kill us. I'm going to do my best to get Davey to focus on me and maybe spend less time trying to hurt you. And just maybe you will find a time when you can make a break for it. Tell your parents, and we'll have a shot at freedom. Don't argue with me. Just do it, okay?"

"But Pete," she started to say.

"No, let's just get this over with. Get our clothes off," I said. I knew Davey wasn't fooling around. He would kill us if we disobeyed him. "Close your eyes and I'll go over by the door and I'll undress. Once I'm finished, I'll wrap Davey's bed spread around me. You do the same, then cover yourself with the top sheet from the bed."

Jerry Kaye was so overwhelmed with stress she didn't protest. She signalled me to get on with it. I went over behind the bedroom door and took a quick peek at Jerry Kaye. Her eyes were closed tight. I finished undressing and walked to the bed. I grabbed the bright blue cover and wrapped it around myself.

"Okay, you can open your eyes. I'm done. Now it's your turn." Jerry Kaye walked to the same corner where I had just disrobed. I closed my eyes. The next thing I knew, Jerry Kaye said, "Okay, Pete, I'm done. You can open your eyes now."

Little Jerry Kaye wrapped in the sheet, looked like a poor refugee from a war zone. I felt so sorry for her. I could have stopped all of this if I had just stepped up several months ago, shown a little courage, told the truth, and faced the consequences. Davey would be in jail, I would have been punished, but I would be free of all of this.

I heard Davey unlock his bedroom door. He marched in with nothing on, wearing nothing but a red turban. This scene—Davey in the nude—was so disgusting I couldn't speak. Jerry turned her head away so she didn't have to look at Davey.

"What's the matter, sister? You've never seen perfect manhood before? look at me. You'll never see a finer specimen. There are many people who would love to trade places with you guys and who would pay good money to be in my company this afternoon. And by the way, lose the wraps. No hiding your perfect bodies behind that silly bedcover and sheet. You guys are beautiful just the way you are. Did you know there are many singles, couples, and families who love being naked so much that they take vacations with others, with no clothes on, in what they call nude ranches? So, get with it. Stop being ashamed of your bodies."

Davey reached over and ripped the bedspread off me and the sheet off Jerry Kaye. There we stood, two shivering nine-year-olds, naked with a monstrous teen leering at us.

"Pete get on the bed face down. Grab the headboard spindles, left hand far left, right hand far right." I did as he said. I lay down on my stomach and grabbed each spindle, wondering what the hell was coming. I looked over my shoulder and saw Davey pawing through the top drawer of his desk. I saw him pull out a large plastic Vaseline tub.

"Jerry Kaye," he said as he took the top off the tub. "I want you to do two things to get ready for our first scene in this afternoon's play. First, take the Vaseline and set it between Peter's legs. Next, grab the Polaroid and stand to the far side of the bed. When I say shoot, you take the picture."

Jerry Kaye did as Davey demanded. She carefully placed the Vaseline between my legs, grabbed the camera and moved to the far side of the bed. While Jerry Kaye was carrying out Davey's instructions, he took a seat on his desk chair. Then he began to masturbate. As his hand started to move faster and faster, he tilted his head back and moaned. In a few short seconds, his hand still stroking his penis, he moved to the bed and climbed on top of me. He placed his knees between my legs. As he kept up his perverted rhythm he shouted at Jerry Kaye. "Jerry Kaye, put the camera down for a second and come over here. Put some Vaseline on your fingers and put a lot of that goo on Pete's asshole and then rub some on my dick."

Jerry Kaye didn't drop the camera, she just held on to it. "Davey you can kill me, but I'm not going to do anything that might help you hurt either one of us. Go ahead, kill me, you sick pervert."

Davey stopped his stroking and looked directly at Jerry Kaye. "All right, you bitch, I'll do the lube myself. You better take a great Polaroid and when I finish with Pete, you're going to pay the price for crossing me."

Davey smeared Vaseline all over my anus and globbed a big finger load on his penis. He restarted his masturbation and quickly had a rigid erection. By now, I'd figured out Davey's plan. There was no way I was going to let him penetrate me. I threw myself to my knees, knocking Davey off me.

"Run Jerry Kaye, run!" I shouted. Just as I uttered my plea, Davey jumped up from the bed and grabbed Jerry Kaye before she could move. He snagged the switchblade from on top of the desk, flicked the blade out and put it against Jerry Kaye's throat.

"Make one move and you're dead. Pete will be next. I will make your ritual demise so dramatic, everyone will think what I did to the cats was baby play. Besides, I don't know where you think you're going, the door is locked."

Davey slowly moved the blade away from Jerry Kaye's neck.

"Now we're going to start all over. I guess we can think of what just happened as an undress rehearsal." Davey laughed wildly at his stupid joke. He looked stupid to me in that moment. An overgrown boy with a red turban on his head and Vaseline dripping from his penis. "First change in our final take is that we're going to make sure Pete will be still and loving what I give him. So back on your stomach, Pete. Remember no trouble because you know what this knife is capable of."

Once again, I surrendered and lay on my stomach on the bed. Jerry Kaye moved out of Davey's line of fire and was crouched against the wall farthest from him. Davey reached into a plastic bin and took out two pair of calf length socks. He came over to me and tied my hands to the headboard spindles. Then he pulled my legs wide apart, binding each to a rail of the bed frame.

"The second thing that's going to be different," he continued, "is I am going to apply the lube myself. Jerry Kaye can't be trusted." Then he looked at Jerry Kaye and said, "Jerry Kaye, grab the camera and get in place to take the shot of Peter and I."

She said nothing, just picked up the camera and moved to her assigned position at the side of the bed.

Davey took his time and applied the Vaseline to his semi-erect penis. He climbed back on the bed and knelt, his legs inside mine. He started a new round of masturbation. Once he was completely erect, he took the tip of his penis and placed it at the entry of my anal canal. He pushed. I screamed.

"Davey, you're hurting me! Please don't do this!" No response. Through clenched teeth I heard him shout, "JERRY KAYE, TAKE THE SHOT!"

I heard Jerry push the exposure button. The Polaroid began its hum and whine. For whatever reason, Davey stopped thrusting farther inside me and took his penis in his hand and continued to masturbate until he came. It shot all over me. Davey rolled off his knees and lay beside me on the bed. With his eyes closed he kept repeating, "Beautiful . . . beautiful . . . beautiful."

By now I was in shock. I reverted to being my nine-year-old self, sobbing while I pleaded for my mother to rescue me. I knew my screams were in vain. I hollered away.

"Help me, Mom! He's killing us!"

"Shut up, Pete!" Davey said. "You know no one can hear you. Even if they did, they wouldn't give a shit. You're aware as well as I am that your parents are worthless. They only care about boozing and killing each other. There's nothing for you and your sister."

I was afraid he was right and so I melted into my tears, all the while my sock bindings were cutting off my circulation.

"Jerry Kaye, come over here. I want to see the picture Petey boy and I starred in." Jerry Kaye brought the camera over. The picture was still in the developing tray. Davey took out the picture, gave it a shake to get rid of any developer that still might be on the image, and looked carefully at it. "Oh my God. This is spectacular," he shouted. "I've got friends back in juvey that will love to see this. I know I can get copies made and I can sell it to magazines for a lot of dough. Great job everyone."

I couldn't believe this was happening to us.

"Jerry," Davey said. "There are scissors in the top drawer of my desk. Get them. While I'm cleaning up, cut Pete loose."

"Davey," Jerry Kaye said. "Now that this is over, can I put my clothes on after I free Pete?"

Davey snorted. "Jerry, what are you talking about. We're just getting started and you are my star in our next scenes. So, don't even think about it. Get those socks cut off Pete and when I come back, we'll set up the next shot."

Davey left and locked us in again. I couldn't stand to look at Jerry Kaye. My embarrassment for both of us drove me into a murky pool of shame. From that day on through the rest of my life, it would forever taint everything I associated with intimate relationships, with the greyness of lost innocence and helplessness. I thought Jerry Kaye felt my guilt and said nothing. She found the scissors and cut the socks from my hands and feet. When she finished, I got up off the bed. I asked her to turn her back and I took a Kleenex Davey had on his dresser and wiped the goo from my behind.

"Okay, I'm done." She turned to me. She was crying and rushed up close to me. "Pete, I'm so sorry he did this to you. I will never forget it and I'm sure when we're finally out of here he will be arrested and put in jail. We both know he's crazy and if something isn't done, he's really going to kill some kid." Then we heard Davey unlock the door. He came in with a hairbrush in his right hand and the switchblade in his left.

He came over to me and brushed my hair with great force for several minutes. Then it was Jerry Kaye's turn. With great care, he ran it through her hair until it shimmered with her long locks spilling over her shoulders with no kinks showing. When he finished, he looked at his handiwork with great admiration.

"Look at you two. Beautiful, ready to star in our next scene." We stood rooted to the spot. "Come on. We're going out in the hallway because we're going to use the linen closet as our new set."

He pushed us out of the bedroom and opened the white pine doors leading into the cavernous closet where his Aunt Peaches kept the few towels, bedding, and such necessary for a single woman to manage her house. In the closet, Davey had set up a living room chair, with armrests and a rich floral embroidered seat. A floor rug he confiscated from downstairs lie in front of the chair. Behind the chair, he'd placed a floor lamp which was giving off a bright light that consumed all the darkness in the closet before Davey's decorating.

"Okay guys, come on in." He pushed us into the closet. "Cool, right? I wanted a set like the pros use to take amazing pictures. So, let's get started. Pete you're going to be the photographer on this first take. Get the Polaroid and stand so you can take a picture of Jerry Kaye and me."

Davey took a seat on the chair, grabbed Jerry Kaye by the wrist, and pulled her down onto his lap. He forced her to sit side-saddle across him. Jerry Kaye was shrieking.

"Davey stop! I can't do this."

"Shut up, Jerry Kaye," he said with an eerie calm. "Look at Pete and smile." Davey took the switchblade he'd been carrying and placed the blade against Jerry Kaye's throat. "Take the shot Peter," he commanded.

I squeezed the exposure button and again the magic camera did its thing and in a few minutes the developed print popped out. He pushed Jerry Kaye off him. While I was waiting for the camera to give birth to another of Davey's perverted views of his sordid sexual world, he readjusted the lamp, moving it more off to the side but somewhat straight on so that lots of light was thrown onto the front of his makeshift set. He took the camera from me, then removed the print from the developing tray and exclaimed, "You guys are amazing. These pictures are super quality."

He put the photo down. "Okay, we're going to do the next shoot. Pete, you're on camera again. I need a few minutes to get ready. Jerry Kaye, when I say now, I want you to come and sit on my lap in a different way. I'll show you."

Davey sat on the chair and closed his legs tight so that his testicles and penis were squeezed upwards in a protruding posture. He then started to masturbate. All of a sudden he stopped, jumped up, pushed Jerry Kaye and I aside and ran out the door, locking it behind him. We could hear some commotion coming from downstairs. And then a voice . . .

"Where do you have those kids stashed you pervert!"

When I heard this command coming from someone, we didn't know it was over.

CHAPTER 20: BITTER TRUTHS

Jerry Kaye and I were rescued and taken to the hospital for physical examinations. Davey was led away in handcuffs by district police. Peaches' house was cordoned off with yellow investigative tape. It was quite the neighbourhood scandal.

Thirty years after that day, I found myself sitting in a darkened conference room at the Mayflower Hotel in Washington, DC. I was in the nation's capital attending an international conference on childhood sexual abuse. I'd travelled across the country to be a part of this important meeting of world experts, not for some work assignment, but rather because of my personal history and intense interest in the latest understanding of why paedophiles abuse children and the efficacy of long-term treatment programs of molested kids. What I was most interested in was the impact of childhood sexual abuse on adults through their lifetime.

There were seminars on paedophile priests, the role parental neglect played in creating a climate ripe for predators, or the parents themselves abusing kids, genetic predisposition of predators, the mechanisms of predatory grooming, the signs of PTSD in abused children, and the seminar I attended, the predictable effects of sexual abuse on children.

There were five presenters on the panel. Two were from Israel, one from Australia, another from Canada, and a representative from America. The experts presented data and slides capturing their research on the effects of sexual abuse on children. Slides rolled by, disgusting pictures of children in all forms of distress from the attacks done to them. I could barely watch these brutal pictures of the poor children that were subjected to the torture of their abusers. What I was most interested in, and the point of that day's seminar, was what were the lifelong effects of such abuse on victims. I took furious notes. The following was what I learned, which was a consensus from all the experts.

FIRST: Sexually abused children experience a cluster of symptoms that in many cases follow them from childhood to the end of their lives. The abuse syndrome doesn't disappear, rather after childhood, these dysfunctional behaviours show up in some cases as significant mental health problems. They may have significant depression and anxiety disorders, poor interpersonal relations resulting in few true friendships and multiple marriages and partners, lack of impulse control showing itself in drug and alcohol abuse, financial problems, eating disorders, and in extreme cases, anti-social behaviour that may lead the abused to becoming abusers in their own right.

SECOND: the cluster of the effects of childhood sexual abuse is highly predictable and translates across almost every culture in the world. This is what clinicians see in patients that have been subjected to sexual torture.

1. Confusion: Kids don't really know what's happened to them. They have an awareness that they have been involved in something out of the ordinary. When the abuser is a loved one, they aren't sure if the attention they received was an act of love, or something more dire.
2. Guilt: Sexually abused kids feel like what's been done to them is their fault–full stop. This sense of guilt leads to adult behaviour that puts an emphasis on pleasing people rather than asserting for what is best for them.
3. Fear: Abused kids live with the utter dread that their attacker will disclose the secrets of sexual play and involvement they have participated in. If the paedophile is a parent or loved one, this fear of divulgement is enhanced many times over.

4. Grief: Abused children stop seeing the world as a safe and friendly place. This sense of loss leads to states of anime and in some cases full blown depressive reactions.

5. Anger: Lots of kids, post abuse, experience bouts of uncontrollable anger. In lots of cases this expression of aggression is aimed at the mother who the kid blames for not seeing what was being done to them and doing nothing about it.

6. Helplessness: Children who are being sexually abused feel helpless to do anything about what's being done to them. As adults, this sense of no personal power can carry over where they allow partners, and even strangers to take advantage of them.

THIRD: Diagnosing these effects is sometimes difficult in children. When dealing with adult abuse, a combination of pharmacology, support group therapy, and talk based counselling, especially Cognitive Behavioural Therapy (CBT) when in the hands of experts can be useful in mitigating abusive symptoms. But with kids, it's different. Talking to them, lack of real understanding and use of pharmacology, and the little likelihood of group therapy all in combination support different diagnostic approaches for children. For example, having a young person write letters to those who abused them and including those who didn't protect them is oftentimes illuminating. Getting kids to draw pictures (like the famous house/tree/person diagnostic) of their abusive experience has been highly effective in gaining deeper understanding of a child's inner experience. Or play therapy where kids are observed interacting with children of their own age, which leads to real time expression of many of the effects I learned about at the seminar.

Over the years, I searched out these opportunities to gain greater understanding of my own plight. I concurred with all the research. No matter how successful you are, once abused always abused. You end up in a grey world of neither alive for full expression, or completely dead out of your misery. I got by beautifully as no one knew my pain and guilt. It was my secret, and if hidden well enough, I could exist without too many devastating negative consequences.

I thought all of us who have been sexually abused, continually play the "what if" game. What if Davey had never raped and abused me? What if my parents would have protected me? And what if I had broken convention, spoke out, and dealt with the consequences, would my life be different today?

These questions lingered with me as I flew west from the conference, back to my academic sanctuary, and a life filled with meaningful possibility. But as we passed over the middle of America, I was drawn back to the last few days I lived in the wake of Davey's vile acts.

Once the cops had Davey handcuffed, they took him away. I would never see or hear about him again. Oh, sure there were interrogations with law enforcement officials and doctor interviews where, naturally, Davey came up repeatedly. But to talk about him outside of official circles, it never happened. With Davey hauled away from The Project, four paramedics rolled up in two ambulances—one for Jerry, one for me. Although we were not visibly wounded except my cut finger and Jerry's nicks on her throat, the child care nurse who helped rescue us explained any kid who had been sexually molested was automatically taken to the hospital in an ambulance for immediate examination.

The nurse helped us back into our clothes and then our moms walked us down the stairs to the front door where the ambulances were parked right outside of Peaches' house.

This was starting to feel like yesterday. It wasn't that long ago that I was taken away in another ambulance to deal with my washing machine suicide attempt.

"Come on, guys, let's get you out the door and onto the gurney so we can get you taken care of as soon as possible," a young paramedic stated. "Let's start with the young lady."

Jerry Kaye's mom opened the door to a huge surprise. There were lots of our neighbours gathered in front of the ambulances, held back by the yellow investigative tape used to control the crime scene. An embarrassed Jerry Kaye stepped onto the front porch with her mom.

The first thing I heard was Benny Tail-Feather's loud voice. "Jerry Kaye, are you and Pete okay? I knew that asshole Davey was bad news. We should have listened to Pete when he told us Davey killed the cats."

"Thanks, Benny," Jerry Kaye's mom said. "We have to get her to the hospital now. She'll talk to you guys in a few days when she comes home." Jerry Kaye was helped down the steps, onto the gurney, and into the ambulance by one of the paramedics. Then the doors closed, and the ambulance left, its siren wailing. Jerry Kaye was on her way to her date with perverted destiny, and it was my fault. I was out the door next, my mom by my side. Before sliding me into the cabin of the ambulance, all the Pirates broke through the yellow tape and were grabbing my hand.

Bill yelled, "Pirates forever!"

Benny bent over and whispered to me, "Pete, we're like brothers. I'm so sorry we abandoned you to that pervert. You're going to be okay. You have to get back really quick. We have a ferocious game of *I Dare You* planned as soon as you're in good shape, ready to kick ass."

"Move aside guys," the paramedic said. "We have to get him out of here so he can get better." He helped my mom into the patient cabin and then they slid in my gurney. After the rescue and all the commotion associated with it, my mom had been relatively quiet. Now she looked down at me as we tore to the hospital approaching our new reality.

"Peter, I'm so sorry. I caused this. I'm a terrible mother. But even though I've made mistakes we have to keep our secret about how your mouth was injured. Can you do that?"

I didn't think the paramedic heard my mom. He was busy fleshing out my intake report. I remained silent. I started one of the first versions of the "what if game" I could remember playing. I was free of Davey now, but what if he had never been dispatched to The Project, icing him while he waited for further sentencing in another case? What if after the washing machine incident, I had been turned over to foster parents? What if my dad stopped drinking? What if I went to live permanently, with my Uncle and Aunt? As I asked these questions, I realized there was no promise in "what if." I had to be content with the stark reality of right now. I didn't know what would happen.

The ambulance arrived at the hospital. We pulled into a dark underground garage and headed for an unloading dock leading into the double sliding doors of the Emergency Room. The two paramedics jumped out of the ambulance, helped my mom out the back doors, then slid me out onto the ER's unloading dock. I lifted my head to check out where I'd landed. I saw Jerry on her gurney with her mom and two female nurses by her side. Then they disappeared through the ER intake doors.

Soon, I was whisked through the same doors that Jerry disappeared through with the same configuration of people, my mom and two nurses. I was taken to a sterile exam room. One nurse left the room while the other moved me to an exam bed. She asked my mom to leave the room. My mom asked why, and the nurse explained it was hospital protocol when dealing with child sexual abuse. My mom reluctantly left, and I was left alone with the nurse. They helped me out of my clothes and into a hospital gown.

"Peter, get comfortable," one of the nurses said. "Dr. Wilson, our chief of paediatrics, is coming to do your physical."

An hour later, Dr. Wilson had poked and prodded my entire body including careful exams of my cut finger, my injured arm, my scarred mouth, and my rectal opening. He called my mom back into the exam room.

"Mrs. Gregg, I've completed a thorough physical exam of Peter. I paid attention to the most significant presentations of trauma. I looked carefully at all his injuries. This is what I found: Pete, for all that he's gone through is healthy. His arm is healing well, the knife cut of his finger is serious, but will heal nicely in about two weeks. The small knife wounds on his throat and arms are going to be fine in a few days. His rectum shows bruising and some small lacerations from forced penetration but will right itself in about three weeks. Frankly the most serious injury that has already healed, but is still a concern of ours, is the dramatic scarring of his mouth. Mrs. Gregg do you have any idea what happened to Peter's mouth?"

"I really don't know what caused Pete's mouth to be in such bad shape," she lied. "He'd gotten into hot sauce I had brought home from Don Miguel's Mexican restaurant. Man, it was blistering hot, but it's the only thing I can think of."

"Mrs. Gregg, that story is so far-fetched to be totally unbelievable. Pete can you tell me what happened?"

"It's like my mom said. I ate the hot sauce with some chips, went to bed and woke up with my mouth on fire. The hot sauce is the only thing I can think of that might have burned my mouth. I don't know what else to say."

"Listen, both of you need to know this. In just a few minutes Peter is going to be interviewed by the district police's special victim's unit. If it's found that you have been lying, Mrs. Gregg, charges could be filed, and Peter might be assigned to social services for foster care placement. Do you get that?"

"I get it, and you don't need to threaten us," she said. "When can Pete go home?"

"Mrs. Gregg, I've figured out why you left your child in the grasp of an obviously disturbed fifteen-year-old paedophile," the doctor said. "It met your needs for parental freedom where you could go on about your life under the illusion Pete was being watched by the criminal, ah what's his name?" Dr. Wilson looked at his notes. "Oh yes, Davey. Mrs. Gregg, you must understand that mothers are their children's protectors, a major source of love and well-being. When mothers go missing, psychologically abandoning their kids, what is left is a young person so desperate for inclusion they will go wherever they can to find a source of social support. Gangs, cults, and yes paedophiles use this void of maternal love to exploit abandoned children. Mrs. Gregg, I'm not sure you are fit to be a mother."

Bombshell!

I expected my mom to explode in a white-hot expression of rage. Surprisingly, she said nothing. Instead of letting Dr. Wilson have it, she got up, tears streaming down her cheeks, and walked out of the exam room.

"You didn't have to be so mean to her, did you?" I asked Dr. Wilson.

"Pete, I'm sorry. You should not have heard what I said to your mom. You and I both know that she lied about the injury to your mouth. I'm sure she did it with some kind of acid to punish you. I was so angry I just couldn't stop."

Before I could say anything, a nurse came into the room and said, "Dr. Wilson, the police officers are here to interview Peter.

They're in a bit of a hurry because they have to see the young lady who was also a victim, along with Pete."

"Okay, Pete. Thanks for letting me do your exam. I have one last thing to say to you before I leave. Tell the truth, even though you feel it might hurt your mom. Your life might depend upon it."

The doctor left and two police officers entered the room, followed by my mom. They pulled up chairs next to my bed, while she remained standing. "How long do you think this is going to take?" she asked. The youngest of the two cops said, "We really can't say, probably about two hours. Why do you ask?"

"As soon as you're finished, I'm taking Pete home. He's going to get better being around his family and friends instead of this Nazi tribunal masquerading as a hospital."

"Mrs. Gregg, what happens to Peter after we finish is a medical question that we have nothing to do with. Pete's release from the hospital is something you will have to discuss with Dr. Wilson and social services. I might also add, though, speaking of social services, they are going to want to come to your home next week so they can do a family evaluation. They will look at Pete's home environment and how, or if, it might have contributed to the forces leading up to Pete's molestation. But now, if you will excuse us."

My mom left the room. I could tell the contrite patina she showed Dr. Wilson earlier was now replaced with a simmering volcano, just waiting to explode. The police officers were polite and gently walked me through my travels with Davey. They took furious notes and every so often they would get up and move away from my bed, standing and whispering to one another so I couldn't hear them.

"Peter, we just have one more thing to cover. Up until now you've done a really good job. We think you've been telling the truth and we're sure those Pirate pals you talked about would be proud of you. But here's what we need to know. Did your mother do something to you that caused the scarring in your mouth? Now remember, you *have* to tell us the truth."

I took a deep breath and when I exhaled I let the lye soap secret spill out of my being. I told them about everything that led up to my mom's attack, the attack itself, my dad's refusal to intervene, and the pleas of my mother for me to lie so that she might not get into trouble and even perhaps me being taken away from her and my dad. By the time I finished, the two police officers were sitting in stunned silence.

Finally, one asked me, "Are you afraid of your mom?"

I shook my head yes, and then I said, "My mom scares me when she gets so mad she can't control herself. Most of the time I can handle how pissed off she gets, but the night she tortured me, so much had happened with me running off without permission to check out the B-47 crash that I can see why she flipped her lid. I don't care what's happened. I do not want to live with any other parents than my mom and dad."

"Peter, we can't help with what happened between you and your parents. Social services will have to make that call."

Then the other officer chimed in. "Thank you for being such a brave young man. You deserve a great life and we hope you get it."

The police officers left my room. It was about nine in the evening and I was completely exhausted. What I heard next was my mom arguing with Dr. Wilson.

"I don't care what you say. I'm taking Pete home tonight. He'll sleep much better in his own bed. His dad and I will take good care of him."

"Mrs. Gregg, I agree with your request and there's no real medical reason to keep Pete overnight, and I know he wants to go home," Dr. Wilson said. "I assure you the investigation of what happened to him is not over, and the family visit by social services next week is critical in plotting a path leading to Peter's health and well-being. I'll sign his medical release to your care, but I want to see Pete in about a week for a follow-up exam. My nurse will give you a call to schedule a time. I also want to make myself abundantly clear. If anything else happens to this little boy that you or your husband may have caused, I assure you, I will do everything in my power to have you both arrested and Pete placed in a foster home. You have my word on it."

My mom was smart enough not to attack Dr. Wilson and his threat. She knew a counter punch would get her nowhere. She left the hallway and came back into my exam room. "Okay Pete, we're going home. Everybody can't wait to see you. I have a special surprise for you, too. Your dad called your uncle, told him everything, so he's coming to see you in the morning. Says he has a very rare silver dollar he wants to give you."

Before I could get up from the exam bed and start getting dressed, she leaned over and in that conspiratorial whisper she asked, "Did you tell the cops the truth about your mouth?"

I decided there had been enough lying and said back to her, "Yes, Mom, everybody knows the truth. That it was your lye soap attack that screwed up my mouth."

"Oh my God!" she gasped. "I don't know what we're going to do. I'm sure I'm in trouble, and they might take you away from us. Look what you've done, Pete! You may have destroyed our family. But there's nothing we can do now. Get you clothes on and let's go."

"Hey, Mom, before we go, have you seen Jerry Kaye? How is she? Can I see her before we leave?"

"Peter, Jerry Kaye has already left for home. I talked to her mother briefly and she told me Jerry was okay physically but was totally devastated over what Davey did to her. Her mom blames you for getting her daughter involved in this mess and insisted that Jerry Kaye never talk to you again."

I was crushed.

CHAPTER 21: ROUTE 66

We drove home in Porsche's aged elegance. "So how did the cops know about Jerry Kaye and I being tortured at Davey's house, and how did you get there so fast? You were supposed to be at your sister's going on a date with your new friend."

"Pete, it's an amazing story. We are so lucky. If a few things had gone another way who knows what would have happened to you and Jerry Kaye. Mrs. McDouglas, who I don't think you know, lives with her husband right next door to Peaches and Davey. Anyway, she was out sweeping her porch when you first came to Davey's house. She heard Davey yelling for you to come in, but immediately became suspicious because she knew Peaches was not home as she had a Sunday afternoon waitressing job. A young kid home alone with a strange teenager was not right as Mrs. McDouglas saw it, but she wasn't sure she should do anything.

"Well, after finishing sweeping her porch, she went back inside her house, but was still concerned. She kept peeking out between the curtains covering the front window to watch if anything else that might be going on. For a while there was nothing. Then Jerry Kaye showed up and went into the house. Mrs. McDouglas' danger signals went into overdrive. Still not sure she should do anything, she replaced worry with hypervigilance and acutely listened for any sounds that might indicate foul play.

"After a while, she heard you and Jerry Kaye yelling for help. That was it for her. She immediately called the police."

"But how did you get there so quick?" I asked.

"Fortunately, for us, Todd, my new friend, had to cancel lunch because of an emergency welding job he had to go on. So, I left your aunt's early and returned home with your sister. When I found you weren't around, I didn't worry. I just thought you were playing with Davey. The next thing I know, two police officers and a nurse were knocking on our door. Standing next to the cops and the nurse was Jerry Kaye's mom and Mrs. McDouglas. One cop told me there was an emergency involving you and Jerry Kaye at Davey's house.

"The youngest police officer told me that you and Jerry Kaye might be in danger. They needed me to identify you and Davey and provide immediate trauma support.

"The rest is history as the saying goes. We were all so lucky. But Pete, I need to say something else before we get home. I think our family is in trouble. I understand how important it was for you to tell the truth to the police officers and Dr. Wilson about how your mouth was injured, and about your dad's drinking and our fights, and how your father and I didn't protect you from Davey. I get why you let everybody know what really happened, but I bet because of what you've said, your dad and I might be in trouble with the police. I am sure some of the authorities are going to do what they can to take you away from us, maybe your sister, too. We have to do something. That's why I called your uncle. He's coming tomorrow morning so we can talk over what a good plan for the future might be."

I couldn't imagine what plans they had for us. I was tired. I just wanted to go to my room and get some sleep.

"You're going to stay home from school tomorrow," she added. "I want you around us while we figure out all of this stuff."

I finally responded. "I'm not staying home. I want to see my friends. I want to talk to Jerry Kaye. And I want to go to school."

"Sorry, Pete, you are staying put. No arguments." I stayed silent, but she continued to talk. "When we get back to the house, let's make sure your dad's all right. I haven't seen him since Friday morning. I assume he's laying half drunk on the couch. After I get him taken care of, we can get you something to eat, and then it's off to bed with you."

I didn't want anything to eat. All I wanted was sleep. When we got home, my mom was having trouble getting my dad off the couch and into their bedroom. Food prep would be a long ways off. I made my way up the stairs to my room and collapsed onto my bed without even taking off my clothes. I fell asleep immediately and soon passed into a deep, dark sleep riddled with bad dreams of Davey raping me again and using his switchblade to cut my throat.

I sat up, startled. It was only three in the morning. I closed my eyes, but I couldn't get back to sleep. I lay awake until seven in the morning. It was time to get up.

I put on some clean clothes. When I looked outside my window, I saw a swirl of leaves, branches, and debris flying by. It was a Midwest blow, like Dorothy's in the *Wizard of Oz*. Not a tornado, but plenty strong to send lots of stuff flying in all sorts of directions. Then I heard the whistle of the wind through our rooftop. It reminded me of ghostly sounds I read about from ships run aground while searching for illicit plunder. I was overwhelmed in this cocoon of evil past, lost in what the future had in store.

I made my way downstairs. My dad was up, but hungover. It was one of the few of his benders that looked like it had the potential to level him for the day. I opened the front door and looked outside. In between the dust and mangled plant life that shot by, I saw the back of the Pirates as they headed to school. It was all I could do to not break rank with my mother's order and run after them to recapture what I'd lost.

I resisted. Who knew what the Pirates thought of me. I was their perverted friend who created a pathway for another friend to be beaten, tortured, and molested.

I shut the door and approached my mother who was steeping tea at the kitchen table.

"When do you think Uncle Jimmy is going to get here?"

"I don't know. I called him again late last night, after I got the puke washed off your dad and put him to bed. I suggested he come late this afternoon so that your father might be in shape to join in our conversation. I assume he'll be here about three."

I spent the rest of the morning rummaging through my books and finished up the last chapter of my re-read of *Call Of The Wild*. As I turned the final page of what was one of my favourite books of all time, I exhaled deeply and wondered how I might manage a new start, a new life, in Alaska. Something about the purity of pristine mountains, courageous explorers, and their noble companions, the sled dog teams, pulled me out of the cesspool of my life. It offered a vision where troubled people could go and reclaim a new existence if their purpose was pure and devoid of the venal scars that forced their migration. Maybe someday I could answer my own call of the wild and become an Alaskan, at least in spirit.

At 2:45 p.m. my uncle burst through the door and into the house. He was in full tornado mode, exploding with energy, and decked out in his finest cowboy duds. He saw me and rushed over to the bottom of the steps where I was standing, grabbed me in a big bear hug and proclaimed, "Pete, are you all right? I swear if I could catch the pervert who did this to you I would kill him. That's the absolute truth."

I squeezed out of my uncle's arms saying, "I'm okay, Uncle Jimmy. Just a little scared, but ready to go back to school and see my friends."

"Okay, look here little cowboy, don't rush it. That asshole nearly killed you! You need to take a little time to rest up before you get back on the bronc, so to speak. And besides, I have a plan I want to try on your mom and dad. A plan that will change your lives. A fresh start with new pastures. There's lots of upside, and the plan will leave all this bad juju behind."

"Where's your dad?" Uncle Jimmy looked in the kitchen. For the first time he caught sight of my dad in all his hungover splendour. "Good God, you look like shit. How many times do I gotta tell you if you keep booze as your mistress, keep whoring around, you're going to die a lonely old drunk with no one giving a shit about you and your miserable life. It's just like when we were kids, you couldn't keep up and replaced common sense with straight-out gluttony. Come on little brother, you're a better man than this."

My dad looked up with his bloodshot eyes, so embarrassed that his lifetime hero, his big brother, had caught him once again, in the depths of his self-loathing.

"Jimmy, you have no right to climb up my ass. I bet you're leaving here, after you straighten us lowlifes out, and are headed for some club and a night with one of your many prostitutes you fuck on a regular basis."

Then my dad started sobbing uncontrollably and rushed from the table. He went upstairs and slammed the bedroom door with such ferocity that it literally shook the house. My mom had been witness to all of this, the most recent saga of the brothers Gregg's love/hate relationship with each other.

"Sorry, Jimmy. He just found out this morning what happened to Pete. He's devastated. Full of sloppy remorse. I think if we give him an hour or so he will rally, but that said, I think we should plow full speed ahead with the plan you and I discussed last night."

I try to blend back into the background, kind of half in and half out of the furnace room. I leaned against the door jam and heard my uncle lay out the details of what he had in mind.

"So, Louise, like we talked last night, Clyde and Joe are going to show up tomorrow with the big diesel stock truck. We'll put the racks on so we can load furniture and all your personal stuff on the truck bed. It will take about a day to load. Once we have all your things on the truck, they'll drive it to Los Angeles and unload, at ah, what did you say the people's names were?"

"Frank and Ruth Young. They're old friends from our army days. I called them last night and told them what's going on and asked if we could stay with them for a while. Put our stuff in storage until we find a place. They were over the moon with joy to see us again. I told them we would be there in about a week."

"Great Louise. Let's get it straight so you can explain the plan to Thomas and Pete. I'm going to give you guys the move, one year's rent, and a weekly allowance of $400 until Thomas can land a job. I want Pete and his sister to come back to the ranch every summer and I will pay for their way there. If you and Thomas decide to make a summer vacation out of a trip to see Florence and I, I would love it. So that's it. We have to get you guys back on track. Life is too short to just set in the rodeo stands you have to get back on and let'em buck."

"Jimmy, I love you," I heard my mom say. "I can't thank you enough. With this move, and your generosity, I'm positive Pete and the rest of us will flourish. Tell Florence I will call her in two weeks, and we can chat about everything."

"Louise, I can't wait for Thomas. I won't take you up on your kind offer for a bed for tonight. I have some business I have to attend to this afternoon, and this evening I'm meeting friends for a night out on the town at the Dynamite Club."

Bam! Just like that, there it was. Look what I'd caused. My time with Davey resulted in blowing up my entire family, where we lived, what we did and the utter loss for me of everything important, especially the Pirates. I knew my mom well enough to realize no argument I might make would have any chance of changing her mind. I was locked in, as The Mamas and the Papas would sing many years later, "California dreamin' is becomin' a reality."

My uncle's big stock truck arrived the next morning. His two ranch hands loaded our furniture and personal stuff into the truck. Luckily, they started after the Pirates had left for school, so I didn't have to explain the reason for our sudden departure. Several neighbours stopped by and wished us luck. I didn't see hide nor hare of Jerry Kaye's mom, nor any of the other Pirates' parents. By about two in the afternoon, the truck was loaded and rumbled out of The Project heading south, then west onto Los Angeles.

While the guys were loading the truck, I finished packing my books, trophies, and other useless, but essential tools of memories of time spent at The Project. One of my most prized possessions, the picture of me in the championship drag racer, got special care as I double wrapped it with towels and spare underwear and placed it at the top of the box the truck hands had given me to pack my stuff.

Once I finished packing, I decided to take a final walk to the cliffs overlooking the river valley. I passed Peaches' house, still wrapped in bright yellow investigative tape. I finally made it to cliff side and looked down on the serene picture of aspens, pines, and the creek running through them. I thought of the games I had played with the Pirates in and amongst the banks and meadows of this polluted, but amazing wonderland that gave poor kids a place to run free and explore their lust for the wild. What it welded most deeply in my memory of the river valley was the afternoon we were playing our game of B-47. The day I yelled, "They're crashing!" in jest and then watched the two gigantic bombers flying in formation above us scream to the earth in flames. Chip Arden and I visiting the great aircraft of war, and their crew's grave site, and the forces this unbelievable accident unleashed onto my life.

As I walked back to our house from the cliffs to join in the final preparation for our retreat from my life, and all that made the last few month's morality play an utter disaster, I decided I would never give up again. If we were to explore a new life in California, then I was going to attack every opportunity I could and leave my parents behind to sort out their life dilemmas. I would choose to live full out.

We packed Porsche with what we would need, in terms of personal stuff and clothing for our trip. We left at about three that afternoon, just in time to see the Pirates returning from school. I waved to them from my side window. Benny Tail-Feather raised a clenched fist, looked directly at me and yelled, "Peter Gregg and Pirates forever."

I clenched my fist back to Benny as Porsche, with my mom at the wheel, motored out of The Project's parking lot and headed south and then west where we would catch the famous Route 66 just as we crossed into Oklahoma. This ribbon of highway would be our vector to Los Angeles with all its fantasized possibilities and pitfalls.

Route 66 runs from Chicago to Los Angeles and has captured the imagination of explorers, like us heading west for a better life. It has been the source of songs and television shows and millions travel from all over the world just to experience the kaleidoscope of the magnificent South West of the United States as viewed from the window of a car.

For the next seven days we passed through the landscape of stark but beautiful deserts, ranch lands, and farms. They dotted the way between the great cities of western lore of Oklahoma, Texas, New Mexico, Arizona, and finally, California. I was mesmerized by what I saw and experienced. There was the famous Blue Whale statue just outside of Tulsa, Oklahoma, and Amarillo's Cadillac Ranch with its ten buried, only fins showing, vintage Cadillacs. We spent the night in one of the wigwam motels which were shaped like Native American teepees that were spread along our westward journey. Then there was the promise of the magnificent Pacific Ocean I'd been reading about.

When we reached Arizona, Dad convinced my mom to add a day or two to our trip so we could head north to visit The Painted

Desert, The Petrified Forest, and most of all, The Grand Canyon. The Painted Desert and The Petrified Forest were interesting and startlingly beautiful. But it was the Grand Canyon that captured my imagination, as it would for the rest of my life. The beautiful reds and purples of the canyon walls stunned me as I looked out over the edge of what felt like the universe of all things. Then thousands of feet below the rim, to see the ribbon of the majestic Colorado River as it rushed to its eventual rendezvous with the Pacific.

Even my cynical mother was blown away with what she was seeing and experiencing at the canyon. She enthusiastically joined in and convinced all of us to take a mule ride to the bottom of the canyon and then back up. Our mule wrangler was named Steve. Steve had a huge red handlebar moustache, and was adorned with a bright yellow, western, pearl snap button shirt, leather chaps over grimy jeans, and well-worn cowboy boots with spurs.

Steve got us mounted on our individual mules, and we headed down the skinniest trail I'd ever seen. As we started, Steve looked over his shoulder at us and yelled, "Guys, don't try to steer your mule. They've been up and down this trail hundreds of times. They're smarter than you and me. They never slip or fall. Just relax and enjoy the ride."

The ride down the canyon was spectacular. We passed gigantic cacti, small animals, and desert flowers in bloom with petals of purple, yellow, ruby red, and deep green. Our mules never missed a step. They were as solid as a rock. Once we were at the bottom of the canyon the power of the Colorado took over. The river's crashing white water, eddies of undertow and still pools, worked in a majestic dance showcasing one of the world's true wonders.

We made our way to the famous Ghost Ranch, signalling the absolute bottom of the Grand Canyon. At Ghost Ranch, we fed and watered our mules and we feasted on a lunch of burritos, tostados, tomato salsa, and fried cactus. Our gringo status showed up and since we were only used to white man's food, we couldn't quite decide if we were fans of Mexican cuisine or not. After an hour or so of hiking, we climbed back on board our trusty mules and headed back up our spindle of a trail to the top of the south rim.

About halfway up, Steve stopped his mule. Our mules followed suit and stopped in unison. Steve jumped off his mule and ran up and to the side of the trail. Just as he got to the trail's edge, a large snake slithered from what little bush was growing next to our pathway. Steve threw several rocks at the critter and it slithered off the path, probably to find another sunny spot in search of lizards and such.

As Steve climbed back aboard his mule, he explained, "A diamond back is the only thing that spooks our mules. Got to get them off the trail before one of our animals is bit or scared to the point of bucking a passenger off. Could be a disaster. No thanks."

We were all thankful he'd shooed the rattler away.

"Last month, on my wedding day, I was bringing a tour back up the canyon, just like us today. I saw another diamondback, coiled on the trail. I threw some rocks at it. It wouldn't move so I went closer, trying to use hand gestures to scare it into getting out of our way. Well, the sum bitch struck and bit me between my thumb and first finger on my right hand. I didn't have a snake bite kit along so all I could do was use my kerchief as a tourniquet and get up to the rim as soon as possible. My hand was as big as a balloon, but with the help of the park rangers and the resort doctor and lots of tequila, I made my wedding on the edge of the south rim, a month ago Sunday. How about that?"

I was impressed with Steve's story. It stayed with me all this time. It provided a cautionary tale for the many times I went back to the canyon. I ran the rim-to-rim foot race and hiked to Ghost Ranch for days of exploration and introspection. Then the best day of all, perched spectacularly on an outcropping hanging over the south rim, on April 9, at four p.m., I stood there with Anita. We were married by the Justice of the Peace from Flagstaff Arizona. It was one of the greatest days of my life.

***

Our life-altering excursion took two days. Once we were back on Route 66, we had to do our best to make up some time. With my dad at the wheel, we put in a gigantic day of driving and made Barstow, California, at about nine that night. The time that it took us to get from Flagstaff to Barstow flew by as we chattered nonstop about our amazing Grand Canyon experience. It was one of the few times I could remember enjoying each other's company as a family, focusing on a mutually experienced positive event.

We found a cheap Barstow motel to rest our heads and made our way to a local diner for a late dinner. Since things had gone so well that day, I decided to take a risk. Before our food was served, I looked directly at my mom and dad who were seated straight across from my sister and me in a red booth.

I asked, "Dad, Mom, I have a question. Are we moving to California because you guys are embarrassed that I was involved with Davey and all of his sexual shenanigans that he used to hurt Jerry Kaye and I?"

Our reason for moving was never discussed with me at any point on our trip up until that night. My mom pursed her lips, not waiting for my dad to say anything. With a strain in her voice, she said, "Peter, we're never going to talk about you, Jerry Kaye, and Davey again. Do you understand? Do not ever bring this awful subject up, now or in the future. It's over. Do you get it? As far as we're concerned from tonight on, Davey never happened. You agree, Thomas?"

"Yes, of course, Louise," he said. "We have to protect one another and push bad stuff out of our lives. Peter, your mom's right, it's over."

Our food was served and these pronouncements by my parents that my question provoked would be the last time any of us talked about Davey raping me and molesting Jerry Kaye. I wasn't sure what to do. I was confused. I could see how fully invested in me as a source of their shame they were. But right then and there I decided this was their problem. I would never let them see how much they'd hurt me through neglect, stupid hubris, and lack of love. I was on my own. There was no other choice. Only I could save myself.

The next morning, we hit the road at seven. I was morose from the discussion last night. It should have been a wildly exciting day with the Pacific looming on the horizon. I skipped breakfast and waited for everyone inside Porsche. Once we were all settled in our seats with Dad driving again, we headed west through the desert where Barstow lay like a shimmering jewel nestled in a sea of sand and cacti. Then it was on into the mountains and passes that guarded the Los Angeles basin, and finally through San Bernardino and its industrial persona. Route 66 pushed west, through the neighbourhoods of Highland Park, Echo Park, Pasadena, Beverly Hills, and then we were there, at the corner of Lincoln and Olympic, Santa Monica, the end point of Route 66, and the start of a new life us all.

EPILOGUE

I never returned to The Project. I never saw any of the Pirates since the wave goodbye as we headed west. To this day, I don't know what happened to Jerry Kaye. And my parents and I never talked ever again of tumultuous times of my ninth year and the carnage that they, and Davey, brought to my sense of self-worth.

We found a place to live near Long Beach, California. We rented a small white bungalow with a small picket fence, in a mixed race, lower class neighbourhood. I immediately got back into school. I went into fourth grade. From my first day on the playgrounds of South East Central Elementary, it was clear I was once again one of the fastest kids for my size and age. The other kid that was as fast as me, was Calvin Stone. Calvin was black, angular and handsome. He was the youngest of five brothers. He and I became friends instantly. Calvin introduced me to a place that literally saved my life–The Boys Club. Every afternoon, once school was over, we would make our way to the club. It was there I met Jessy James Sherman, a bald, black man, about fifty, with a heart of gold. He coached our football skills, mentored us on how to study and be good students, how to be respectful kids, and generally taught us the art of growing up to be good men.

In addition to friendship and our mutual exploration of skills taught us by Jessy James Sherman at the Boy's Club, Calvin brought me into the fold of his loving family. Calvin's mom and dad treated me like a long-lost son. Calvin's brothers were abusive, fun, and protective, all at once. Skin colour was never a question. What mattered was that I was a good person and I was Calvin's friend. I spent every free moment I had at Calvin's.

Calvin and I played football on the same team from our fourth-grade Pop Warner days, up until our senior year in high school. Calvin was always the quarterback and I was always the wide receiver. We were a great tandem and both highly recruited out of high school by major colleges, with full ride scholarships as part of any possible agreement. Calvin went to a university in the Midwest and became an outstanding college quarterback. After four years of record-setting play, he was drafted by one of the east coast NFL teams, and played for eight years, four of which he was all pro.

I stayed on the west coast and enjoyed a moderately successful career as a wide receiver and defensive back. I was always too small to even think about playing in the NFL. The Canadian Football League (CFL) at a time was interested in my talents, but I decided I wanted a job instead of more football.

I went to work, using my degree in economics, at a major film studio and theme park and became a young and up-and-coming executive. Eventually, I left the world of media management and went back to school and earned my PhD in behavioural sciences. My doctoral dissertation, *Getting It On With Jesus*, won several awards for graduate student research. I went on to a career in university teaching and leadership consulting, which ended this year because of my health crisis.

My dad, who we hoped would change once we moved to Los Angeles, carried on in his old ways of weekend binging, bar hopping, and chasing women. Two years after I left home at sixteen to pursue my football and college career everything changed. My dad was drunk and driving around lost, late one foggy Saturday winter night. He ran a red light and crashed into a young women's car. The accident sent the young woman to the hospital and my dad went to jail. After a week behind bars, my dad was released to the custody of his boss at the large aerospace firm where he worked. Mr. Sterling was my dad's boss and at the time of sentencing he divulged to the court that he was a lifelong, every day, member of Alcoholics Anonymous (AA). He said the only way he would be responsible for my father's release was if he agreed to join AA, become an everyday member, and work with Mr. Sterling as his sponsor.

My dad made this agreement with both the court and Mr. Sterling and it changed his life forever. He never had a drink again and went on to develop an AA program for prisoners at a penitentiary close to where he and my mom lived.

***

It was a Southern California June morning. I was fifty-two-years old and about to give the eulogy for my dad's funeral at the large downtown Methodist Church. I was never able to forgive my mom or dad for what I thought was their enabling of Davey and his rape of me and the molestation of Jerry Kaye. I had written them out of my life. Now I was back.

My sister had called me the day of Dad's heart attack and I rushed from my home in Canada to be by his bedside. I got to the hospital in time to help my family make the difficult decision to enter a Do Not Resuscitate (DNR) order. Then I watched him die in my arms, a frail old man.

I expected a few mourners at the funeral like my immediate family, and family members from out of town. As the time for the service grew near, I was blown away. All the pews in this large religious facility were filled to the brim. Well-wishers spilled out the large brass front doors, onto the entry porch, and a few people congregated on the sidewalk.

After the service was over, I paid thanks and best wishes to all those that took their precious time to celebrate my dad's life. I heard stories of thanks from some of the prisoners his AA program helped. There were young women with their parents recounting his generosity and the loving spirit he demonstrated in his work with a young women's organization. There were also hundreds of guys–young, old, black and white–his pals who treasured his friendship.

To this day one of my great regrets is not finding the grace of forgiveness to open a space where my dad and I could have formed a relationship. The man I knew was not the humble servant I heard about that day. My hurt was so deep I couldn't let it go. Because of that, I ended up with no dad. If I had been kinder, I might have experienced the man so many others told me about that morning.

There is a caveat, though. In the deep psychoanalysis sessions I underwent as a graduate student, my wise therapist simply pointed out that my dad never said he was sorry for all that had happened to me. He had never told me he loved me. Not once did *he* pick up the phone to talk to me. I guess there was room for my rationalization, but in the end, I knew better, and I could have done better.

Over the next few years my Uncle Jimmy, my Aunt Florence, and my mom all died in rapid succession. For whatever reason, I was asked to eulogize all three of these close family members. My mom's funeral was the largest of the three and had the same outpouring of admiration. There was gratitude stemming from her work managing a hi-tech assembly line and the thanks and respect those who worked for her gave as they said goodbye. Like my dad, she had also gotten involved in the young women's organization. They worked together on many projects which helped cement their relationship in the later stages of their lives. There was an outpouring of love and gratitude emanating from many young women and their parents.

I did not communicate much with my mom from the time I left home up until the last few weeks of her life. I spent those remaining days reminiscing with her over the events of our lives, together and separate. I wanted to ask her about Davey and the lye soap but thought better of it and let it pass. My relationship with my mom was so ambivalent and complicated that I did not experience the same regret as I did with my dad, for my disappearance from our relationship. In fact, I think the distance I created with her was a healthy but painful necessity.

My Uncle and Aunt's funerals were a little rodeo, Mardi Gras and Irish Wake all rolled into one. I guess the kindest description of these events would be Irish whiskey soaked in cowboy culture. The funerals for my uncle and aunt were parties.

***

About seven years before my father died, I was in Washington DC meeting with old friends from a large foundation I'd been doing consulting work for. The foundation assignment had been an action research project studying the societal impact of the so-called industrial democracy project as practiced in the Norwegian fishing industry. I'd spent five years on the research, primarily in Oslo and numerous Norwegian fishing villages. What I'd been looking at was what happens when an industry relinquishes hierarchical management structures and replaces them with all aspects of participatory democracy down to the shop level. In the Norwegian experiment, workers owned shares in their companies, sat on boards of directors along with industry elites and government ministers, and at the same time, employees elected peer foremen and managers who would lead their efforts.

I had delivered the findings of my research to the foundation. Worker democracy had moderate positive correlations with a decline in employee alcoholism, child and spousal abuse, employee turnover, and higher rates of productivity. Surprisingly, it also resulted in greater participation in other democratic institution such as greater municipal voting rates, and for some, a willingness to run for public office like school board.

To celebrate the completion of the project, the foundation sponsors invited me, and several of my Washington DC friends, to lunch. They told me to pick, so I chose Frank and Mustafa's. Frank and Mustafa's was a legendary DC grill and watering hole, a favoured place to gossip and cut deals by the city's high profile media players, politicians, lobbyists, lawyers, and the notorious, elite K Street Bandits, and often hardball deal makers.

The six of us were sitting at a table when I heard a loud booming voice that grabbed everyone's attention.

"HEY GREGG . . . HEY 82 . . . GET OVER HERE . . . WAY TOO LONG!"

It was Calvin. I couldn't believe it. We hadn't seen each other in many years. My table mates were awestruck. Here was this all pro NFL defensive back giving a shout out to their friend. I jumped up from my seat at the table and started towards him. Calvin beat me to the punch and literally ran from his table. We met each other halfway. We grabbed one another in a powerful bear hug. Calvin had tears running down his cheek and so did I. We found an empty table, excused ourselves from our lunch companions, and spent the afternoon catching up.

Calvin was married to Darlene, his college sweetheart. They had three kids, a boy and two girls, and they lived outside the city in what I remember as one of the more exclusive neighbourhoods in DC. After his retirement from the NFL, Calvin had built a very powerful and lucrative land development company. He had forty people working for him, and had been asked, even groomed a bit, to run for congress in his district. He said he wasn't interested. He told me his greatest accomplishment was the work he'd done as a national board member of The Boys and Girls Club of North America.

"It's an amazing organization, Pete. I feel the time I spend there is really making a difference. Hey! Want me to fix you up so you can get involved on the West Coast?"

I didn't respond to Calvin's question and instead asked him, "Calvin do you miss football?"

"Not one bit, Pete. I love my life, I have a great family, and my work is challenging. I'm a happy man. What about you? Where you been all these years?"

I launched into my story: my academic and professional accomplishments. Calvin couldn't believe that my proper title was now, Dr. Gregg, Professor of Behavioural Sciences, and international consultant. I even told him about Davey. I finished off with my short history as an out-of-control ladies' man, and most painfully, the neither explained, nor understood, fracturing of my relationship with my son.

"Jesus, Pete you've done a lot. I can't believe how much courage you showed, never letting the Davey cat out of the bag. It must be painful to deal with what happened with your son. If it were me, I don't know if I could handle one of my kids walking away for no reason. No talk, just gone—man that's cold. I must say, I heard my mom comment on several occasions. 'Pete's a wounded boy,' she had said. 'Something has happened to him that he can't talk about. That's why he spends so much time with us. He knows we're a family with love, and you can see him just soaking in our kindness for one another'."

Truer words had never been spoken. Calvin's mom was right. It was her and her family, especially her, and the love she wrapped around me, that allowed me to weather the storms of my California life from fourth grade to my senior year in high school.

Finally, the manager at Frank and Mustafa's kicked us out. Calvin and I walked arm in arm through the front door of the restaurant. It was getting dark and we could see the lights of Georgetown to the west, the Grand Potomac River to the south with Key Bridge spitting the Virginia commuters on to the highways leading home to Alexandria and Fairfax County. Calvin invited me over to meet his family the next day. I explained I couldn't as I had to fly back to California the next day.

We said goodbye. We gave each other a kiss on the cheek, knowing that our paths would never cross again. There was too much water under and beyond the bridge.

As I write these words, I know there will never be friends like Benny Tail-Feather, Jerry Kaye, and Calvin, ever again in my life.

My summation of the arc of my history, once beyond the trauma of my parents and their misfortune to have children when they did, and Davey's sickness, can be summed up in my attempt to be a good man. Putting my life aspirations in a few words is hard for me so I must borrow from the Forty Fourth President of The United States, Barack Obama. He was asked, what message from his life did he hope to leave his children and grandchildren. He said:

Be Kind

Be Useful

President Obama echoed my sentiments exactly. He stated this credo in a much more succinct and elegant way than I ever could have hoped.

No matter how hard it was for me from The Project until today, I have strived to be kind and in some small ways, been useful. Many times, I failed, but I hope most of the people I have encountered in my life will agree at some level, kindness and usefulness are hallmarks of the experience they have had with me.

Today, my life is full, filled with the love of those around me. I await my fate with thoughts, not of remorse, or the seeker of pity, but as a person blessed to have lived a full and consequential life.

Dr. Peter Gregg

P.S. One of the primary reasons I wrote Lost Boy Found was that just before I started the book I had been diagnosed with a terminal disease and given only two years to live. This shocking event motivated me to not leave this world without telling my story, and perhaps helping all of those dealing with child abuse to act even more aggressively to save children.

In the two years it took me to write Lost Boy Found, a new experimental drug that increases longevity and mitigates physical symptoms, came to the Canadian market and I was the first patient included in this non-placebo study.

It's been a year since I started the new drug and I am feeling much better these days.

ACKNOWLEDGEMENTS

First, my wife Anita Dosaj deserves my everlasting thanks for her patient review of my work, her constant encouragement, and a willingness to marshal the resources needed to complete my book. Anita read every word, providing feedback and encouragement, delving into the darkest parts of my life with unflinching love and loving me through all the hurt and guilt my experience provoked.

I want to thank my amazing publisher, Tabitha Rose, and her excellent publishing house: Life To Paper Publishing. Without Tabitha there would have been no book as it was her continual encouragement, tenacious spirit, and generous coaching that moved this project forward to completion. It was one of the best days of my life when Tabitha concluded I had a book not only worth reading, but also it might make a difference in some lives.

Then, there is Darcy Nybo of Artistic Warrior. As my amazing editor worked through the story, she had to live through the very difficult experiences I described here. Lesser mortals might have wilted under the perversion these scenes described, but she did anything but wilt. She kept my story and my voice true and authentically me. Thank you.

I want to thank my mates at Success Lab. You know who you are. Thank you for helping me stay true and keeping at it when all was very dark, and it would have been easy to pull the plug.

Lastly, I also want to thank my wonderful fact and cultural details editor-Clare Duckett. Clare is an amazing scholar and fact checker. It was her careful work that made sure my fifty-year-old memory of my circumstances were true to the world of the early 1950's in the Mid West of the United States.

Dr. Peter Gregg, October, 2019

ABOUT THE AUTHOR

Dr. Peter Gregg grew up in the mid-west of the United States, moving to Southern California when he was ten. Dr. Gregg is an internationally recognized behavioral scientist—writing, researching, and teaching in the fields of social influence and counter cultures. He received his PhD from the University of Southern California and did post graduate work at the University of California at Los Angeles. He's taught at some of North America's top universities and has contributed a new form of serious research as well as writing-narrative non-fiction to explain and explore complex social and leadership issues for non-academic audiences.

In addition to his academic work, Dr. Gregg also acted as a highly respected leadership coach and consultant. He has helped executives from a number of North America's most innovative corporations achieve their most important life and professional goals.

In his younger days, Dr. Gregg also worked as a young executive for a theme park and started his career there as Rangoon Pete on The Jungle Cruise. It is still one of his most favorite jobs.

Dr. Gregg won a university scholarship to play football.

Today, he lives with his wife, Anita, in the shadow of the magnificent Canadian Rockies, in Calgary, Alberta, Canada.

LOST BOY FOUND

A FINAL THOUGHT

I wrote Lost Boy Found to help build awareness of readers to the pain and suffering of kids who experience parental abuse, child sexual molestation, and rape. Now, I would like to ask for more than awareness. I would implore all of you, that if you experience either in your own family, the family of others, within your schools, churches, and your kid's organizations children with overtly, or hidden the signs of molestation and abuse, that you go to the authorities and report your concerns.

It is far better to err on the side of a mistaken report than it is to sit by and watch a kid be destroyed - or even murdered - at the hands of a predator. As the saying goes: *If you see something. Say something.*

Let's end the worldwide destruction of our children in our lifetime!

Manufactured by Amazon.ca
Acheson, AB